the food and wine lover's guide
to melbourne's bays and peninsulas

australia

Hardie Grant Books

the food and wine lover's guide
to melbourne's bays and peninsulas

restaurants • wineries • people • places • produce • recipes

lucy malouf

introduction by max allen
photography by simon griffiths

First published in 2001
by Hardie Grant Books
Private Bag 1600
South Yarra, Victoria 3141
Australia

Copyright © in text: Lucy Malouf
Copyright © in images: Simon Griffiths, except those credited on p142.

All rights reserved. No part of this publication may be reproduced, stored in a retrieval system or transmitted in any form by any means, electronic, mechanical, photocopying, recording or otherwise, without the prior written permission of the publishers and copyright holders.

National Library of Australia
Cataloguing in Publication Data:

Malouf, Lucy 1962 -
the food and wine lover's guide to melbourne's bays and peninsulas

Includes Index

ISBN 1-74064-032-2

1. Restaurants - Victoria - Melbourne
2. Dinners and dining - Victoria - Melbourne
3. Wineries - Victoria - Melbourne

1. Title
647.959451
Cover design by Andrea Gill
Text design by Elizabeth Farlie Design
Index by Faye Dunleavy
Map by Christina Miesen
Printed and bound in Singapore by Tien Wah Press

This book is an initiative of
Melbourne's Bays and Peninsulas

LUCY MALOUF

Lucy Malouf is a Melbourne-based food writer. She contributes regularly to *Food and Drink* in Melbourne's *Herald Sun* newspaper, and writes on a freelance basis for the *Australian* and *Australian Gourmet Traveller*, as well as a number of food and wine-based websites. She is also a restaurant reviewer and feature writer for *Mietta's Eating and Drinking in Australia* and *The Age Cheap Eats Guide*.

Lucy Malouf is the co-author (with chef Greg Malouf) of the best-selling cookery books, *Arabesque* and *Moorish*.

SIMON GRIFFITHS

Simon Griffiths is a Melbourne-based photographer of food, wine, gardens, interiors and travel. He created the visuals for the best-selling *Saluté* with Gail and Kevin Donovan. He regularly travels overseas on assignments for magazines and publishers. He also collaborated with Paul Bangay on *The Defined Garden* and *The Boxed Garden*. His next book project is *Maggie's Table* by Maggie Beer.

MAX ALLEN

Max Allen is the wine columnist for *The Australian Magazine*, drinks editor for *Inside Out* magazine and a regular contributor to wine and food publications around the world. He is the author of numerous books, including *The Food Lover's Guide to the Great Ocean Road* and *Crush, The New Australian Wine Book*, both published by Hardie Grant.

The Food and Wine Lover's Guide

- Werribee
- You Yangs
- Geelong
- Corio Bay
- Portarlington
- Indented Head
- St. Leonards
- Queenscliff
- Barwon Heads
- Point Lonsdale
- Great Ocean Road
- Bass Strait

Melbourne's Bays and Peninsulas

- Melbourne
- St Kilda
- Brighton

Top of the Bay

Port Phillip Bay

- Frankston
- Mt Eliza
- Mornington
- Dromana
- Rosebud
- Sorrento
- Rye
- Arthurs Seat
- Red Hill
- Main Ridge
- Hastings
- Somers
- Flinders
- Cape Schanck

acknowledgements

Thanks to all those people who made researching and writing this book so much fun. First and foremost, to Fiona Hardie at Hardie Grant and Roger Grant of Geelong Otway Tourism, who set the wheels for the project in motion and to Heather Millar, who stopped them falling off along the way! Secondly, to Simon Griffiths, for his fantastic photos, which bring the places and stories within this book to life so vividly. Thanks also to my editor Foong Ling Kong for her endless patience and invaluable advice.

I am also grateful to the family and friends who offered me hospitality and gave me pointers along the way. In particular, I'd like to thank Ben and Bobbie Bowen in Geelong, who filled me in on my own personal family history as well as that of the region. Also, heartfelt thanks to Steve Warne, who so generously offered me accommodation and advice while in the Mornington Peninsula.

Finally, thanks to the food and wine people I met on my travels, who patiently told me their stories, who encouraged me to sample their wares and who invited me into their homes and entertained me way above and beyond the call of duty!

contents

Foreword	12
Introduction	17
Mornington Peninsula	23
Foodshops & Producers	25
Wineries	48
Eating Out	59
Top of the Bay	71
Williamstown	72
South Melbourne	75
Albert Park	79
St Kilda	80
Brighton & Beyond	87
Bellarine Peninsula and Geelong	95
Foodshops & Producers	97
Wineries	108
Eating Out	114
Directory	136
Index	140 & 141
References and photo credits	142

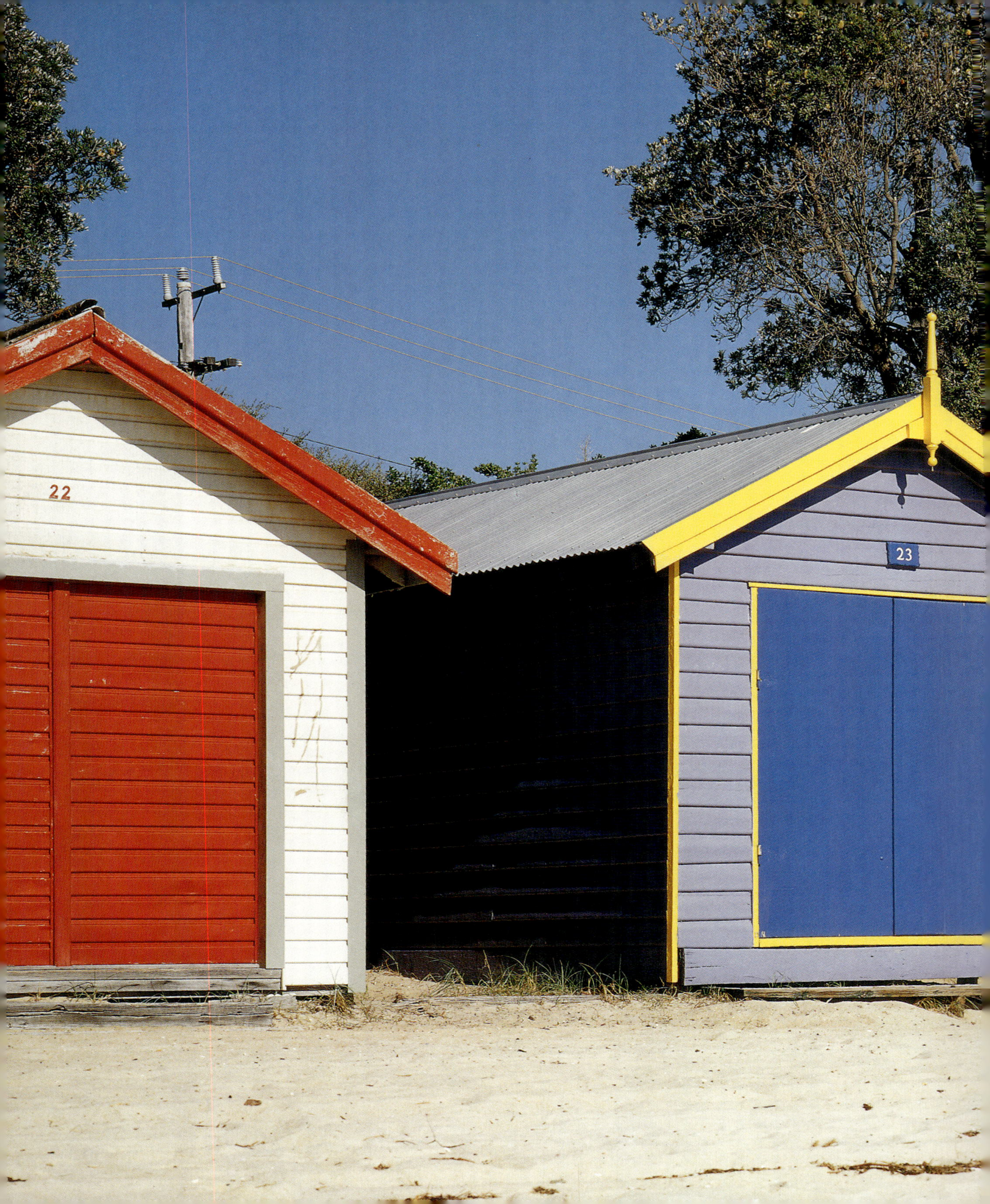
22
23

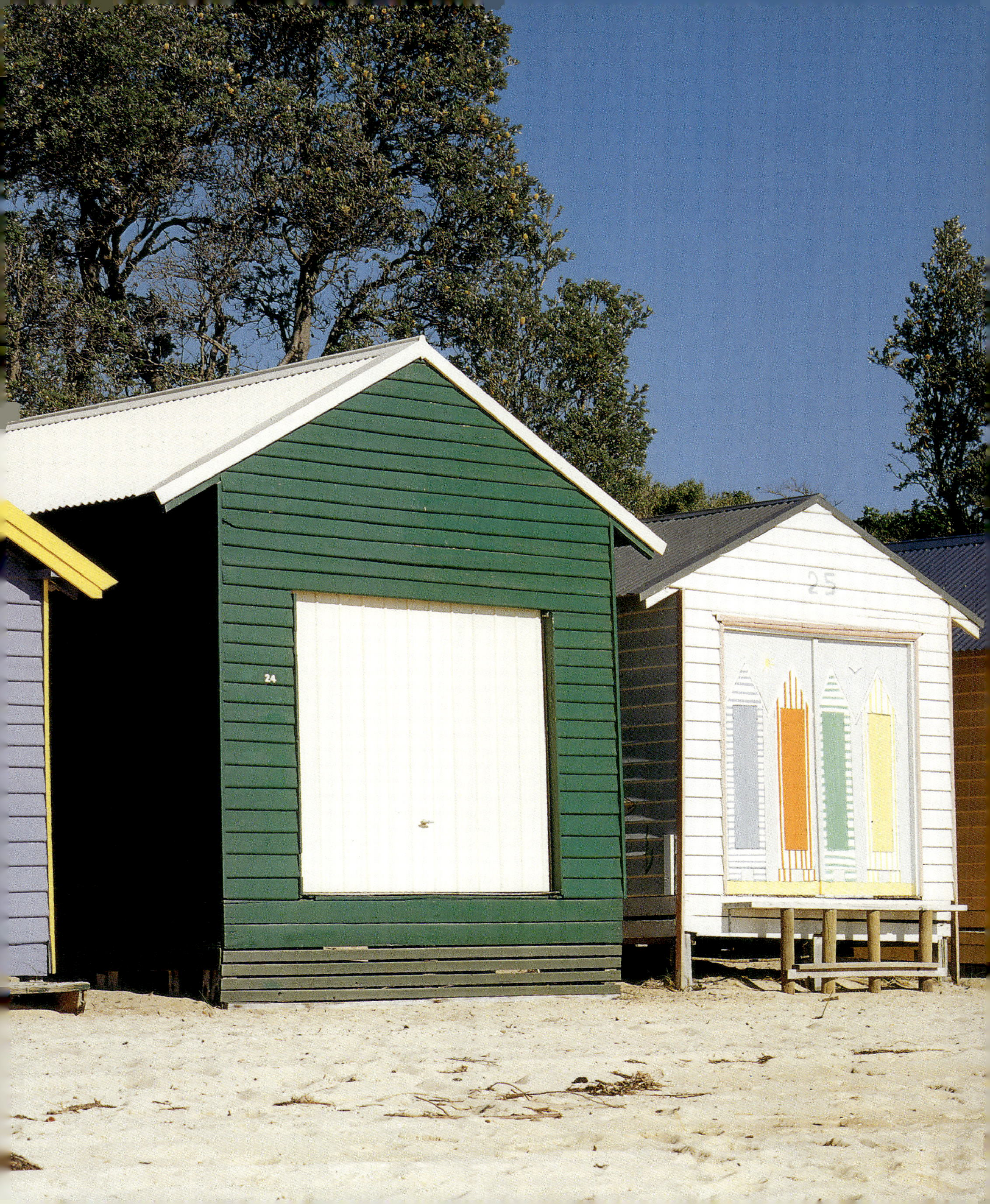
24
25

FOREWORD

You can keep your revolutions in cloning and nano-technology and genetic engineering. They don't interest me in the slightest. What I'd really like the boffins to start working on instead is a way to squeeze more hours into every day. Because then, and only then, will we be able to fully enjoy all the wonderful food and drink – especially the drink – being made and served in and around Melbourne.

In the meantime, we'll have to content ourselves with trying to cram as much of it as possible into twenty-four hours. Which is precisely why books such as this exist: to point you in the best directions and make sure you maximise your enjoyment.

This is the second Food Lover's Guide to be published by Hardie Grant. While I was researching the first – *The Food Lover's Guide to the Great Ocean Road* – a couple of years ago, I felt that there were so many other parts of Victoria – Australia, for that matter – that were begging for a similar treatment. And one of the most obvious candidates was the fertile ground that starts where the Great Ocean Road stops: the wonderful sweep of Port Phillip Bay, stretching away to the east.

I have to be honest and say that I was slightly concerned when I heard that this second guide would include the Bellarine Peninsula and Geelong. Hadn't I already covered those two regions in my first book? (I thought, full of the preciousness of the author.) Isn't there enough to be written about in the bayside suburbs of Melbourne and on the Mornington Peninsula to fill a book without doubling up?

I needn't have worried in the slightest. For a start, as with all guides, mine was almost out of date even before it was published. The food and wine industries are volatile; perhaps dynamic is a better word. People move on. Old places close down. New places open. And nowhere is this more true than in Geelong and on the Bellarine Peninsula. Australia is witnessing unprecedented growth in food- and wine-related tourism, and you can really feel the energy down there. Indeed, after just two years the area was sorely in need of an updated guide, even bearing in mind that a revised edition of my first book had in fact been published.

Not only that, but any author – especially one as passionate about her tucker as Lucy Malouf – will have her preferences, her own favourite secret places, and respond differently to the efforts and produce of various individuals. Send two writers to the same restaurant and they can write wildly different reviews, depending on their tastes, experience and idiosyncrasies.

This is precisely what Lucy has done. From Queenscliff right round to Sorrento, she has taken a very personal journey and written about the people, plates and pinot noirs that have pleased her. This is not meant to be an exhaustive list of everything that's happening (although most things are covered), but more a starting point – an inspirational, mouthwatering, evocative story, with equally mouthwatering, evocative photography by Simon Griffiths that will inspire you to get up, get out and visit the places yourself.

Crucially, though, it's not all passionate

Previous page: Bathing boxes on the beach at Dromana.

enthusiasm. Not everything is rosy in the restaurants and farms of Melbourne's bays and peninsulas, and Lucy is not afraid to point this out. She rails against the sub-standard food and sub-standard service that can still be found all too frequently, especially in popular bayside resort towns. And she offers alternatives by pointing to the people who do things well, and explaining why and how they do it.

I like to think I know how she must have felt, driving what seemed like endless kilometres in search of the next flavour hit. Much of the time you'll come across places you already know, or have read about, or even seen on telly. But occasionally you'll walk into a kitchen or winery or shop and your nose will immediately know – before your brain can even register it as a conscious thought – that you've found it. And invariably, your nose will be right: the person who greets you is warm, passionate and just as interested as you are in the next mouthful of something delicious.

It always comes back to people. Lucy gathers invaluable insight when she's talking with the people who make all this happen, usually over a plate of food or glass of wine in unique and wonderful settings. This is the combination – people making the most of the place where they live – that excites me too.

The Mornington Peninsula can be a difficult place to grow grapes. Too many grape growers and winemakers there have been seduced by the romantic beauty of the place, or are chasing the dollar returns that the rest of the Australian wine industry seems to be offering at the moment. But these few committed people have the energy, passion and drive for quality to realise the region's potential.

It's the quiet pioneering commitment of Nat and Rosalie White at Main Ridge Estate, the entrepreneurial vision of Garry Crittenden at Dromana Estate, the cheeky brilliance of Rick McIntyre at Moorooduc Estate, the deceptive calm of Lindsay McCall at Paringa Estate, the professional attention to detail of Tod Dexter at Stoniers and the sheer manic irreverence of Kathleen Quealy and Kevin McCarthy at T'Gallant that produce some of the region's most character-laden and enjoyable wines.

Up in the bayside suburbs of Melbourne, it's brilliant chefs in smart-night-out restaurants such as Karen Martini at the

Melbourne Wine Room and Robert Castellani at Donovans alongside smaller, more accessible local places that service communities – places like St Kilda's immortal Galleon Cafe and Elwood's Blue Tongue – that make Melbourne's gastronomic life as richly rewarding as it is.

And in Geelong – both the city and the region – the establishment of smart new restaurants like Sempre are adding to the already enviable achievements of quality-driven people like Randall Pollard, who left the famous Bannockburn Cellars soon after I wrote the Great Ocean Road book and now runs one of Australia's best independent wine shops, Randall the Wine Merchant, and George Biron, the wonderful chef who contributed so much to that book but closed his country restaurant, Sunnybrae, soon after its publication.

Biron is currently working on the food side of a grand new Geelong winery called Pettavel (after one of the nineteenth-century pioneers of the district), scheduled to open in late 2001. It's an indication of how the food and wine industry in this part of the world is booming when new wineries can attract enormous amounts of interest and even publicity before they've even made a drop of wine.

Another – perhaps the best, certainly the most symbolic – example of this excitement of the new is the wonderful Shadowfax winery at Werribee, part of the Mansion Hotel and Joseph's Restaurant complex, tucked in behind glorious (and gloriously restored) Werribee Mansion.

Although winemaker Matt Harrop and viticulturist Andrew Tedder source grapes for Shadowfax from a number of established, proven wine regions around Australia – including Heathcote in Central Victoria and McLaren Vale in South Australia – they have also broken totally new ground (literally) by planting a vineyard next to the winery, in Werribee's rich red soil. As far as I know, it's the first time wine grapes have been grown in the district – certainly in modern times.

The last time I was down at Shadowfax, just a few weeks after the mad flurry of vintage activity had subsided, I walked through the quiet barrel hall tasting the young wines with Matt, revelling in the citrus and mineral flavours of Yarra chardonnay, the rich, dense, dark inky tannins of Heathcote shiraz.

And then Matt drew a sample of deep purple liquid from the last barrel and squirted it into my glass. It was the first ever Werribee shiraz, and I was one of the first people from 'outside' to taste it. For an instant, I felt like I was really participating in a moment of history . . . but then the enticing spicy berry smells of the wine grabbed my attention and before I knew it, I'd drunk every last drop.

The question now, then, is: where next? Which region of Victoria – of Australia – will be put under the gastronomic spotlight? Somewhere new and full of promise for the future? Or somewhere old, established and full of the traditions of the past? I for one can't wait to find out.

MAX ALLEN

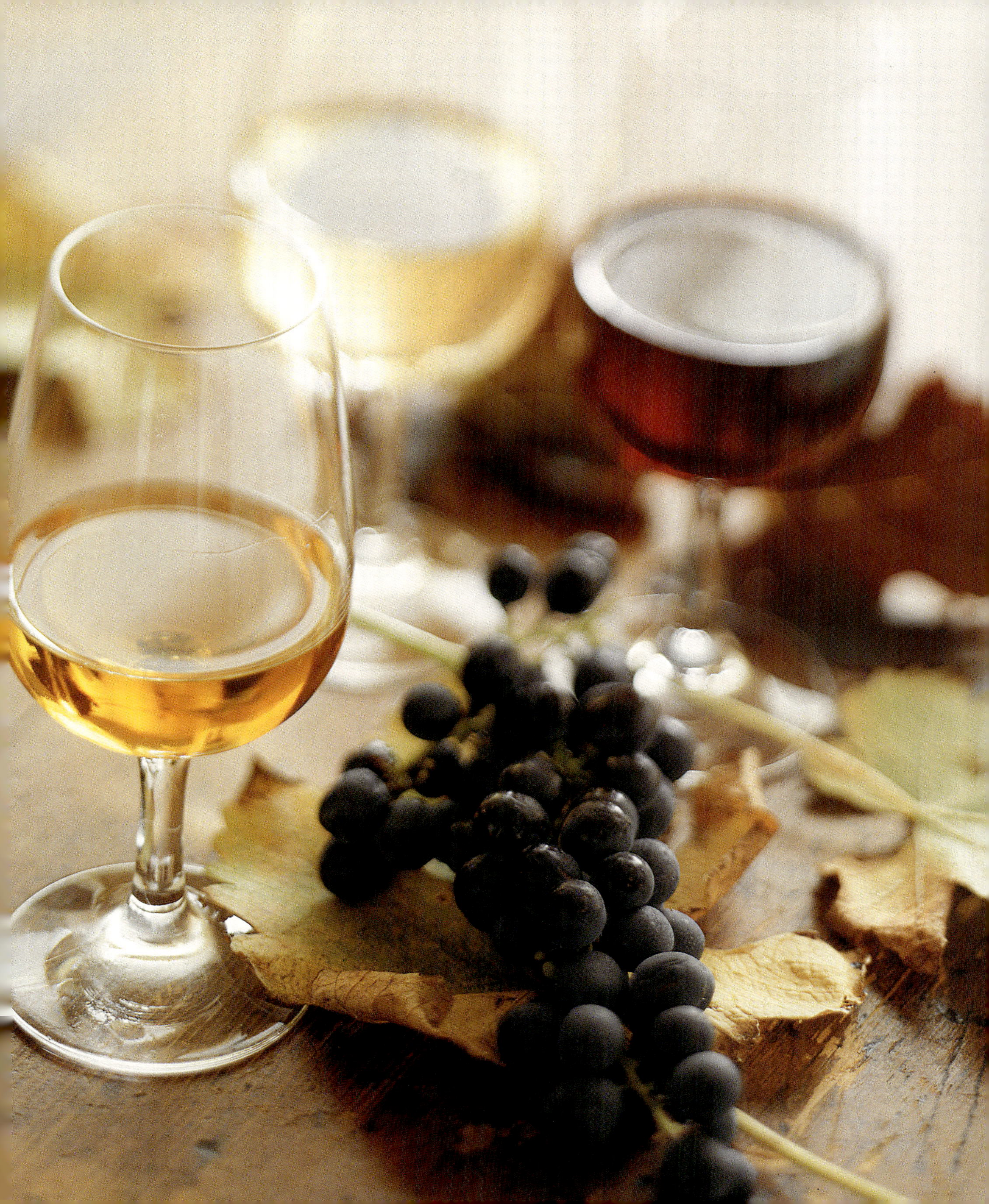

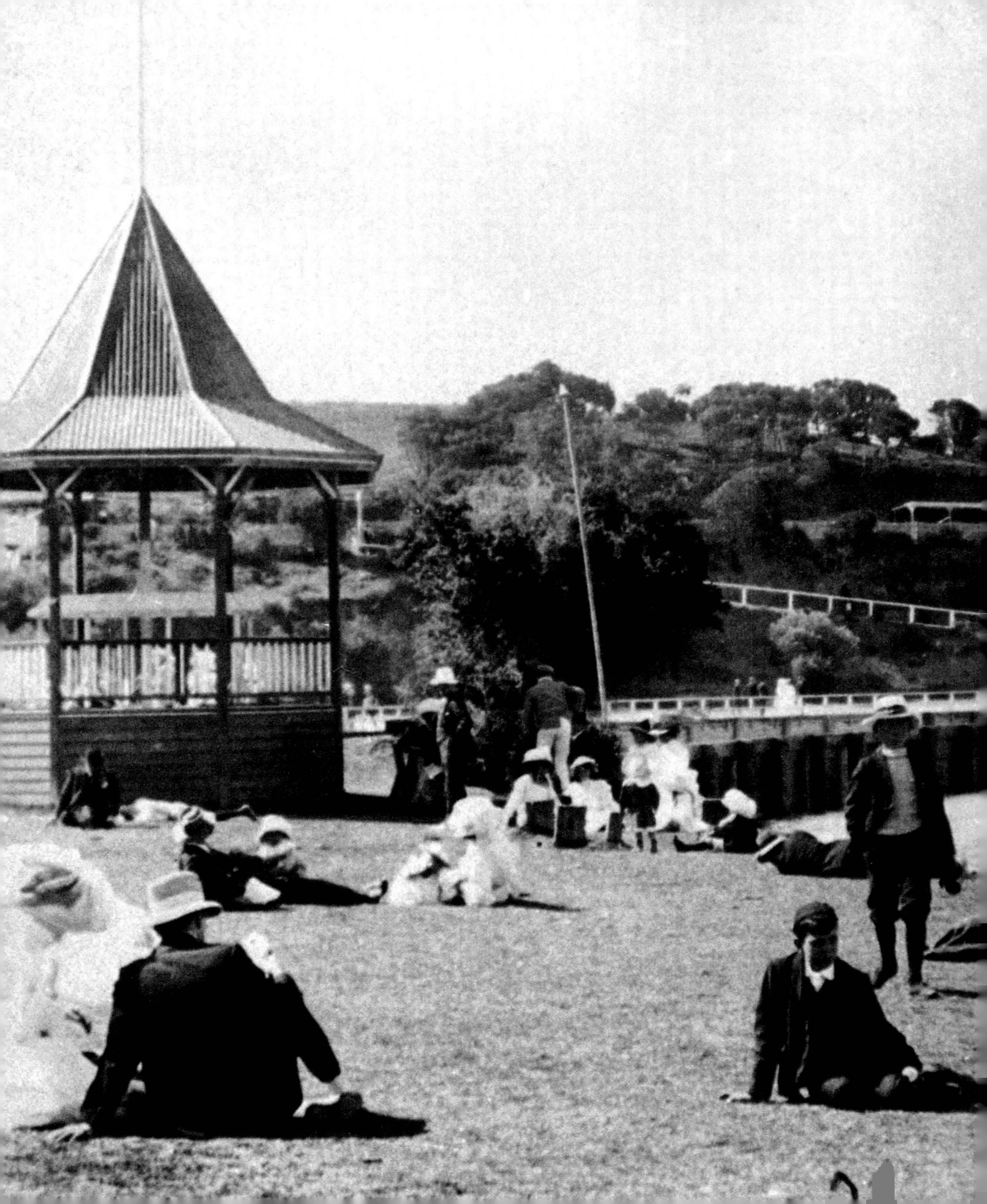

INTRODUCTION

Food and wine. Wine and food. The two go undeniably, inevitably and triumphantly together. Throw travel into the equation and you have an irresistible package. For me, holidaying has always been about much more than the museums and art galleries I visit, the beaches I lie on and the countryside I explore. More often than not, it is the food and wine I consume along the way that add enjoyment, and bring colour and dimension to my memories.

I know that I'm not alone – in recent years Australians have become a nation of food and wine lovers. It's no wonder, then, that these elements have become such an integral part of tourism in this country. Eating and drinking are no longer considered peripheral to our holidays, but have become a crucial part of the whole tourist experience. This in turn has stimulated the growth of an industry in its own right.

Food and wine tourism is considered such an important drawcard nowadays, that most tourist authorities around Australia have established specific food and wine development initiatives. In Victoria, for instance, the last decade or so has seen an explosion in food and wine tourism activities. Within and around Melbourne, there are now endless opportunities for people to discover good things to eat and drink and to explore the very regions where they originate.

Another sign of this increased interest in 'regionality' can be seen in new ventures such as the very successful Regional Food Trail in the Yarra Valley, and in publications such as *The Food Lover's Guide to the Great Ocean Road*, *The Age Good Food Guide* and *From The Farmgate*, which have sent countless people off in search of culinary adventure around Victoria. And then there are the thirty-plus food and wine festivals held annually around the state to educate and inform hungry citizens. The largest of these, the Melbourne Food and Wine Festival, has become a 'must' in every food-lover's diary.

Which brings us to Melbourne's bays and peninsulas. Most of us are only too well aware that the city itself is a hive of food-related activity; less well known is just how much wonderful food and wine stuff is happening around the bay. I must confess that writing a food and wine lovers' guide to the area was, at first rather a daunting prospect. Geographically it's a lot of land to cover, encompassing two major towns and two big holiday regions. But, as I soon realised, the area is also very close to the city. Every place profiled in this book is within an hour and a half of the CBD, offering endless opportunities for day trips, weekends away or a longer touring holiday. And with the development of a new hourly ferry service between Sorrento and Queenscliff, a round trip is not merely possible, but the very easiest way of getting from one peninsula to the other.

One of the great things about researching this book has been discovering how well loved these regions are, and by so many people. Nearly every Melburnian has holiday memories of one or other of the peninsulas. In my own family, for instance, we have home movies of my mother as a child, paddling in the shallows of the beach at Rosebud. My father's family were from Geelong, so his holidays were spent at

Previous page: View of the front beach and band rotunda at Sorrento, circa 1900.

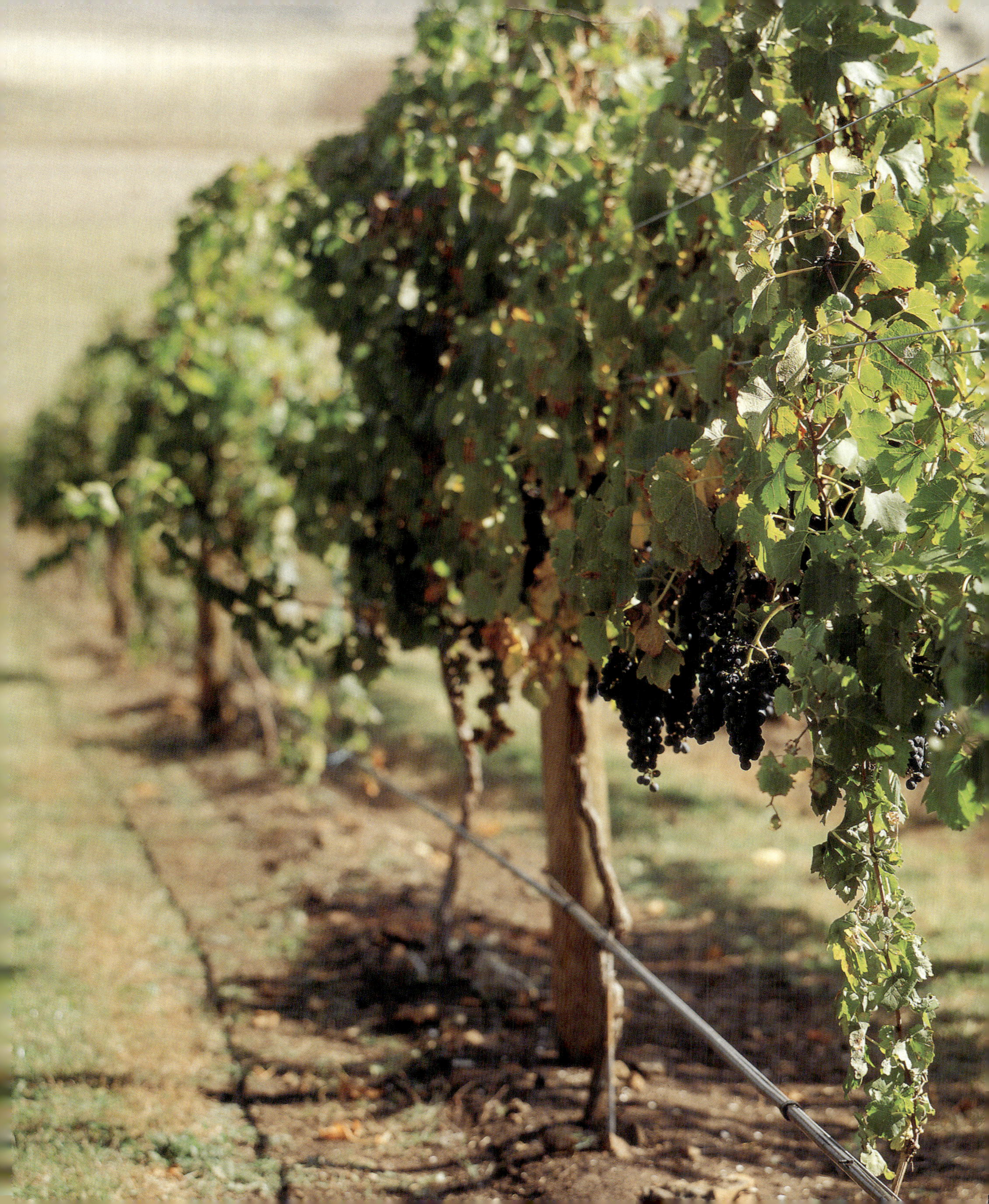

Indented Head and Point Lonsdale. And the memories are still being created; despite the lure of distant pastures, the Mornington and Bellarine peninsulas are still the main holiday destinations for many Melbourne families.

I've loved, too, having the chance to meet so many people who are truly passionate about their lifestyle and produce. Some have been living in their particular part of the world all their lives, and their daily work carries on the tradition established by generations before them. Others are relative newcomers, who have made a conscious choice to leave the hurly-burly of the city and move to the country full-time. But the thing they have in common is an absolute commitment to what they do, and I feel privileged that they have generously shared their stories and passions with me.

Finally, this is not intended to be a comprehensive guide. Rather, it is the result of my own travels and experiences over the years, and reflects my own perceptions and biases. What I have tried to do is paint a picture of the way food and wine traditions are evolving in these parts of the country, and tell the stories of the people and places I've particularly enjoyed visiting. It may not include everything you want to know about food and wine in Melbourne's bays and peninsulas, but I hope it will reveal enough to make you want to begin your own voyages of gastronomic discovery.

I hope that, like me, you will experience the thrill of discovering delicious things in new and sometimes unlikely places; that you will find that small local market nestling under the gum trees in dappled sunlight, or the berry farm at the end of a dusty laneway, or buy spanking fresh fish from a wooden shack on the beach. One thing is certain: around Melbourne's bays and peninsulas, there is always another delight for the tastebuds waiting to be discovered just around the next corner.

Right: The beach at Ocean Grove.

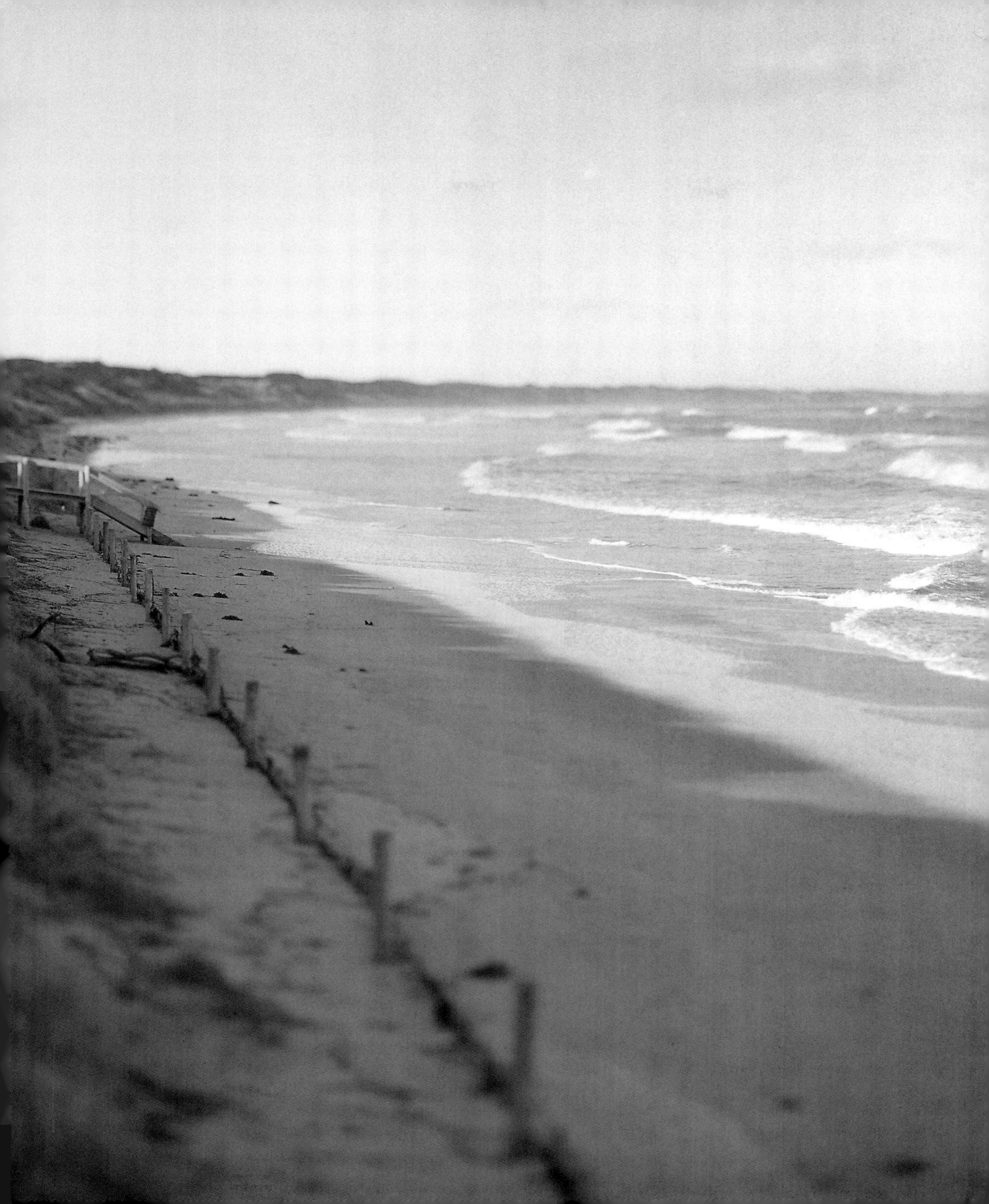

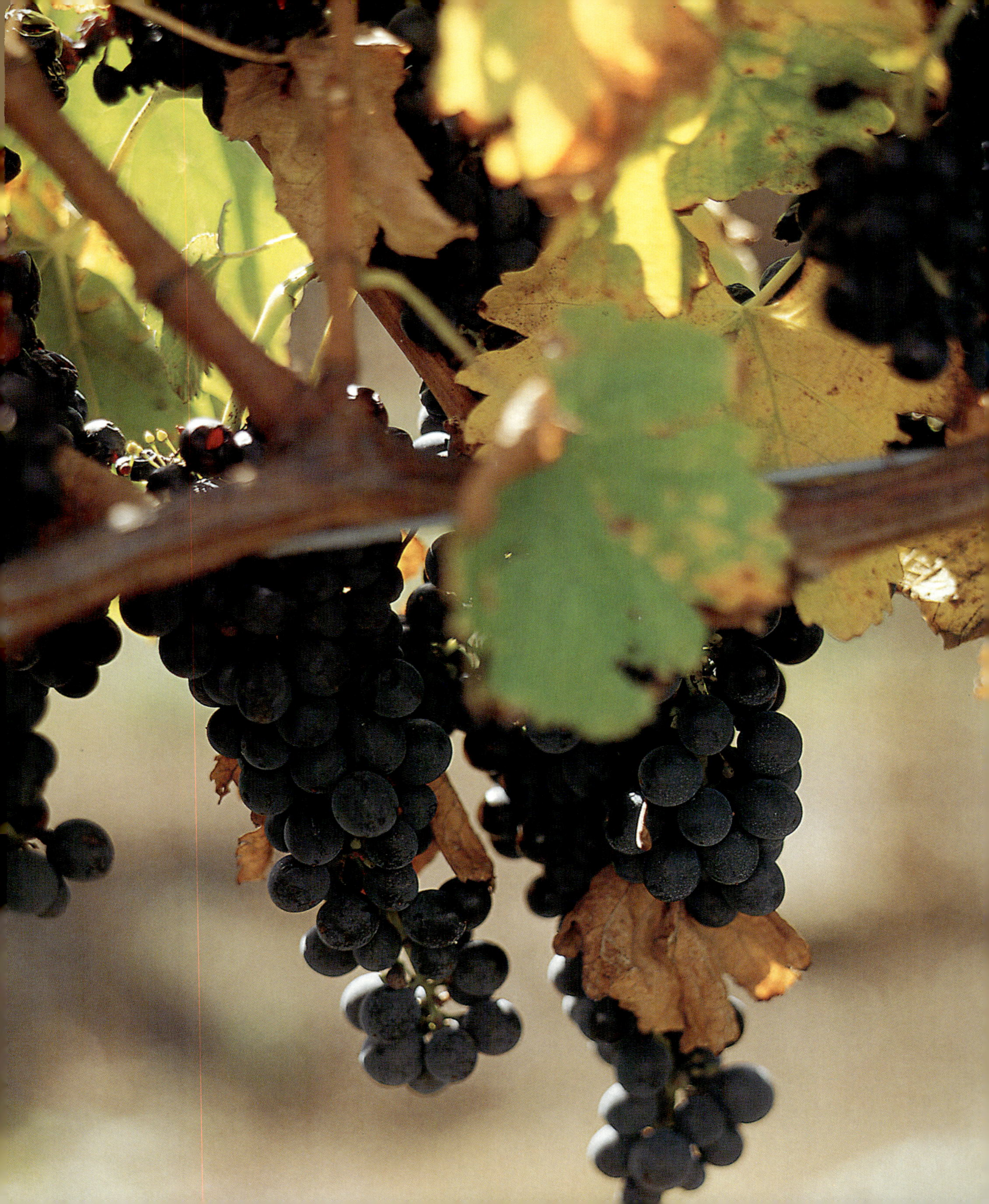

MORNINGTON PENINSULA

It's so easy to be seduced by the Mornington Peninsula, a place that seems to offer everything one might need as an antidote to the fuss and bother of modern city life. Here, the climate is agreeably temperate, the pace of life is slower and more contented, and the countryside is of almost indescribable loveliness.

I have been visiting the Mornington Peninsula for nearly twelve years now: for relaxing long weekends at Somers and Sorrento, and eager trips with friends to explore the region's burgeoning food and wine industry. The fact that you can hop in the car and be at Red Hill within the hour makes the peninsula an enormously attractive option for a weekend away. It is also the holiday destination par excellence of many Melburnians, who every January make the annual pilgrimage to the caravan at Rye, the beach house at Flinders or the mansion with its million-dollar views just outside Portsea, and lose themselves in the sun, surf and sand.

Above: Perrott butcher's shop at Hastings, circa 1900.

The peninsula has always been popular with those who love the beach, surrounded as it is on three sides by the waters of Port Phillip and Western Port bays, and Bass Strait. Long stretches of sandy beach line the crescent-shaped sweep of Port Phillip Bay, which is dotted with little bays and rocky coves. Along the dramatic coastline between Point Nepean and Cape Schanck, cliffs of dark volcanic rock tumble down to meet the wildly pounding surf, and further north, around Hastings, natural wetlands and mangroves offer residence to a vast array of bird and marine life.

Inland, the countryside is just as diverse. Closer to the city, the terrain is warmer, flat and fertile – perfect grazing land for the surprising number of cattle and horse studs that abound. And then there is Red Hill, where the land is indeed rich and red, and the hills and dales provides ideal slopes for vineyards and newer crops of avocado, macadamia nuts or olive trees. At Arthurs Seat, the wooded peaks of the State Park provide a dramatic backdrop to the coastal resort towns, and towards the south of the peninsula are gently rolling hills, where the grass is a vibrant emerald green.

Time after time, while driving around the peninsula to research this book, I found myself thinking 'Wouldn't it be great to live here?'. To escape the city and find a quiet little wooden beach house overlooking Western Port Bay, or a small acreage up in the hills where I could grow my own vegies – organically of course!

I am not the only one to have had such thoughts. The peninsula is full of teachers, doctors and stockbrokers, disillusioned by city life, who have done just that. These are the people who are largely responsible for the frenzy of viticultural activity around the place – today, there are around 200 vineyards and forty-plus wineries on the peninsula. And these, too, are the people responsible for changing the face of the peninsula in many other ways.

Broad-acre farming – for which the land was never really suitable – has all but disappeared in the Mornington Peninsula. Instead, a plethora of small boutique farming businesses have sprung up. This diversity of agricultural activity is nothing new. Indeed, much of the innovative character of the region's agriculture today is due to the legacies of the area's pioneering past: the Mornington Peninsula has a tradition of specialised farming and livestock breeding that stretches back to the middle of the nineteenth century.

It didn't take long for the early European graziers to realise that peninsula land was not well suited to the pastoral dream. Much of the land was forested, which meant it had a low stock-carrying capacity. By the mid-1800s the region's large pastoral runs were subdivided into ever-smaller acreages, and the cattle and sheep farmers decamped to Gippsland and Victoria's Western District. After this brief pastoral era, the region's natural resources became of greater interest. The bark from native forests was stripped for use in tanneries in Van Diemen's Land and Melbourne; she-oak and messmate trees were felled and hauled by bullock trains to the Mornington jetty and sent on to Melbourne by boat; cement works sprang up to burn limestone from the lime quarries around Point Nepean to make mortar for Melbourne's building industry.

By the 1860s, with much of the native forest cleared, the way was opened up for small crop farms of wheat and oats and, more importantly, orchards. The soil and climate, particularly around the Somerville area, were ideal for fruit growing, and the region soon filled up with pioneering orchardists and nurserymen who planted cherry, quince, pear and apple trees. By the early 1900s apples from the area were being shipped all around Australia and as far as England. And by 1930, John Bunning and Sons had the largest fruit tree nursery in the southern hemisphere, and sent their saplings to New Zealand, South America and even India. Hardly surprising, then, that the area around Somerville, until the 1960s, was known as the fruit bowl of Victoria.

With all that water around, one would also expect fishing to have been a key activity on the Mornington Peninsula. In the very early days whalers and sealers were the first Europeans to establish contact with the Bunwurrung Aboriginal people. Many of the coastal resort towns started life as small fishing villages: snapper and couta were fished from Port Phillip Bay; Chinese fishermen settled Flinders in the hunt for crayfish and mussels; and at Hastings, King George whiting, flathead, mullet and shark were caught in Western Port Bay.

With a history of food cultivation as rich and varied as its landscape, it seems only natural that the Mornington Peninsula should have become such a hive of food- and wine-related activity just waiting to be explored.

FOOD SHOPS AND PRODUCERS

Think of agriculture in the Mornington Peninsula, and more likely than not the first thing that springs to mind is grapes. And that's fair enough, given the explosive growth in viticulture in that part over the world over the past five years or so. But the Mornington Peninsula is about much more than winemaking. Its cool, mild climate and variety of soil types provide the perfect foundation, too, for an extraordinarily diverse range of agriculture. Today the new boutique farming and produce businesses are not just a significant part of the region's economy, but are increasingly becoming tourist attractions in their own right.

As you drive around the hilly hinterlands and the lush lower plains you simply can't avoid the evidence of all this rural activity. The countryside spills its wares out onto the roadside, with signs tempting visitors to stop and pick strawberries, or to pop in for fresh farm eggs, just-picked corn and pumpkins. There are cherry growers and cheese makers,

FLINDERS
FARM
TOMATOES
Red Hill
Cheese
Gunnamatta Gold
Handmade on the Mornington Peninsula
Red Hill
Cheese
Portsea Picnic
Handmade on the Mornington Peninsula
ELLISFIELD FARM
MERRICKS
CUMQUAT
MARMALADE

apiarists and avocado farmers, bakers and berry growers. You can find organic salad leaves and tomatoes; and close to the sea there are small shops where fishermen sell the day's catch. All this abundance is also put to excellent use in the many local cafés and restaurants, but the likelihood is that, as you travel around the Mornington Peninsula you won't be able to resist loading up the car with the goodies that you discover.

For me, much of the fun in taking to the road in search of culinary adventure is that I always seem to end up getting lost. The day usually starts well enough: I set off with a map and a plan, but before long my attention will be diverted by a signpost. I take a turn and before I know it I find myself beetling along a windy dirt road lined with native trees and cypresses. And for me that's where the magic lies – in the sunlight filtering through the leaves, and the silence all around (apart from the distant 'boom' of a bird scarer from a nearby winery), and in not knowing quite what I'm going to find just around the next bend.

If you are pushed for time, there are a couple of excellent ways of doing your own, more condensed voyages of discovery. Just about every Saturday you'll find a market somewhere on the peninsula, where local producers and farmers gather to sell their produce. The best known and best attended is the Red Hill Market, but my favourite is the one at Emu Plains, located romantically under the stringybarks next to the racecourse.

Another good place to head for is the Red Hill Cool Stores. For anyone seriously interested in finding out about produce from the Mornington Peninsula, this is the place to start. Run by local artist, Gill Haig, the Red Hill Cool Stores was set up specifically to showcase the art and produce of the area. Gill and her knowledgeable and helpful colleagues are well tuned to what goes on in the region and also sell a wide range of tempting goodies. There are jars of jams and jellies, chutneys and relishes, preserves and honey. The fridge is crammed full of wines, cheeses and homemade pasta sauces; in the freezer are superb ice-creams from Sunny Ridge Strawberry Farm; and dotted around the place are mounds of locally grown avocados and the delicious Flinders tomatoes.

The food culture of the Mornington Peninsula might not be as well developed or organised as in some other areas of Victoria, but things are changing. The newly formed Mornington Peninsula Gourmet has a mission to put the Mornington Peninsula on the foodie trail, and the farmers and producers themselves are passionate about what they do. For now, though, all you really have to do is ask a local like Gill to find out everything you need to know.

Red Hill Muesli

Peter Einsiedel and his wife Jodie lived just down the road from the farm where I was staying, and I drove up to their front door after breakfast one Tuesday morning. Jodie was just off to work (she runs the catering facilities at the nearby Stables Conference Centre), but Peter was ready to sit down and chat. It being a Tuesday, most of the muesli mixing had been done the day before, and he was in for a day of labelling. But he seemed perfectly happy to brew up some coffee and tell me his story instead.

We sat at the table in the spotless living room sipping contentedly. Glancing around, I could see no sign of anything resembling muesli or its making.

'I do it all in the shed at the bottom of the garden,' Peter explained, which startled me somewhat. What about hygiene and food-handling requirements? Later on, when we ambled down the garden to check out the operations side of the business, the 'shed' turned out to be a super-modern, clean and well-organised affair, hardly the ramshackle wooden shack I'd imagined.

Left: A basket of 'goodies' from the Red Hill Cool Stores.

'It's a bit of a problem,' Peter admitted. 'We never know quite what to call it. I do get a bit worried when customers ring up with an order and Jodie tells them I'm in the shed mixing. It just sounds too amateurish and a bit unhygienic. But I don't really like to call it a factory either. That's way too over the top, and besides, I don't want to lose the homemade, small-scale feel of the stuff.'

Homemade and small-scale the operations might be, but Peter clearly runs a tight ship with his muesli. Having started off making 150 to 200 bags a week on his rostered days off from teaching at the local high school, he now works full-time at the business and fills orders for 600 to 800 bags of muesli a week, which keeps him quite busy enough, thank you very much.

'I get new customers ringing up wanting to order my muesli all the time,' he said with a bit of a sigh. 'But to be honest, I'm perfectly happy with things as they are. If I took on any more work I wouldn't be able to manage on my own, and it wouldn't be fun any more. Plus, I'm a bit of a perfectionist. I like to do things my own way, and it's important for me to get my arms into the mixing bowl and feel the balance of the ingredients.' With this last remark I noticed the merest hint of a fanatical gleam in his eye.

Eventually I ask, 'Why muesli?'

Peter chuckled. 'As much as I hate to admit it, the muesli was actually Jodie's idea. I guess we've always been a bit alternative and health conscious, and we always made our own muesli at home,' he said. 'You know how it is. Most of the stuff you buy in the shops is crap, and you'd really be better off eating the box.'

But the real impetus for turning things into a business came seven years ago, when a friend who ran the hugely popular Red Hill Market offered them a stall there. All they had to do was find a product to make and sell. Muesli fitted the bill perfectly, and before long Peter was selling his five varieties at the other markets around the Peninsula and delivering to most of the local B&Bs. Then he started delivering to Melbourne so that desperate holidaymakers could have their favourite breakfast food back in town. Today, top delis such as Phillippa's in Armadale, Pete 'n' Rosie's at the Prahran market and Leo's in Kew all stock Red Hill Muesli.

I'd actually been eating Peter's 'Traditional Muesli' all week as my host had left a bag in the kitchen and told me to try it. 'This is really good stuff,' he had said. And he was right. One of the irritating things I find about muesli is that all the good bits seems to sink to the bottom of the bag, and it's only the lucky last who gets all the yummy pieces of apricot, sultanas and crunchy nuts.

Not so with Peter's muesli. The even distribution is all in the mixing (the 'arms in' approach), and each of the muesli recipes, from 'Traditional' to 'Roasted Almond' or 'Hazelnut', to the chocolate-laden 'Wicked', has been carefully devised over the years to meet the Einsiedel family's strict criteria. Each muesli has a generous balance of top-quality fruit and nuts to oaty ballast. Peter uses Australian produce wherever he can, and naturally, only ever the very best quality.

As I was leaving he gave me a little lecture about sultanas. 'I only ever use five- to six-crown sultanas,' he said. 'They're a work of art, you know – plump and juicy even without milk. Most commercial brands of muesli use inferior sultanas. Your average two-crown sultana really is a very mediocre product.' As I waved goodbye I noticed that the gleam was back in his eye.

Red Hill Cheese

On my first eager investigation of the produce at the Red Hill Cool Stores, I was excited to spot a range of promising looking cheeses piled up next to the white wines in the fridge. I consider myself something of a cheese freak – and many locally made

Right: Cheesemaking at the Red Hill Cheesery.
Bottom left: Trevor Brandon.

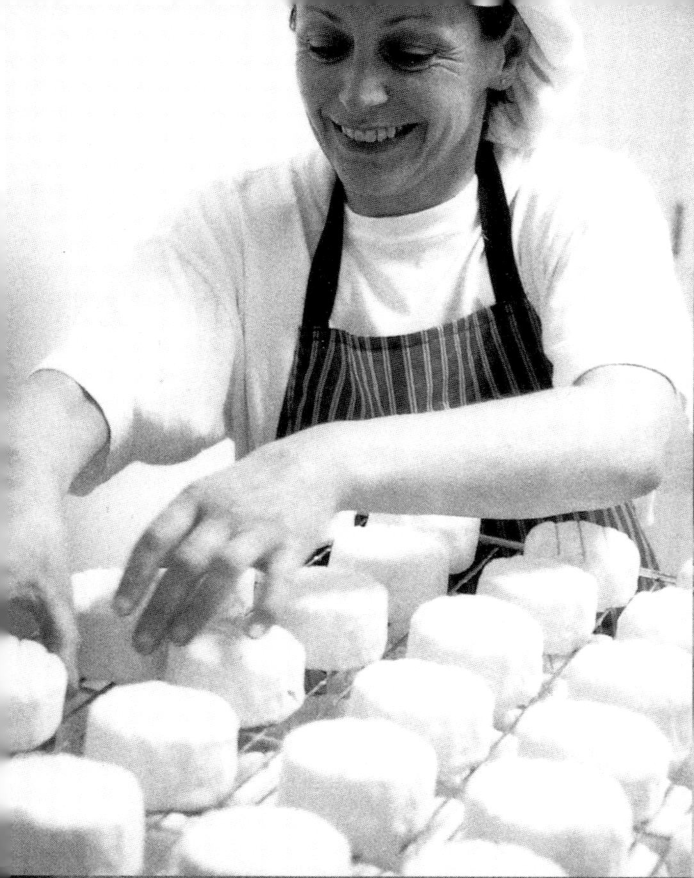
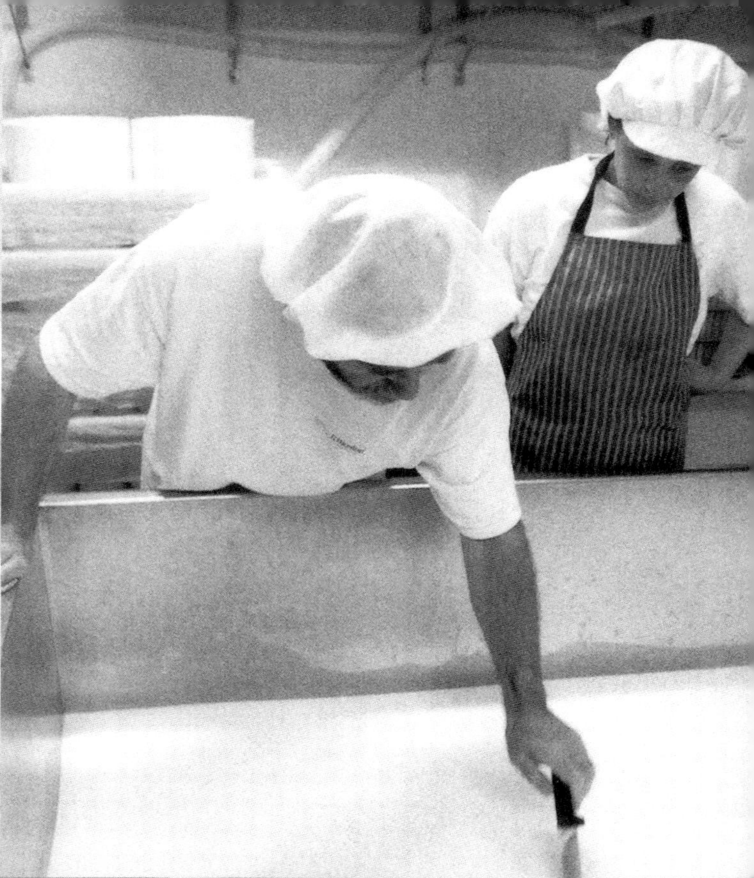
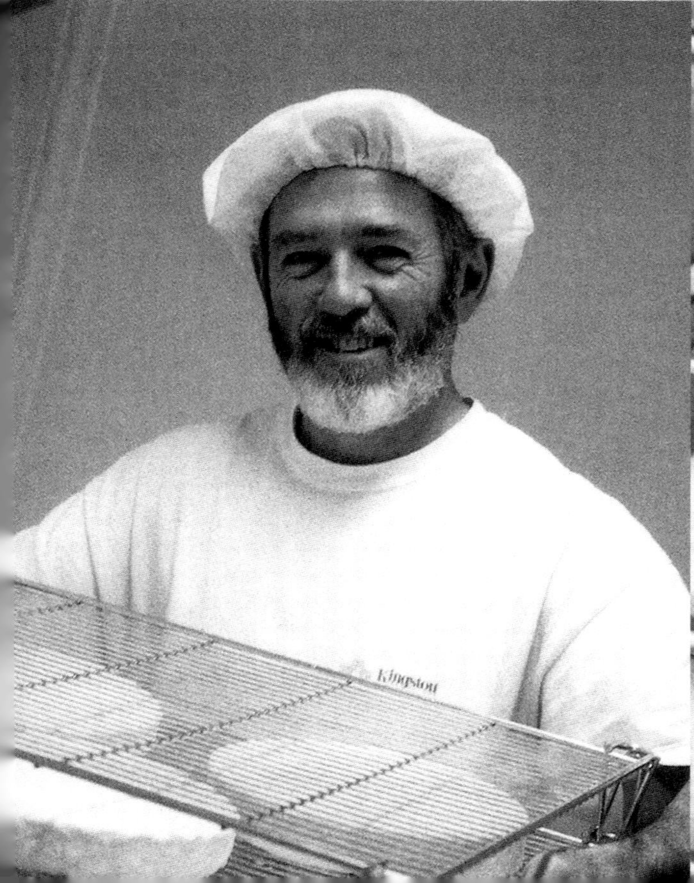
Kingston
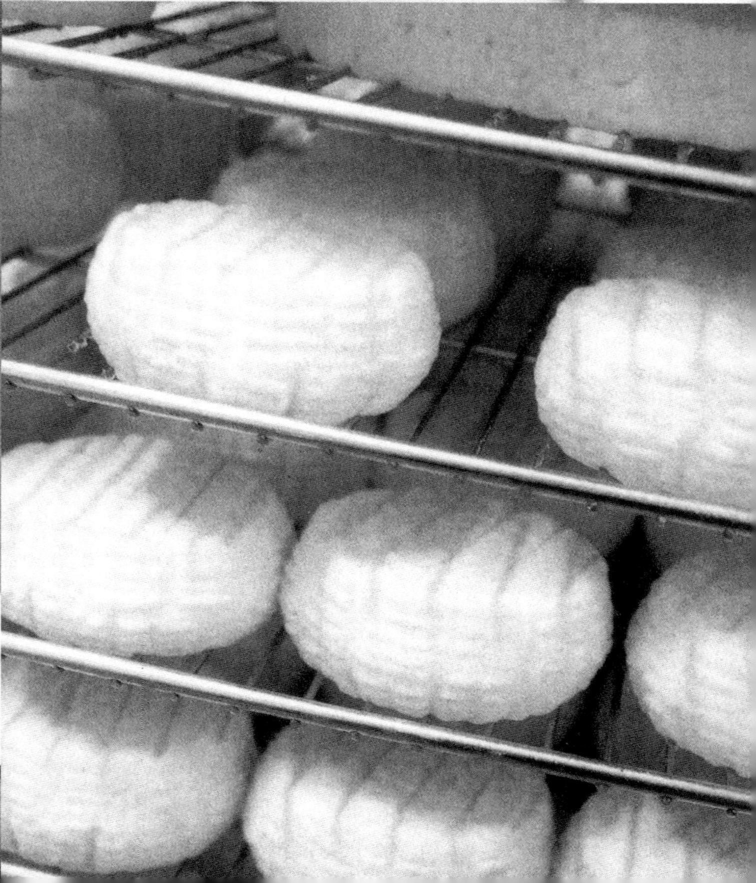

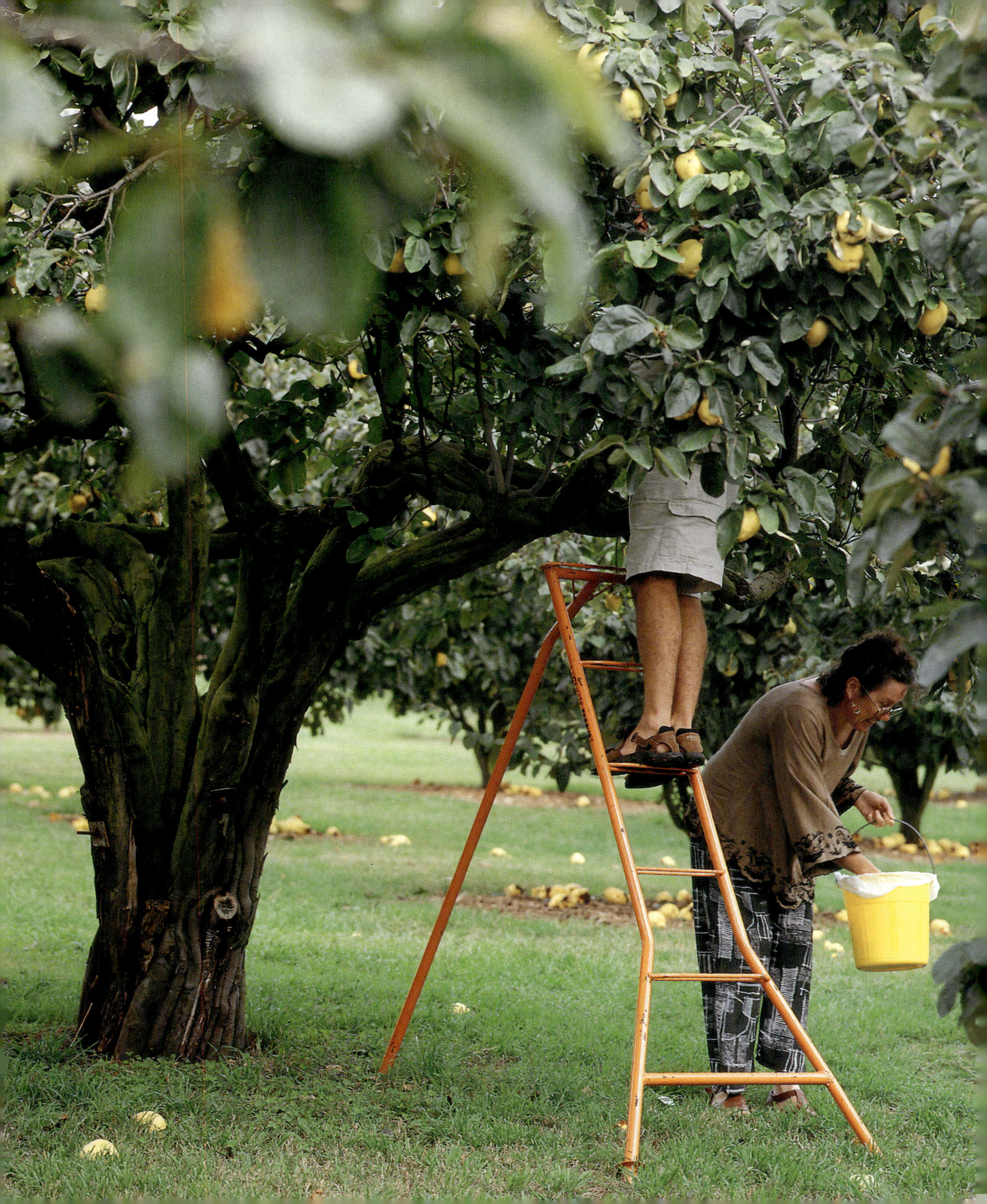

Victorian cheeses are my favourites – but the smart red, black and white Red Hill Cheese label was new to me.

'What's this then?' I asked, peering at the cheeses. With names like Portsea Picnic and Flinders Feta, their provenance was obvious. But who made them? How come I'd never seen them before? And were they any good?

A telephone call and a day later, I set off to visit Jan and Trevor Brandon, who ran the small, modern Red Hill Cheesery next to their bush-surrounded home in a quiet corner of peninsula hill country. As I drove down a dusty dirt road, the sun came out and filtered attractively through the tall gum trees. A middle-aged couple who'd been staying in the Brandons' B&B cottage were just checking out. Jan was seeing them off, so Trevor made me a cuppa and we sat on the sunny veranda to talk about cheese making.

Trevor was a lean grey-haired man, with rosy-apple cheeks and nice crinkly wrinkles around his eyes. He had a slightly serious air about him, and it came as no surprise to learn that he had a scientific background, and a particular interest in food microbiology. He and his wife Jan moved to the peninsula in the late 1960s, initially to Frankston, which even then had something of the feel of a Melbourne suburb, and was somewhat at odds with their self-sufficient, back-to-the-land approach to life. It was when the pumpkins they'd planted in their backyard started to run into the neighbour's garden that they knew that it was time to bite the bullet and move on to a more seriously rural property.

The Brandons had been living in their current home for over twenty years, and had the settled, contented air of people at peace with themselves and their surroundings. They had kept three-quarters of the land as native bush, but also grew oranges, apples, cherries and hazelnuts along organic and environmentally friendly lines.

'We leave the native grasses to run wild between the trees,' said Jan. 'They encourage natural predators, you see. We leave the insect-eating up to the native birds and never use sprays.'

Trevor brought out a cheeseboard and Jan started slicing off pieces for us to taste. We sat there for a while in the warm sunshine, savouring the differences between the two St Brandons: a soft fresh goat's cheese, and an aged version, its stronger, saltier brother. Then we tasted Misty Creek, a soft, creamy camembert-style cheese and Gunnamatta Gold, a washed-rind milk cheese, which was perfectly gooey and appropriately pongy.

I leant over to inspect an interesting knobbly lump of greyish cheese. 'Ah, that's a new one called Pulpit's Rock,' said Trevor. 'Actually it started out as one of our mistakes!' I scooped up a morsel, savouring its sea-air tang, and letting the firm crumbs dissolve slowly on my tongue.

I was struck yet again by the curious dilemma of the cheese maker. On the one hand, it is such a rigorously controlled and scientific process, requiring meticulous attention to cleanliness and hygiene in order to get the fermentation process just right. But on the other hand, the flavour and texture of the resulting cheeses owe as much to the weather and the flora that happen to be floating around in the air at the time as to technique. It all seemed so arbitrary. But in the end it is the encouragement of these endless small variations in the product that puts the small, handmade cheeses into a different class from the sweaty, plastic-wrapped, dreary efforts of large-scale commercial manufacturers.

Something else was bothering me. To make cheese – on any scale – you need milk, and dairy farming on the peninsula has been in a swift decline in recent years, with

Left: Picking quinces at Ellisfield Farm.

the very last local dairy closing at the end of 1998. The Brandons' own land was neither suitable nor large enough for them to become dairy farmers themselves, so it was clear that they would have to look further afield. Finding milk to match their exacting organic and biodynamic standards took them to Gippsland for their cows' milk, and even further for the goats' milk. It meant a six-hour round trip every week to fill up their mini-tanker and drive back to the peace and quiet of Red Hill. Talk about dedication to their craft. What started as a simple weekend hobby for Trevor had over the years become an all-consuming passion, taking over first their kitchen and eventually their entire lives.

Once he realised that the cheeses he was making really were good, Trevor started to share them with friends. 'You know how it is. You get invited over to dinner and need to take something along.'

So, when he retired from teaching a couple of years ago, they decided to go full-steam ahead. They built a carefully planned small cheesery next door to the house, and serious men in white coats came over to check that it met all the appropriate food-making standards. I peered in through the windows at vast stainless steel vats, spotless white-tiled floors, and steel racks stacked with cheeses at varying degrees of maturity. There was something reassuringly orderly about everything.

The Red Hill Cheese company had the feel of a business still in its infancy, and I learnt that Trevor had only been making his cheeses commercially for just over a year, and had restricted his output to local restaurants and the Red Hill Market (which explained why I hadn't seen it before). But even in that short time the cheeses had met with outstanding success.

'We seem to have another restaurant ringing us every week asking for our cheese,' said Trevor proudly. And lots of local delis and smart city shops have been badgering them for the product too. But the Brandons are not to be rushed. 'We're really still feeling our way a bit. We're just not making enough to be expanding too fast, so they'll just have to wait.'

I was relieved to learn that they were beginning to explore the possibility of mail-order for their cheeses, which might go some way to filling demand from city folk. I popped into the tasting room before I left and stocked up on a round of my favourite Portsea Picnic – 'Perfect for picnics with a peninsula pinot or chardonnay. Won't ooze in the picnic basket!' The label helpfully informed me that this particular piece would be at its peak in a fortnight's time. Now, the only challenge would be to see if I could wait that long . . .

Ellisfield Farm

All around the Mornington Peninsula are small farms and market gardens selling their wares by the roadside, from farm shops and at U-Picks. On the drive down from Melbourne you can buy free-range farm eggs, local honey, fresh herbs, salad leaves, organically grown vegetables and orchards of fruit. And in the summer months you can gorge yourself on blueberries, strawberries, raspberries and cherries.

The countryside is deliciously rich and fertile and was known for many years as the fruit bowl of Victoria. But the crops being grown today are not what they used to be. Apples, pears, cherries and other stone fruit were once the economic mainstay of the region, but today, many of the old fruit orchards have disappeared, and in their place a brave new world of grape growing has sprung up.

But those people who have stuck to the traditional crops are finding that they can

Right: Barry and Liz Pontifex.

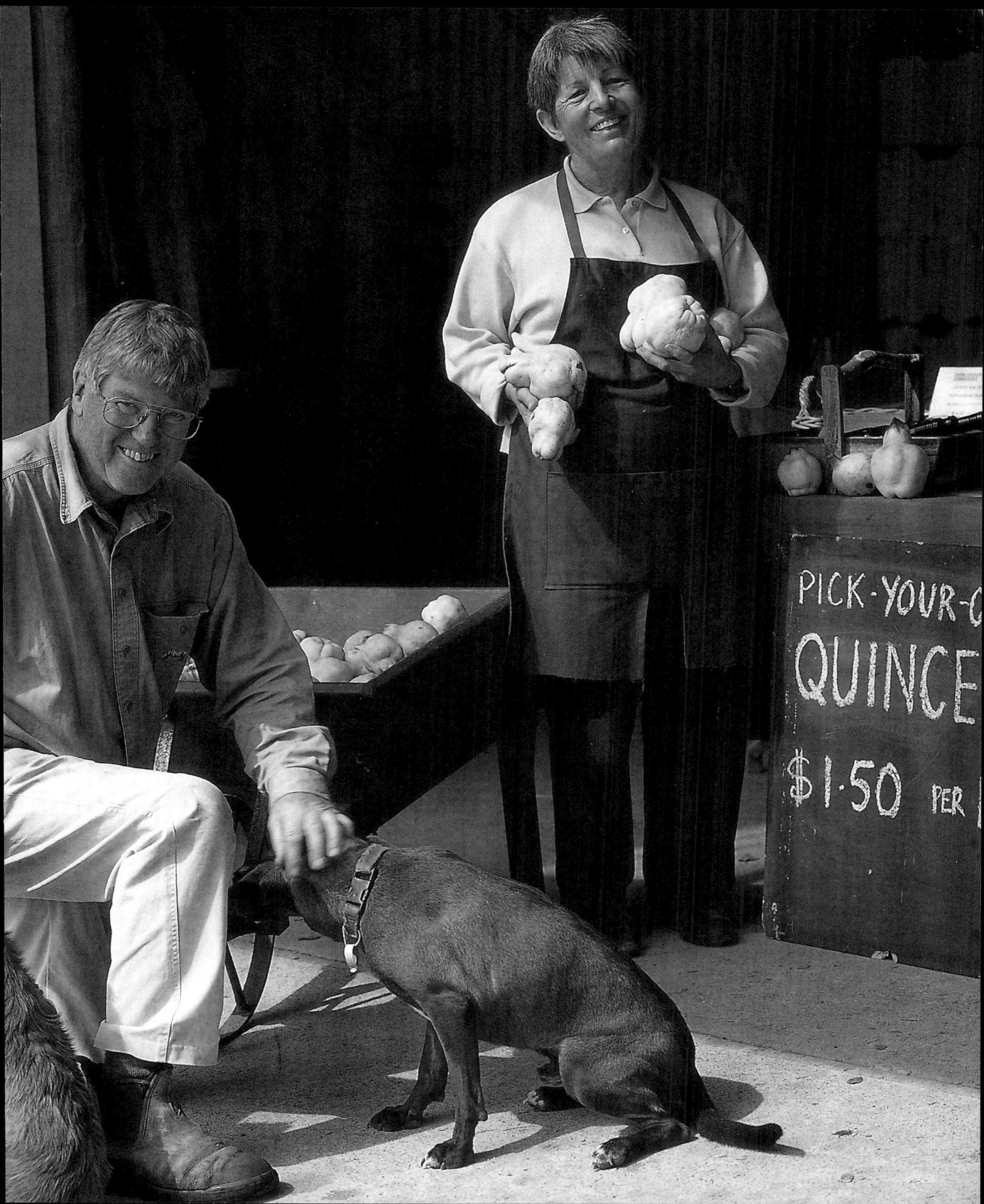
PICK-YOUR-
QUINCE
$1·50 PER

barely keep up with demand. One of my very favourite places on the peninsula is Ellisfield Farm, which is owned and run by Barry and Liz Pontifex. They moved to the region twelve years ago when the kids left home.

'We thought about retiring,' said Barry, 'but ended up buying a working farm instead!'

When they took it over, Ellisfield Farm had a small orchard of productive cherry and quince trees, but the main business was field-grown native flowers. The Pontifexes dutifully carried on with the protea business for a few years, but soon realised that it was the pick-your-own cherry business that offered the greatest potential.

At first, Italian families from Dromana, Mornington and Mount Eliza would come to pick the farm's sweet cherries. These were people who just kept on turning up, year after year, as regular as clockwork! But then they noticed another group of people appearing. It started one weekend four or five years ago, when a Polish lady turned up to pick the sour black morello cherries. The following weekend the cars kept rolling up, more and more of them. The word had spread like wildfire through the Polish community, and soon other Eastern Europeans – Russians, Czechoslovakians, Hungarians, Croatians – started beating a path to their farm gate. 'One weekend, over a thousand people turned up,' said Barry. 'We nearly had a fit!'

Ellisfield Farm is about more that morello cherries, though, and it is far from being a hobby farm. Barry and Liz are very serious when it comes to their business, and are constantly developing new and different horticultural methods and plant crops to take the best advantage of the farm's rich red volcanic soil and its favourable north-facing slope. As well as the cherries, Barry and Liz also sell quinces (which sell like hot cakes in autumn), and they are experimenting with damson plums, French prunes, chestnut trees, avocados, wheat and barley grass and gooseberries – all boutique crops. And, if that wasn't enough, they also run a thriving B&B business.

Over the past five years or so, the Pontifexes have expanded the small original orchard of 150-odd morello cherry trees to well over 2000, and these make up around half of the pick-your-own fruit business. Barry and Liz can't keep up with the demand for their sour cherries. Local restaurants are clamouring for them – Sasha Esipoff, the Russian chef at nearby Poffs', Herman Schneider from Arthur's Seat Restaurant, and Jill McIntyre from Jill's at Moorooduc Estate all take whatever they are given. As for the pick-your-owners, they just keep on coming!

Bryant's Organic Vegetables

All around the Mornington Peninsula you find people getting on with the business of growing things, and doing it their own way. And this means, increasingly often, that their produce is pulled from the ground, or plucked from the branch, untainted by pesticide or forced by artificial aids into unnatural perfection – and certainly none of it is genetically modified.

Rosemary and Graham Bryant have been growing vegies this way for the past thirty years or so. Back when they started out nobody really even knew what 'organic' meant. 'Many of our neighbours thought we were a bit odd,' said Rosemary, as she slipped a bunch of pretty pink rhubarb in with a customer's order. 'These days, though, everyone wants organic produce.'

Everyone certainly wanted Rosemary Bryant's organic produce, that was clear. In the half-hour or so that I'd been standing chatting to her, a constant stream of cars had made their way down the driveway to the small farm shop, and by the door a

Quince and Almond Tart
ELLISFIELD FARM

Preheat the oven to 200°C.

To make the pastry, put the sugar, butter, flour and salt into a food processor and pulse until the mixture resembles breadcrumbs. Add the egg and egg yolk and around a tablespoon of iced water (or enough to form a paste). Knead lightly and roll into a ball. Flatten slightly and wrap in cling film and refrigerate for 30 minutes.

Butter and flour a 25-cm loose-bottomed flan tin. Roll the pastry out on a lightly floured surface. Line the tin with the pastry and prick all over with a fork. Refrigerate for a further 20 minutes. Bake blind, lined with paper and dried beans, for around 10 minutes, until the crust is set. Carefully remove the paper and beans and cook for another 5–10 minutes until golden. Remove from the oven and allow to cool.

To prepare the filling, peel, core and cut the quinces into quarters. Save the peelings and the cores and wrap these in a piece of muslin. Put the sugar and water into a saucepan and warm until the sugar has dissolved. Add the quince pieces with the muslin-wrapped cores and the lemon slices and cook gently for at least 4 hours (or overnight if you can). Let the quinces cool in the syrup, then drain the fruit on paper towels. Discard the peel and cores.

When ready to bake the tart, preheat the oven to 180°C.

Cut the quince quarters in half and arrange on the tart base. Beat the eggs with the additional 1/2 cup sugar, and when thick, mix in the flour and almond meal. Melt the butter until dark golden in colour and mix into the eggs, stirring well. Fold through the almonds and pour over the fruit in the tart shell. Bake for 25 minutes. Serve warm with pouring cream.

Serves 8–10

INGREDIENTS

PASTRY

2 TEASPOONS ICING SUGAR

125 G CHILLED BUTTER, DICED

250 G PLAIN FLOUR

A PINCH OF SALT

1 EGG

1 EGG YOLK

FILLING

3 QUINCES

2 CUPS SUGAR

500 ML WATER

2 SLICES LEMON

2 EGGS

AN ADDITIONAL 1/2 CUP SUGAR

1 TABLESPOON PLAIN FLOUR

1 TABLESPOON ALMOND MEAL

125 G BUTTER

2 TABLESPOONS SLIVERED ALMONDS, TOASTED UNTIL GOLDEN

Heirloom Cherry Tomato and Basil Tart

HARVEST CAFÉ AT HERONSWOOD

INGREDIENTS

HOMEGROWN TOMATOES SUCH AS PINK CHERRY, SUNDROP, YELLOW PEAR AND TOMMY TOE ARE BEST FOR THIS RECIPE. SEED PACKETS ARE AVAILABLE FROM DIGGERS SEED COMPANY.

PASTRY

150 G PLAIN FLOUR
A PINCH OF SALT
75 G UNSALTED BUTTER, DICED
50 G PARMESAN, GRATED
1 EGG YOLK
2 TABLESPOONS CHILLED WATER

FILLING

250 G FETTA
250 G BLACK OLIVES, PITTED AND CHOPPED
3 HEAPED TABLESPOONS ROUGHLY TORN FRESH BASIL LEAVES
500 G MIXED HEIRLOOM CHERRY TOMATOES

To make the pastry, place the flour, salt and butter in a mixing bowl and rub together with your fingers until the mixture resembles breadcrumbs. Stir in the parmesan and add the egg yolk and water. Mix to form a dough, then turn onto a lightly floured bench. Pat into a round, then wrap in cling film and refrigerate for at least 15 minutes.

Butter and flour a 28-cm loose-bottomed flan tin. Roll the pastry out on a lightly floured surface. Line the tin with the pastry and prick all over with a fork. Refrigerate for a further 20 minutes.

Line the pastry with baking paper and fill with beans, rice or pastry weights. Bake the pastry for 10–15 minutes, remove the paper and beans and cook for another 5–10 minutes until golden. Remove from the oven and allow to cool slightly. Lower the oven to 180°C.

To make the filling, crumble the fetta into a mixing bowl and mash with the olives and basil. Spread the filling over the pastry shell. Pile the tomatoes on top and bake for 15 minutes, until the skins have burst and the tomatoes are browned. Remove from the oven and allow to sit for about 10 minutes before serving. This tart is delicious with a wild rocket and toasted pine nut salad.

Right: Historic Heronswood House.

mountain of neatly labelled shopping bags was waiting to be collected.

Around the cool airy shed, produce was neatly displayed in bins around the walls. There was a great pile of pumpkins, sweetcorn in their silken cocoons, the last of the season's beans and cucumbers, and plump bunches of beautiful long carrots. Rosemary slid open the coolroom door to reveal a huge rustling wall of leafy greenery. I identified spinach and silverbeet, vibrant peppery rocket, frilly lettuces and a mountain of exotic Chinese greens such as tatsoi, wong nga bok, Chinese cabbage and broccoli.

Through the window across the farmyard I spied a couple of pigs and a wriggling, squirming mass of little piglets. 'They're our waste-management system,' smiled Rosemary. 'And we use ducks as pest control. They eat up all the slugs and beetles.'

There's often a perception that organic fruit and vegetables stack up really poorly appearance-wise, compared with the unnaturally large, bright and shiny stuff you find in supermarkets. But everything here looked fabulous. 'Everything comes straight out of the ground into the shop,' said Rosemary. 'We clean it up and then it's there for the customers. And of course, we only sell what is in season at the time. In a way you have to take pot luck, because when we run out, we run out!'

You say Tomato, I say Tommy Toe

I have a confession to make. I've never really like tomatoes that much. The ones I've prodded and picked at in my salad bowl over the years have always seemed furry, soggy and bland-tasting, and hardly worth the effort. But since visiting the historic Heronswood property just outside Dromana, I've changed my tune. Heronswood is owned by Clive and Penny Blazey and is home to Diggers Seeds, which specialises in

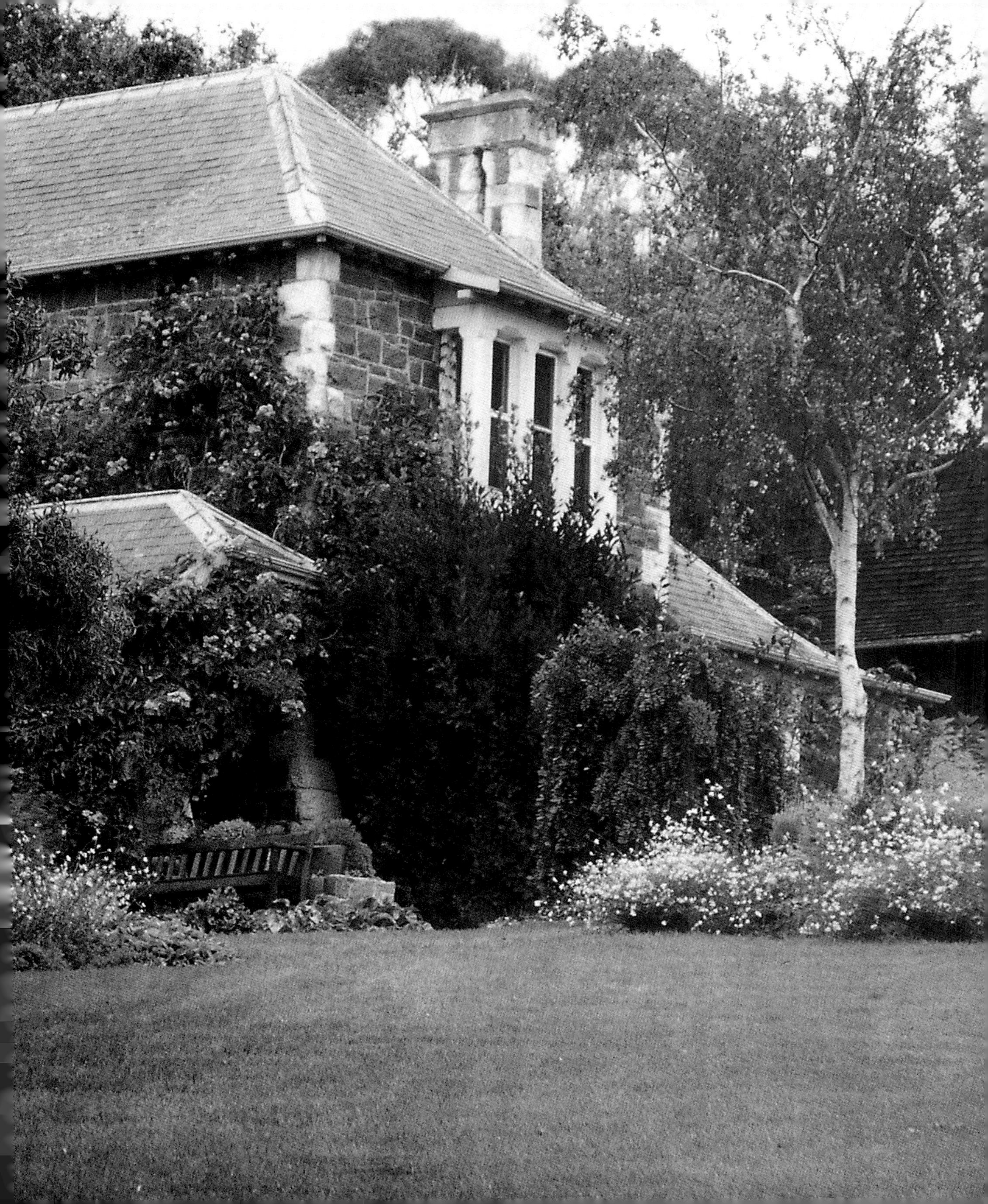

hard-to-find heirloom varieties of all kinds of vegetables and plants. It was there, one fine sunny day in late February, that I experienced my tomato epiphany.

The drive down from Arthur's Seat, as usual, made me catch my breath. At each turn of the road I was distracted by glimpses of a sparkling blue sea, so it was with a sigh of relief that I pulled up safe and sound outside lovely Heronswood house. Lisa Kinsella, who manages Diggers Seeds, was there to show me around the beautiful grounds, pointing out trees and plants of interest as we passed. I was particularly impressed by the miniature vegetable garden, where I learnt that I could feed myself for a year (with 244 kg of vegetables) from one 10-metre by 1-metre garden plot. This was good stuff – I could do this in my own pocket-handkerchief-sized inner-city garden!

And then we reached the tomatoes, ducking under the protective netting to inspect the crops. My first startling discovery was that they were not all uniformly round and red. This mess of higgledy-piggledy fruit was like nothing I'd seen before: a bewildering range of colours from orange, yellow, green and white as well as shades of pink and dark purple. Some even came striped. Just as wondrous was the range of shapes and sizes – from tiny and currant-like to great monsters resembling beefhearts, onions and capsicums.

Lisa picked off a couple of tiny Broad Ripple Yellow Currants and handed them to me. 'These are the smarties of the tomato world,' she said. I popped them in my mouth and squished them, creating little explosions of flavour.

As we wandered down the rows, she reeled off more names. 'These are Tigerellas,' she said, pointing out an apricot-sized, yellow-striped fruit. 'These are Amish Paste, from America. They're one of the most delicious for salads and cooking. And these are Tommy Toe – they consistently rate sweetest and best flavoured in our taste tests.' Other beauties were Black Russians, Green Zebra, Beams Yellow Pear and the wonderfully named Mortgage Lifter.

Back at the delightful Harvest Café we sat and enjoyed a coffee. I was interested to learn that nearly all the produce for the colourful Mediterranean-style dishes came from the Heronswood gardens and from other organic growers close by. Besides cooking food for the café, chef, Sharnell Lawrence makes a range of herbed oils, vinegars and preserves, and on festival weekends her picnic hampers are all the go.

'Running a completely seasonal menu is really quite a complicated exercise in garden and kitchen management,' said Lisa. But several years of meticulous observation and note taking have led Sharnell and Lisa to develop a workable plan for the café. One of the most popular dishes is the Diggers Harvest Pizza. In winter it might come topped with Jerusalem artichokes, crunchy hazelnuts, gruyère and spinach. In summer it is likely to be smothered with roasted eggplant, capsicum and caramelised onion, with fetta and basil pesto. The cake selection looked pretty good, too. I was particularly interested in the old-fashioned lemonade scones. 'It adds a nice sweetness, and the bubbles make for a nice light airy scone,' explained Sharnell.

On my way out I stopped off in the shop to see what I'd need for my miniature veggie garden. An entire room seemed to be devoted to tiny packets of seeds. I was quite taken by the little Shishitou capsicum (a good fryer), and some little orange Turkish eggplant. Other names that caught my eye were lemon cucumber, five-colour silverbeet, sweet chocolate capsicum, Easter egg radish, even sex without strings beans!

That night, back at the farm where I was staying, I made myself a little Tommy Toe

Right: Heirloom produce from Heronswood and the Harvest Café.

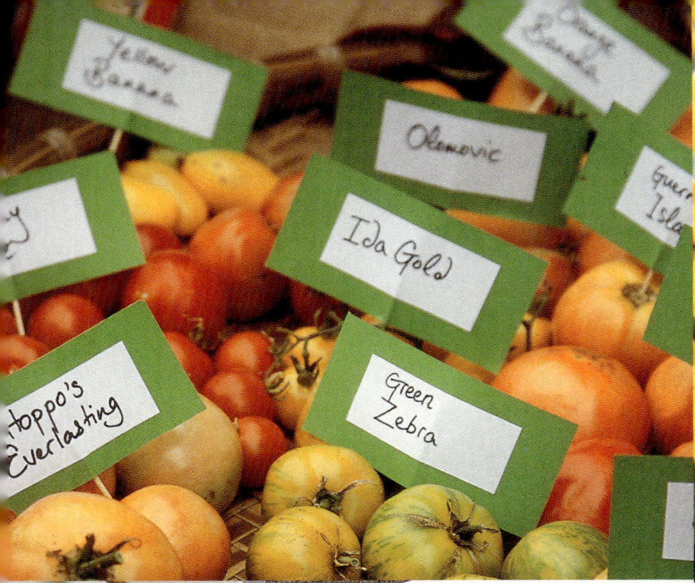
Yellow Banana
Olomovic
Ida Gold
Green Zebra
Everlasting
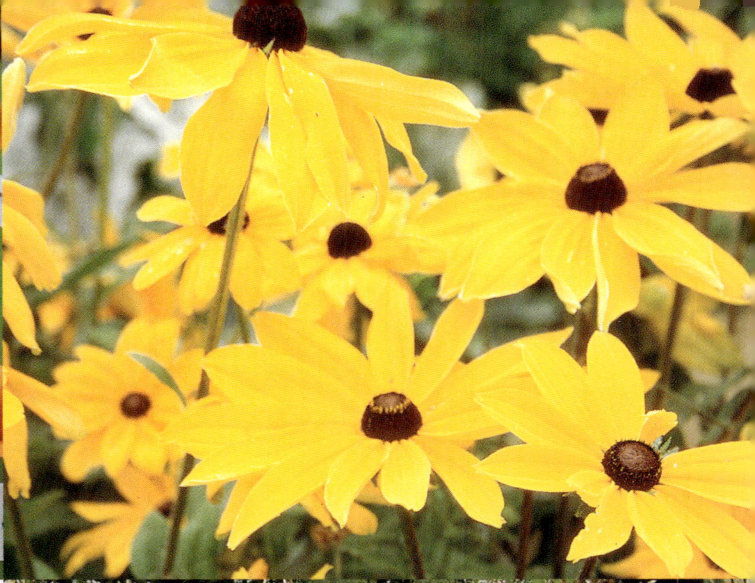
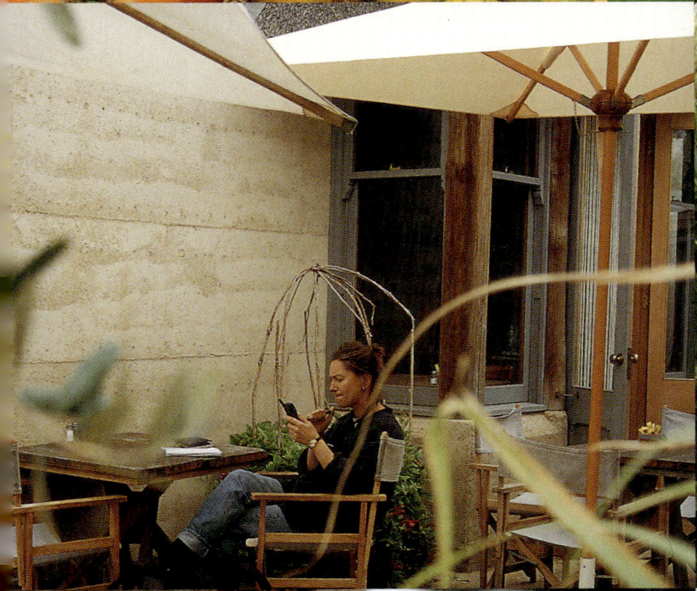
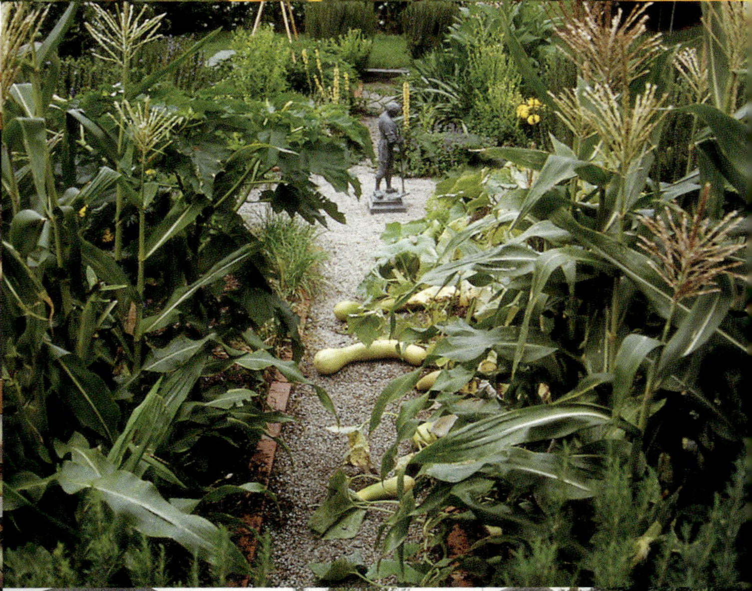
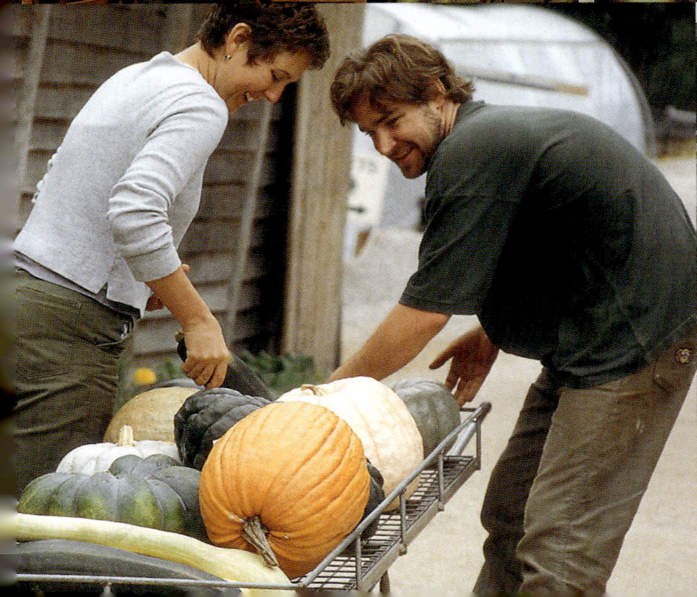
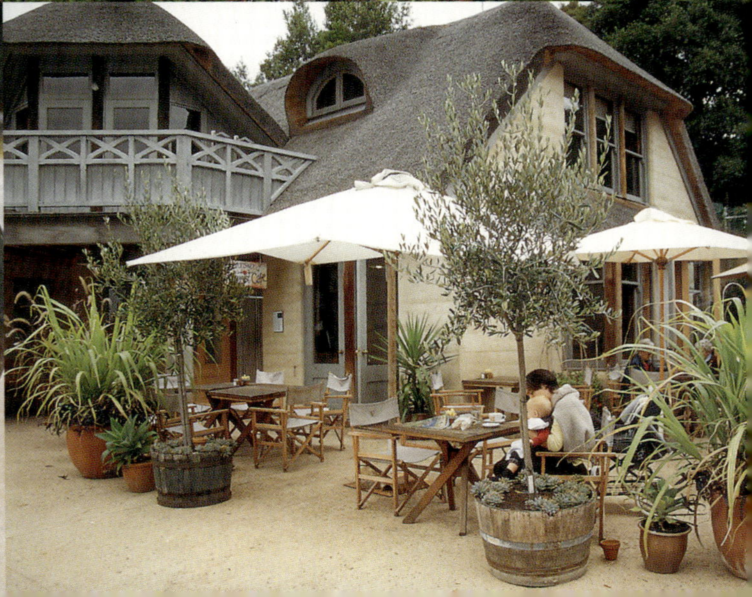

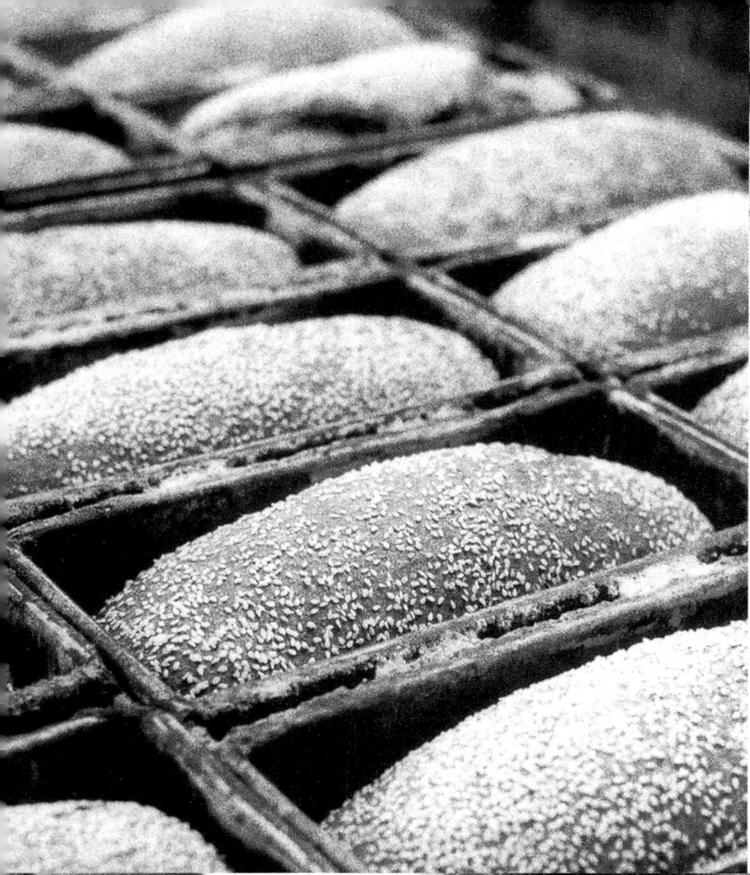
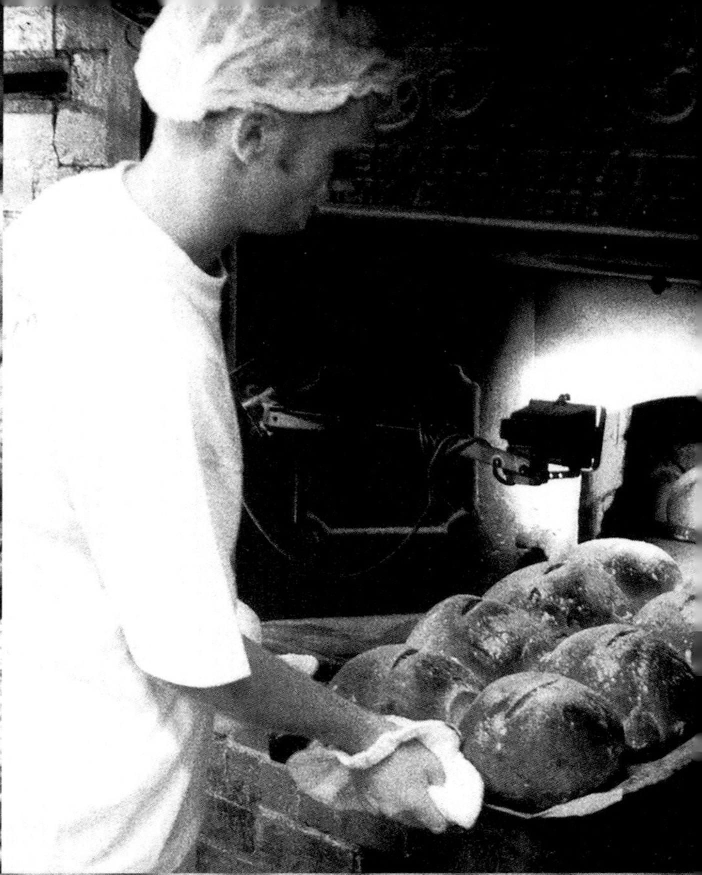
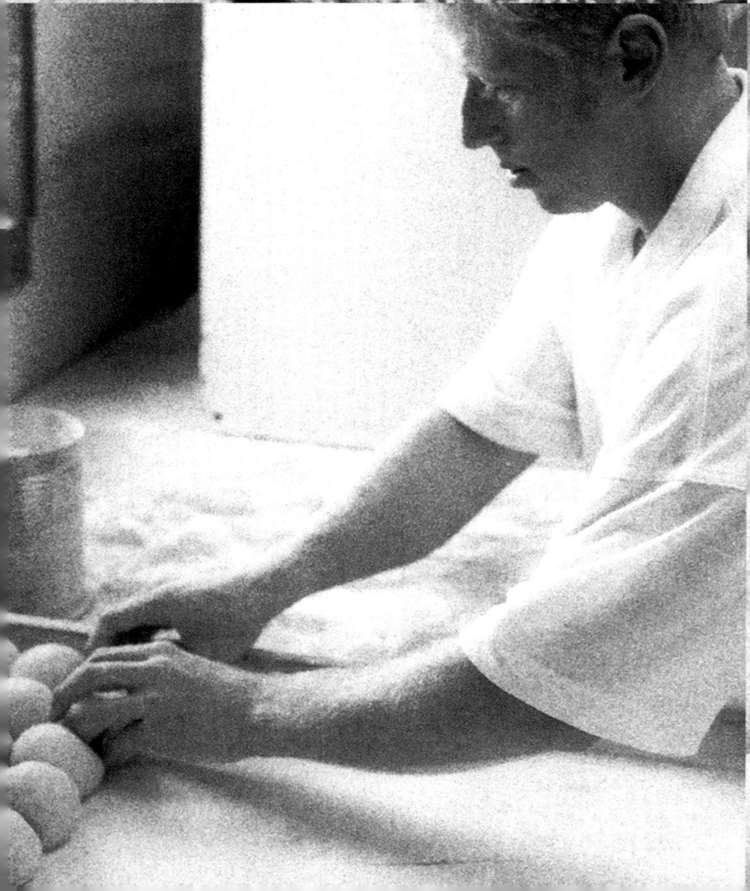
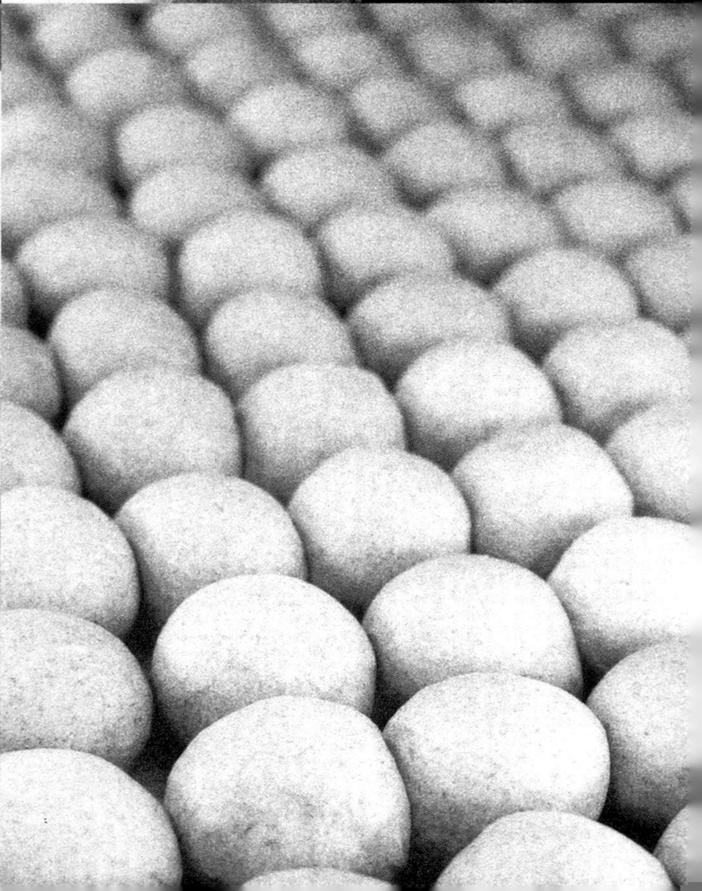

salad. I added some of the intensely fragrant basil growing in the kitchen garden, poured myself a glass of the wonderful chardonnay from neighbouring Paringa Estate and sat on the veranda watching the light fade from the sky. As I savoured the intense sweetness of the tomatoes I could hardly believe that there had ever been a time when I didn't think that these were the best food in the world.

The Fabulous Baker Boys

It seemed as if I'd been sampling the Baker Boys bread all over the Mornington Peninsula, and had developed quite a passion for their ciabatta. Most of the good restaurants in the area serve John's bread, as do the delis. And I soon discovered that I'd eaten Baker Boys bread in several top Melbourne restaurants too.

I found John Mentiplay, one of the Baker Boys, catching up with some orders at his small bread shop in the Rosebud shopping strip. It must be said that the shop is nothing flash – it looks just like any old Aussie bread shop in any suburban shopping precinct. But look a bit more closely at the loaves stacked up behind the counter, and you begin to get a feel that there might be something a bit special about the bread after all.

John Mentiplay is a startlingly young-looking 31 years old, with his Scottish heritage freckled all over his face. His grandfather and father were both bakers, and John and his brother Paul defied their wishes by following in their footsteps, albeit in a slightly less hands-on fashion. (Neither of them actually bakes these days.)

You get the feeling that John has always been a bit of a dynamo. He started up his first bread shop in Brighton ten years ago, to complement the family business in Rosebud. After stints in Italy he discovered ciabatta, and was determined to bring it to Melbourne.

'I don't care what anyone says. I was the first person to bake ciabatta in Melbourne,' said John firmly.

I asked John what made a good loaf. 'Come and see,' he replied, heading off to the kitchen. I trotted after him as he led me past trolleys stacked with oven trays in anticipation of that night's batch, then past giant mixing machines (one full of flour, waiting for its sourdough starter to be added), past what looked like a small mountain of flour sacks ('about half a week's supply'), to a wide, gleaming, five-deck monster of an oven that appeared to fill the entire back wall.

'To bake good bread, you definitely need good quality equipment, and this is the Rolls-Royce of ovens,' John pronounced, eyes sparkling. 'It came from France and cost an arm and a leg, but it's a joy to use.' He opened up one of a bank of glass doors and peered lovingly in.

We walked back past the flour and mixing machines, and John stopped to prise the lid off a plastic bucket. 'Have a whiff of that!' he said. I dutifully stuck my nose into the bucket and a whoosh of beery aromas hit the back of my nostrils. This was the 'sponge' – a bubbling spongy mass of yeast, water and flour that was to be added to the flour to make ciabatta.

The sourdough breads don't use yeast as a raising agent, but a leaven – a naturally fermenting substance that can be anything from potatoes to sultanas. John showed me an attractive-looking oval loaf, with a shiny hard curl of a crust over the top.

'That's our pinot sourdough,' he grinned. 'I made the starter using a bunch of grapes I pinched from the vines over at Lindenderry!'

The raw ingredients are important in a good loaf of bread. 'European bakers would kill for Aussie flour,' John said. I was surprised, but John insisted that it was so. 'Most of the flour in Europe isn't nearly as good as ours. Their

Left: Breadmaking in the wood-fired oven at Flinders.

gluten and protein content is much lower, so the doughs take much longer to mix, and they don't have the flavour.'

John picked up a large loaf of ciabatta. It was the long familiar slipper shape, flattish, with an attractive floury crust. He broke it open and we both peered at the result. It gave off a sweet, nutty bready aroma.

John gave me a loaf to take home with me. I hastily said my goodbyes and hurried to the car. Once safely inside (it wouldn't do to have my greediness spotted!), I pulled the loaf out of its bag and broke off a piece. Yes, it was just the way I liked it – the crust was firm and chewy, and inside, the crumb was olive-oil-moist, yet light, airy and full of the distinctive large holes. I popped the piece in my mouth and savoured the tangy, yeasty flavour. And then, being the sort of person who believes you can never have too much of a good thing, I ate the rest of the loaf on the way home!

Flinders Bread

Although bread has been baked at Flinders since the 1880s, there are a lot more loaves coming out of the original wood-fired oven today. The bread is travelling a lot further afield than it did back then, too; these days you don't have to live on the Mornington Peninsula to recognise the distinctive Flinders Bread logo. Their range of gourmet cottage-style breads are known and loved all around metropolitan Melbourne and as far away as the Bellarine Peninsula on the other side of Port Phillip Bay.

For this, we have to thank the Hawley family, who bought Flinders Bread around five years ago. Before then, the bread was really only known around the Mornington Peninsula – but over time it began to be discovered by holidaymakers, and soon there was a growing demand for the Flinders Bread range up in Melbourne.

Jan and Barry Hawley are actually not bakers at all, but businesspeople who somehow found themselves owning two bakeries. It all began fifteen years ago when they bought the Country Life Bakery, a smallish Melbourne-based bakery specialising in health and dietary breads. Having continued to expand the distribution of this range all around Australia, the Hawleys were thrilled when the opportunity to buy Flinders Bread presented itself.

Since taking over Flinders Bread, the Hawleys have roughly tripled production, so that you and I can enjoy it up in Melbourne, and elsewhere around Victoria. Sadly, not all the bread can be baked in the original oven down at Flinders. These days around half of the range – the higher-volume, straightforward white, wholemeal and multigrain bread – is made in the smart new modern bakery in Dandenong. But gourmet breads, like the tomato and black olive bread, dark rye, walnut and kibble wheat, and the famous wholemeal fruit cob are still baked in the original wood-fired oven.

Last year, the family added another string to their bow, when they took over the popular Main Street Deli in Mornington. This place has a constant stream of customers for its excellent Mediterranean-style food. It has a terrific range of pies, pasties and quiches, and stocks my favourite Kez's cookies. As well as doing great business in take-home tucker, it's also a great place to stop for coffee and cake, or for a lunchtime sandwich or pie. Naturally, it also sells the full range of Flinders breads.

Houghton's Fine Foods

Many people had told me about Houghton's Fine Foods, so I parked the car and wandered down Mornington Main Street one busy Wednesday morning to investigate. It was market day, and the streets were lined

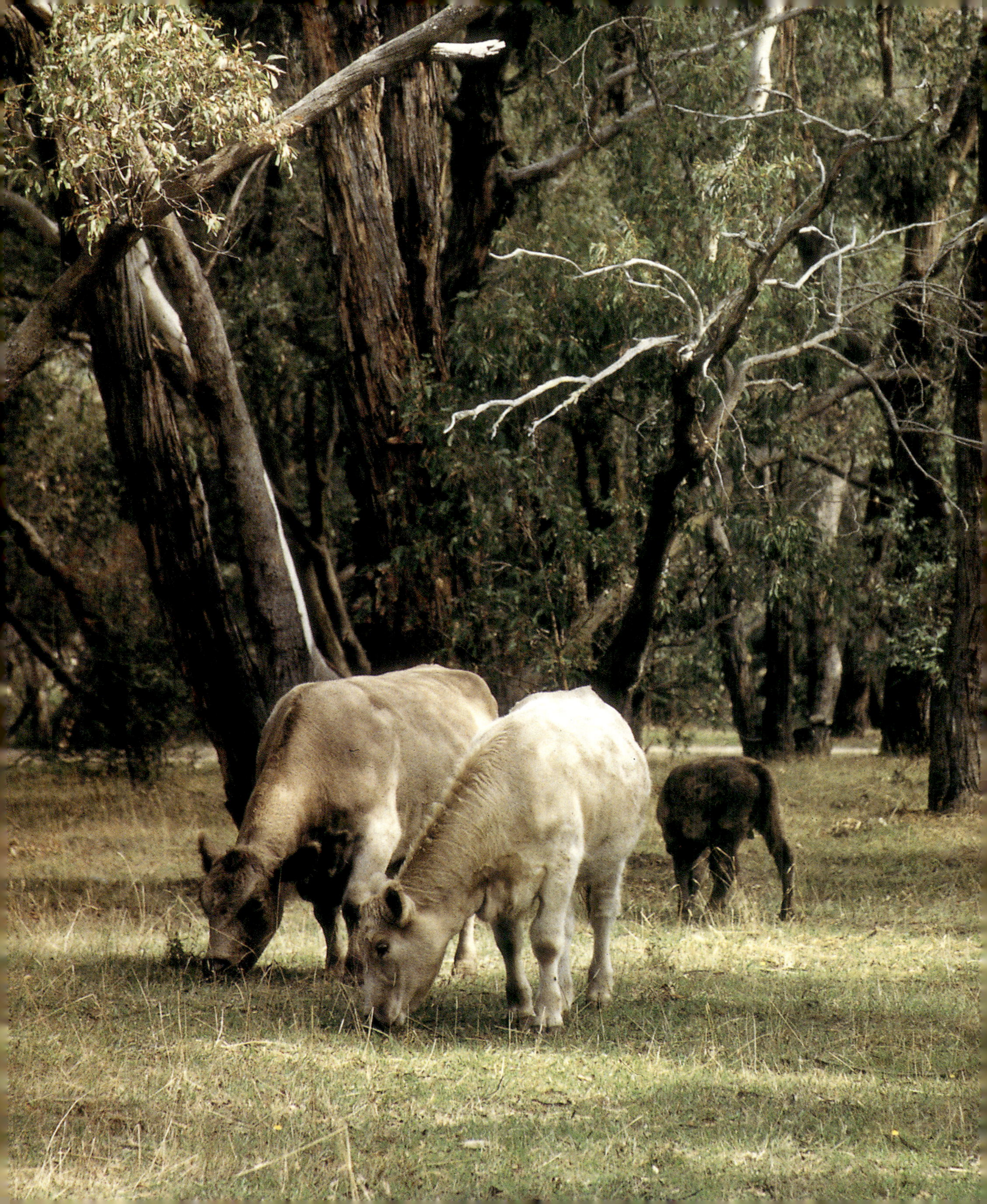

with stalls selling everything from scented candles and women's underwear to free-range eggs. It was one of those unexpectedly hot autumn days, and the good folk of Mornington were out in force to make the most of it.

Houghton's Fine Foods was a lovely surprise. Tucked just off the main street, it was one of those classy-looking modern delis, clean and bright and full of all kinds of ultra-desirable and beautifully packaged goodies. There was a display of brightly coloured cookware in one corner, a trendy cookbook lay casually open on the central table, and exquisitely arranged bottles of olive oils, vinegars and all kinds of homemade pickles, preserves and jams crowded the shelves.

But behind the counter was where things really started looking interesting. There was the usual range of fine-looking cold meats, pâtés and cheeses, but Houghton's has become famous for its fantastic range of take-home foods, and I could well believe that it was the number one place for holidaymakers to stock up on the way down to the beach house. Whether you wanted an array of designer goodies for the Portsea neighbours to nibble on when they come over for drinks, or just some good tucker to feed the family, Houghton's seemed to be the place to find it.

Beside me, a spivvy young man in shirtsleeves was buying the makings of the evening's dinner. 'I've got a young lady coming over,' he explained to the girl behind the counter as she ladled some Florentine sauce into a tub for him. I had my own dinner in mind, and surveyed the bounty spread before me. I could well understand why this kind of food had become so popular. After all, nobody wants to have to cook every night, especially on holiday. And why would you bother with a greasy hamburger or soggy pizza when you can have roast pumpkin and chickpea salad or Mediterranean vegetable lasagna instead?

I tried to decide between the delectable-looking range of homemade savoury pastries and quiches, or the yummy looking pasta sauces. The salmon patties looked plump and inviting, too. Eventually I opted for Thai chicken curry ('this one walks out the door') and couldn't resist a slice of rhubarb and sour cream cake. A girl has to keep her strength up, after all.

Tim Mirabella

When I first visited Hastings on a sunny midsummer Saturday afternoon, the local fishermen were up in arms. They were protesting about the Environmental Conservation Council's controversial plans to establish a series of marine national parks around Victoria, which would be off-limits to commercial fishermen and have a potentially devastating impact on their livelihoods.

Life as a fisherman around Victoria's bays and inlets has never exactly been easy. If they're not copping flak about depleting the state's marine stocks (recreational fishers take at least the same amount), or the damage they're doing to the environment (introduced species and pollution have proved to have a far worse impact), then there is always the threat of bad weather preventing them actually getting out there. It almost makes you wonder why anyone would want to be a fisherman at all.

And then you meet someone like Tim Mirabella. He's young, energetic and passionate about fishing. He comes from Western Port's oldest fishing family and can't remember ever wanting to do anything else. As a young boy he spent all his holidays with his grandfather (another Tim Mirabella) out fishing and helping in the small shop. Later on, he travelled and fished some more, even working on some of the huge prawn trawlers up off northern Queensland before returning to the Mirabella heartland at Hastings, and carrying on the family fishing tradition when his grandfather retired.

Today Tim Mirabella works on his own out in the deep, fast-flowing waters of Western Port Bay. He's out at all times of the day and night, depending on the weather, the tides and seasonal patterns. More often than not, he will set off at sunset to fish overnight, returning at dawn just as you and I are sitting down to our cornflakes. It's a haunting image: one man, out there at sea, all alone, surrounded by all that heavy, pressing blackness of night. Beneath him, the frighteningly dark, impenetrable water. It's a real 'man against nature' thing.

'It does take a certain type who wants to be a fisherman,' Tim agrees. 'I suppose you could say we're the last people to be living a true hunter-gatherer lifestyle.'

Some of his fishing is done close to shore using seine nets, but more often than not he'll head a bit further out and set mesh nets to catch snapper, gummy shark, rock flathead and King George whiting to sell from his small shop on the Frankston–Flinders Road just outside of Hastings. (Look for the 'golden arches' – Tim's shop is a couple of hundred metres down on the right.)

These days, Tim Mirabella is finding that more and more of his time and energy is taken up with the political issues plaguing the fishing industry. I asked him how he came to be involved with that side of things. He laughed a little ruefully before pausing to consider.

'Well, it's as simple as this,' he explained. 'My wife and I, and my little girl Dominique, all love to eat fish. In fact, we eat it most nights of the week. We're lucky, because it's the stuff I pull straight out of the sea, so it

Baked Western Port Mullet
TIM MIRABELLA

Preheat the oven to 200°C.

Brush the fish fillets with a little of the olive oil and season with salt and pepper. Brush an oven dish with the remaining olive oil and add the fish, skin side down.

Combine the dill, parmesan and breadcrumbs. Sprinkle the lemon juice onto the fish, then scatter the dill mixture over.

Bake for 10 minutes or until the fish is firm. Serve with salad and new potatoes.

Serves 4

INGREDIENTS

4 FILLETS OF GREY MULLET, EACH AROUND 180 G

50 ML OLIVE OIL

SALT AND PEPPER

A GOOD HANDFUL OF FRESH DILL, ROUGHLY CHOPPED

60 G GRATED PARMESAN CHEESE

40 G FRESH BREADCRUMBS

JUICE OF 1 LEMON

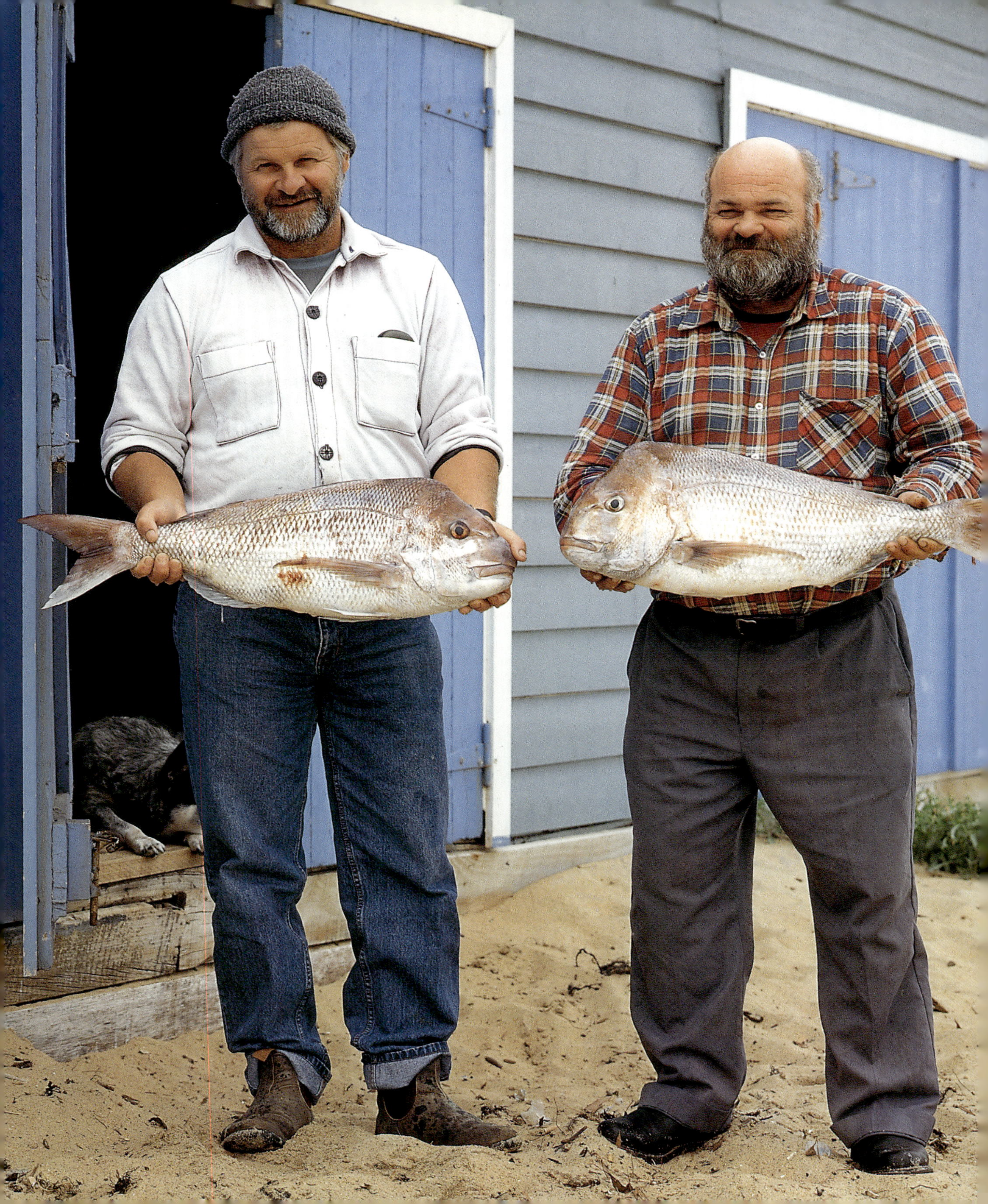

couldn't really be fresher or tastier. But the point is this. Even if I wasn't catching it myself, I'd still want to be eating it, and I want Dominique to be able to eat fresh fish when she grows up. So I just have to do what I can to make sure the industry survives.'

Having enjoyed so much of the wonderful seafood from Melbourne's bay waters, all I can say is thank heavens for people like Tim Mirabella.

Neville & Dalton Hutchins

Now here's a challenge: on a sunny day, stand on the clifftop just north of Fisherman's Beach at Mornington and cast your gaze out over the bay. If you are lucky, from out of the corner of your eye you might just catch a flash of quicksilver, or spot a faint dark shadow beneath the blue. And there it is: that elusive shoal of garfish or mullet, or even precious King George whiting. Apparently it's as easy as that to find the fish, or at least that's how Neville Hutchins and his brother Dalton do it, anyway.

They've had lots of practice. The brothers have been fishing from that very spot since they were small boys helping their grandfather on his boat, and over the years have learnt all there is to know about this part of Port Phillip Bay. They know the tides and the currents, they know the rocks and channels, and they know all the secret hiding spots of the fish. So, as long as the weather holds up, you can be sure of getting fantastic fresh fish from the Hutchins' blue shed down at Fishy's Beach.

Flathead, whiting, flounder, Australian salmon, mullet, garfish – all of these are caught close to shore using large seine nets. It makes sense, doesn't it? Instead of chasing a shoal of fish all around the bay, why not let the fish come to you? That's the way the Hutchins brothers do it. First, thanks to Neville's eagle eye, they locate the fish.

Dalton takes over then, carefully rowing the boat out in a wide semicircle around the shoal, lowering the net out over the side as he goes. Then, it's simply a matter of slowly and gently hauling the flip-flopping, slippery silvery catch onto shore.

That's the way Port Phillip Bay fishermen like the Hutchins family have been doing it for nearly 150 years. Some things have changed, particularly when it comes to equipment. These days the brothers communicate with a two-way radio rather than the elaborate system of whistles and hand signals their grandfather used. Their nets are made of light nylon rather than high-maintenance cotton, and the boats are of aluminium, not wood. But when it comes to the actual daily business of catching fish – and the types of fish themselves – things are exactly the same as they were when the Hutchins family first started their fishing business down at Mornington back in 1860.

Today, Neville and Dalton are part of a dying breed of small commercial fishers who sell their small catch from their own small shop on the beach. Most operators would say that there is only money to be made when you fish on a much larger scale. Which is what many of them do, delivering their catch directly to the big city wholesale markets such as Footscray in Melbourne. This leads to a truly ridiculous state of affairs. How can it be, when we live in a country predominantly populated at the water's edge, when we are still blessed with a bountiful and huge variety of fantastic seafood, that it is so hard to buy good quality and truly fresh fish? And that is true even when you live by the coast and the fish is being pulled out of the water under your very nose?

But the Hutchins brothers are the exception that proves the rule, and thank goodness for them. You can be guaranteed

Left: Neville and Dalton Hutchins with the morning's catch.

that in their tiny shop the fish will have come straight out of the sea, more than likely that very morning. So when you next drive through Hastings, look out for their red-and-yellow sign by the roadside and stop to check on the catch of the day.

WINERIES

It might not have such an impeccable heritage as a wine region as some other places around Victoria, nor is it home to as many of the 'big players', but there's no doubt that the Mornington Peninsula has come of age. When you drive around the area today, it seems as if you can hardly turn a corner without being directed to yet another cellar door. Things look so busy and well established that it's hard to believe that all this activity has really only happened in the past few decades.

But the story of grape growing in the Mornington Peninsula is quite different from other regions around Victoria. Unlike the Yarra Valley and Geelong, for instance, it was largely settled by solid Anglo-Saxon stock, who didn't have the same tradition of daily wine consumption as European settlers elsewhere. Which is not to say that grapes were completely unknown. There were some very small plantings around the peninsula in the nineteenth century (in 1886, Dromana wine even won an honourable mention in the Intercontinental Exhibition) but by the 1920s, most of them had been abandoned. In the 1950s members of the Seppelt and Seabrook families (who had holiday houses on the peninsula) also planted a few trial vineyards, but they were destroyed by bushfire in 1967.

The real story of winemaking in the Mornington Peninsula begins again in the 1970s, when a few wine fanatics began to see the potential of the region as a cool-climate grape-growing area. The first to arrive was Baillieu Myer, who planted a small vineyard at Elgee Park. Hot on his heels were Nat and Rosalie White, who started up the peninsula's first winemaking operations at their small Main Ridge vineyard.

The late 1970s and 1980s saw additional vineyards pop up around the Mornington Peninsula, as more and more people were bitten by the cool-climate wine bug. Brian Stonier planted vines at Merricks Estate, followed by Garry Crittenden at Dromana, and Richard and Jill McIntyre at Moorooduc. The trickle started to turn into a flood in the late 1980s and 1990s, with the arrival of other serious players such as Stephen Hickinbotham, Kevin McCarthy and Kathleen Quealy at T'Gallant, and Jenny Bright at Red Hill, and the Mornington Peninsula began to establish a real name for itself for its cool-climate pinot noir and chardonnay.

Over the past five years or so, the region has seen explosive growth. Since 1996 the total area planted has almost doubled; the 1996 harvest was 1260 tonnes, and the 2000 harvest was around 3500 tonnes. Conservative estimates put the value of Mornington Peninsula wine for that vintage at around $35 million. There are now over forty wineries on the Mornington Peninsula and more than 174 vineyards, and still the vines go in. Not only is the Mornington Peninsula a serious player in the Australian wine industry these days, but it has also become an integral part of the region's economy. The grape-growing and winemaking industry is a major employer in the area and has become increasingly intertwined with the area's status as a tourist destination. The region even has its own ambassador in the form of the Mornington Peninsula Vignerons Association, whose mission is to promote the profile of the Mornington Peninsula and market it as a leading producer of high-quality cool-climate wines.

However, there is still a long way to go. Of

the two million visitors to the Peninsula every year only five per cent visit wineries, which must surely be one reason why more and more wineries are adding other attractions such as cafés and restaurants to the cellar door.

It is interesting to speculate as to where things are heading for Mornington Peninsula wines. Many local players talk of an increasing divergence in the size of the participants. Some are making single-mindedly for the big time. Red Hill Estate and Dromana Estate are both gearing up to be 1000-tonne wineries; Stoniers is now partly owned by Petaluma. Others, like Main Ridge, Osborn and Winbirra remain determinedly small, single-vineyard operations.

One thing that is certain: the quality of wines coming from the Mornington Peninsula is gaining increasing recognition for excellence. And good wine, plus good food, plus fabulous scenery equals more tourist dollars for the region. Which can only be a good thing.

Main Ridge Estate

There are many reasons to be in the Mornington Peninsula in autumn. For a start, it's less crowded than in the height of summer. Secondly, the countryside is spectacularly beautiful at this time of year, all gold and amber and burnt sienna. It's also vintage time, which means that the feeling of excitement (or tension) in the air is nearly palpable.

I drove over to visit Nat and Rosalie White one glorious afternoon early in April. As I made my way along the small country road to their winery, a strong autumnal sun was shining and the landscape was dipped in a warm golden wash. The region was a hive of activity – nets were coming off and grape pickers were arriving by the carload. Up at Main Ridge, one of the highest and therefore coolest vineyards on the peninsula, they were enjoying a brief moment of peace – the calm before the storm.

'We're always one of the very last to pick,' said Rosalie, as we sat on the terrace looking out over one of their small blocks of pinot noir. The Whites were planning to start picking that weekend, and were keeping an anxious eye on the weather. The past few weeks had been a time of constant checking and testing. Nat and his daughter Annelise, who helps manage the vineyard, had been out that morning snipping off a few botrytis-affected bunches they'd spotted on the chardonnay grapes. And then there were daily checks of baume (sugar) levels, to try to pinpoint that crucial start time, and to give Nat a feel for the likely flavours that would end up in his wines.

Nat and Rosalie White are vintage veterans, with Main Ridge Estate being the Mornington Peninsula's first commercial vineyard and winery. Like many Australians, the Whites first discovered and fell in love with wine while travelling around Europe as young newlyweds. They were particularly taken with the cool-climate wines of Burgundy, and when they found themselves living in Mt Eliza early in the 1970s, couldn't help but spot the similarities between the two regions.

They decided to take a punt on a passion, and bought a small eight-acre plot of land on a promising looking north-facing slope up on Main Ridge. Money was tight, so the Whites planted the vines and built the winery themselves. Back then there wasn't even access to their place, and everything had to be brought in through the neighbour's apple orchard. Luckily, Nat eventually put in a road (putting his training as a civil engineer to good use) so that people could come to visit the winery.

Nat is quite clear that their vineyard is modelled firmly on Burgundian principles, where the truly great pinot noirs are made by

Over page: View across Stonier's vineyards to Western Port Bay.

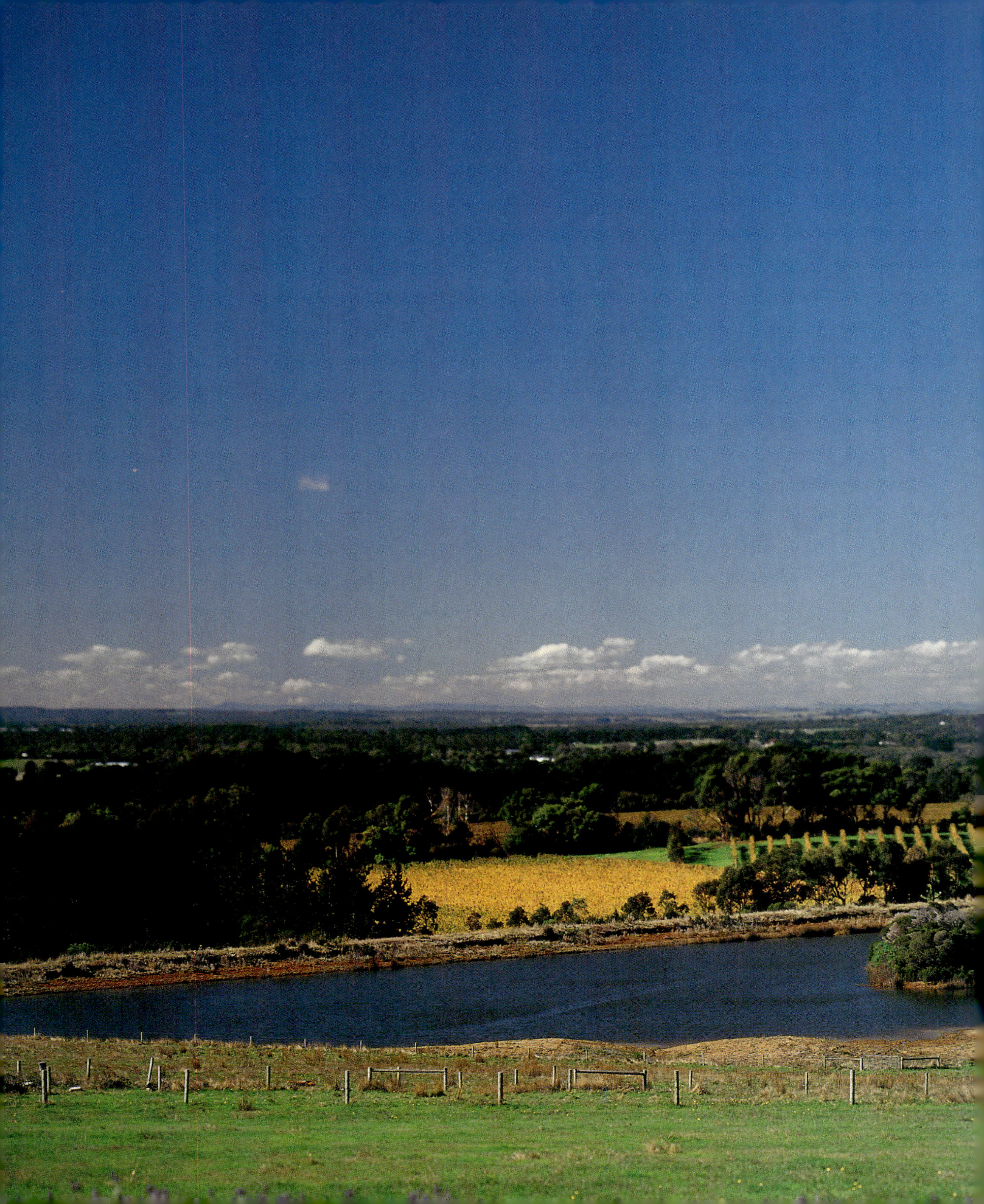

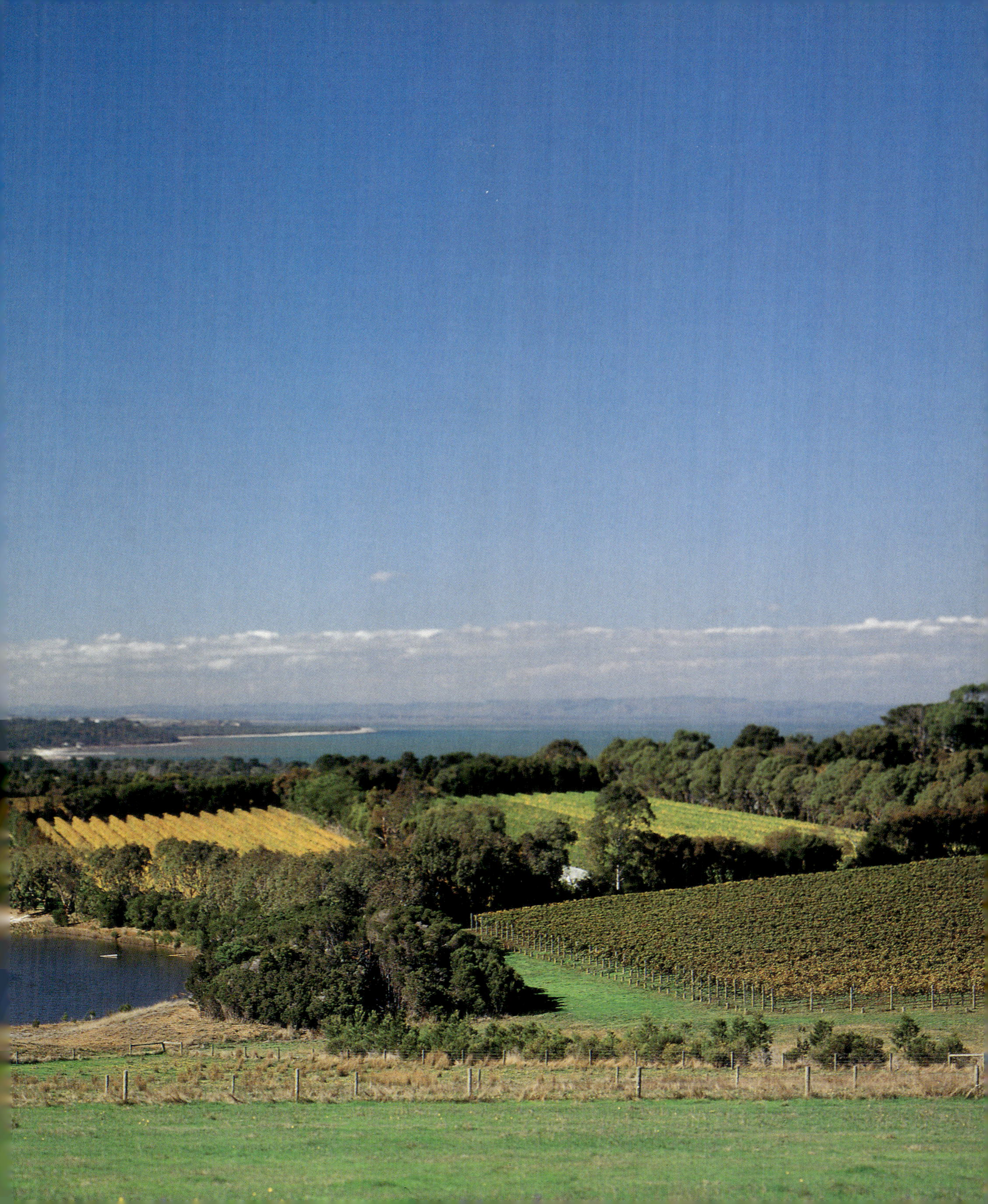

dedicated individuals on tiny plots. Growing grapes and making wine in this type of cool, marginal climate is a risky business, and vineyard management is extremely labour intensive. Not only does the weather pose a challenge, but it is also much harder to achieve the balance between wood, leaf and grape, and enough sunlight exposure than in warm-climate regions.

At Main Ridge, the Whites only grow the classic cool-climate grape varieties, pinot noir and chardonnay. Earlier plantings of cabernet and cabernet franc have been pulled out, as Nat believes that they are better suited to warmer sites. He also believes that his vineyards truly have to be coaxed to reach their full potential. That means meticulous attention to detail – Nat and Annelise conduct almost daily leaf-picking, expensive and elaborate trellis-management systems (they use the Scott Henry split-canopy method)–and a willingness to accept small crop yields.

'We crop at about one to one and a half tonnes of fruit per acre,' said Nat. 'Compare that with industry standard levels of around five for a regular chardonnay.'

All this attention requires commitment. For Nat and Annelise, managing their eight acres of vines is a full-time job and they are actively working in the vineyard every single day. The industry norm requires one person per twenty acres. These kinds of statistics must give his accountant heartburn, but Nat is adamant. 'I'm just not interested in the big-business approach to grape growing and winemaking. For me it's about making interesting wines and having an interesting life.'

And how does all this effort translate into the final product? At a recent pinot tasting in Melbourne, the best of the New World compared very favourably with the best of the Old World. All the more so when you consider the relative prices: the grand-daddy of them all, the Domaine de la Romanée-Conti, came in at around $900 a

Above left: The Stonier Winery.
Above right: Winemaker Todd Dexter at the Stonier Winery.

bottle – and didn't even make it into the top three. Nat White's 1999 Half Acre Pinot Noir might not have made it into the top three either, but it was judged to be one of the best of the Aussie entries, and at around $50 a bottle, seems exceptional value.

Stonier Wines

Vintage is a tense time for winemakers: the question of when to start picking the grapes is one of the most important decisions they have to make, particularly in cool-climate regions like the Mornington Peninsula. Too early, and the grapes wouldn't have had a chance to develop the full intensity of baume (the sugar levels that translate into the flavours that end up in the wine); too late, and they run the risk of rain or other bad weather, which can ruin a vintage altogether.

It's a delicate balance, and the weeks leading up to and during vintage involve a complicated timetable of running between vineyards, testing, tasting, picking, crushing, fermenting and finally barrelling. And naturally, the bigger and more scattered the vineyards are, the more complex the whole process is.

Asking a winemaker to make a prediction about the current vintage is an even more delicate issue. Todd Dexter, respected winemaker at Stonier Wines, and veteran of 24 vintages, seemed pretty happy but was cautious in his response.

'Things are looking OK,' he said hesitantly. 'It's been a bit like 1998. We've had a long hot summer with big cropping levels, so ripening has been a little slower than expected. On the other hand, the sun we've had means that flavours have concentrated nicely. It's been relatively disease-free, and the conditions for picking right now are fantastic.'

We both looked out through the wide open doors of the winery, at the sun-brushed hill of vines that stretched out behind. 'At an early guess I think we're looking at a pretty good year,' he ventured a bit more confidently. 'We've got all the chardonnay in and most of the pinot. My early feel is that we're looking at good flavours and structure. With any luck it will be one of those lucky years when we have both good quantity and quality.'

Stonier was one of the first vineyards to be established on the peninsula by publisher-turned-vigneron Brian Stonier and his wife Noel back in 1977. Over the years, the vineyard has expanded dramatically from the first small block of 600 vines to today's spread of over 40 acres of high-quality chardonnay, and pinot noir grapes. A further 10 acres are given over to other varieties such as cabernet sauvignon, cabernet franc and sauvignon blanc, but it is for their outstanding, multi-award winning Reserve chardonnay and pinot noir that Stonier has gained its reputation of one of the most widely respected wineries in the Mornington Peninsula.

These benchmark wines demonstrate just what can be achieved in a cool-climate region such as the Mornington Peninsula, where the surrounding sea makes its presence ever felt. Stoniers is located near Merricks, on a high ridge of well-drained volcanic soil, but Todd Dexter and vineyard manager Stuart Marshall also have around ten contract growers to supervise, at carefully selected sites ranging from Cape Schanck to Moorooduc. Vineyard management is clearly all-important, and Todd and Stuart work hard to select good-quality clones and employ various canopy management systems to control vigorous vine growth and optimise exposure to sunlight.

As well as viticultural discipline in the vineyard, crops in this type of cool climate often have to be reduced to what might be deemed elsewhere absurdly uneconomic levels to concentrate the fine delicate flavours. This is particularly so for capricious

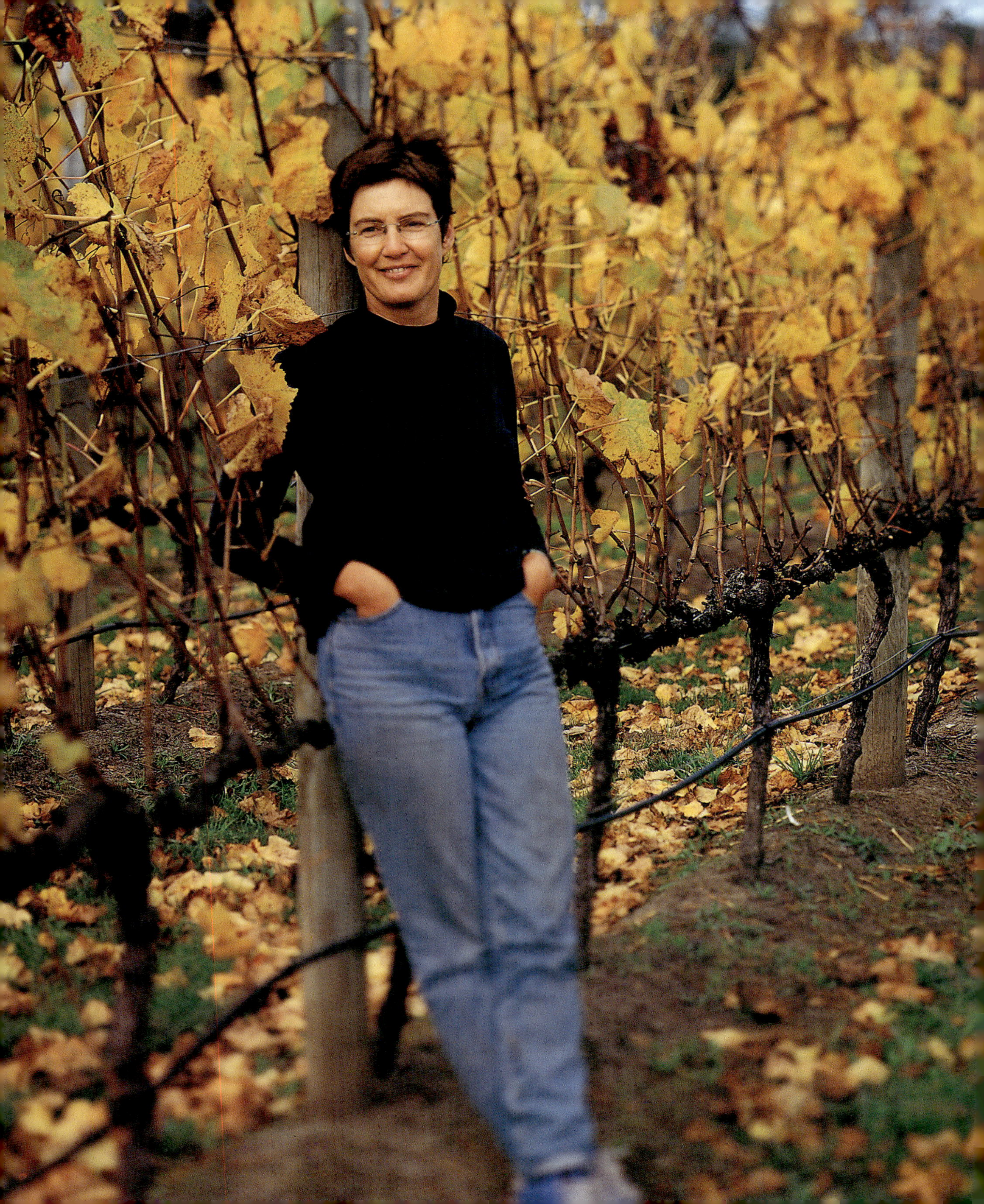

varieties such as pinot noir, which at Stoniers are cropped at around three tonnes per acre, compared with five or so for chardonnay.

When the crops are safely gathered in, the kid-glove treatment continues back at the Stonier Winery. Most of the Reserve chardonnay and all of the pinot noir grapes are barrel fermented and also undergo a second malolactic fermentation. Only the best French oak barrels are used.

But the rewards of growing grapes in this type of challenging environment are manifold, as a tasting session at the Stonier cellar door made abundantly clear. I began my tasting gently, with a Stoniers Standard Chardonnay 2000, which had plenty of straightforward honeydew flavours, and a nice balance of body, freshness and acidity. This was good drinking wine, the perfect accompaniment, perhaps, to a good piece of local whiting.

The Stoniers Reserve Chardonnay 1997, by comparison, was a completely different animal, and it was easy to see why this has been a consistent award winner. It is widely considered to be one of the best wines from the peninsula: a rich, butter-toffee wine, with hints of sweet melon and a smooth, seamless finish.

The Reserve Pinot Noir 1998 was also exceptional – a deep, intense wine of great length, with plummy depths, a hint of pungent mushroom and a soft oak finish. I closed my eyes and let my imagination wander. All I needed to complete my happiness was some food: a nice piece of duck, perhaps, or a wild mushroom risotto would fit the bill nicely.

After my tasting session, I took myself outside to sip and sit in the late afternoon sun, and watch the shadows lengthen across the vineyard. All that was left for the day was to think about dinner.

Dromana Estate

Garry Crittenden has always had big ideas for wine in the Mornington Peninsula, and over the past twenty years he's been one of the driving forces in the region. As a result of his studied and meticulous approach to viticulture and winemaking, and his marketing genius, the Dromana Estate winery makes some of the best known wines in Victoria. Week after week, people come by the busload to taste the range at the cellar door, to eat simple, tasty food in the popular café, and to enjoy the delightful surroundings.

While most grape growers and winemakers around the Mornington Peninsula are happy to operate on a small scale, Dromana Estate has not been scared of climbing into the 'big boy' league. In recent years the Crittenden family has been busy buying wine assets and planting large new vineyards around the peninsula, getting involved with joint ventures in the Yarra Valley, and, to fund this flurry of expansion, they have also hit the headlines with a public listing on the stock exchange.

It all seems a very long way from those pioneering days in the early 1980s, when the

Left: Winemaker Judy Gifford among the vines at Dromana Estate.

wine industry in the Mornington Peninsula was but a twinkle in the eye of a few prospective vignerons. Garry Crittenden was one of them: back then, he was a horticulturalist with a plant nursery business, but he had a keen interest in wines, and a yen to grow grapes. He was one of the first people to recognise the climatic suitability of the Mornington Peninsula for producing cool-climate wines and in 1982, after extensive research, he selected his spot at the slightly warmer, lower part of the peninsula, and planted his first vines.

It was undoubtedly his background in horticulture that shaped his approach to vineyard management at Dromana Estate. The vines are a work in progress. Garry and his viticultural team are constantly experimenting with different methods of propagation and cropping, and with trellising and canopy management systems.

This open-minded and experimental approach also extends to the grapes he grows, which these days are a veritable smorgasbord of varieties. Under the flagship Dromana Estate label, which uses purely peninsula fruit, he also makes the expected range of cool-climate wines, as well as cabernet, merlot and shiraz (using fruit sourced from his own vineyards in warmer, flatter terrains). Since April 2000, he has also had access to the high-quality fruit from Mornington Estate (previously owned by Hugh and Isabel Robinson, and now brought into the Dromana Estate fold).

Garry has never been one to miss an opportunity. In the early days, when much of his time was spent travelling around Victoria consulting for other vineyards, he found that he was constantly coming across good-quality parcels of fruit looking for a home. One thing led to another: he started buying, and before long the Schinus label was born. Over the years the range has been trimmed from around twelve varieties to three: a sauvignon blanc, a chardonnay and a merlot, made from grapes sourced from central and northeast Victoria. The distinctive and well-made Schinus range has a well-deserved reputation as reasonably priced premium wines.

Garry is also known as a pioneer in the production of wines from Italian grape varieties. Historically, most Australian winemakers have gone down the French route, but Garry was seduced by the contrasting qualities of good Italian wines. Since 1992 he has been experimenting with different varieties and has now built up one of the best known ranges of Italian varietal wines in Australia. The Garry Crittenden 'I' range uses fruit mainly grown in the King Valley in northeast Victoria, and includes the classic red varietals barbera, dolcetto, sangiovese and nebbiolo, as well as a dry white arneis, a rosé and a Piedmont-style riserva.

And it doesn't stop there. There's no point in having hundreds of tonnes of grapes if you don't have the ability to crush them. In the near future, the Dromana Estate winery will have a new home at Tuerong Park, a little further up the Dromana Valley. By vintage 2002, the company will have around 200 acres of the Mornington Peninsula under crop, and a brand-new winery capable of crushing around 1000 tonnes of fruit.

It might not be on quite the same scale as the monster wineries in other parts of the country, but for a region that is still only in its infancy, this is certainly a quantum leap in winemaking capacity. We can all look forward to exciting times ahead.

T'Gallant

There's something seductive about eating at winery restaurants. Partly it's because vineyards are usually located in impossibly gorgeous locations, but mainly it's because you know that the food has been designed as much as possible to fit into its rural vineyard surroundings. And there is nothing

Right: Weekend fun at T'Gallant.

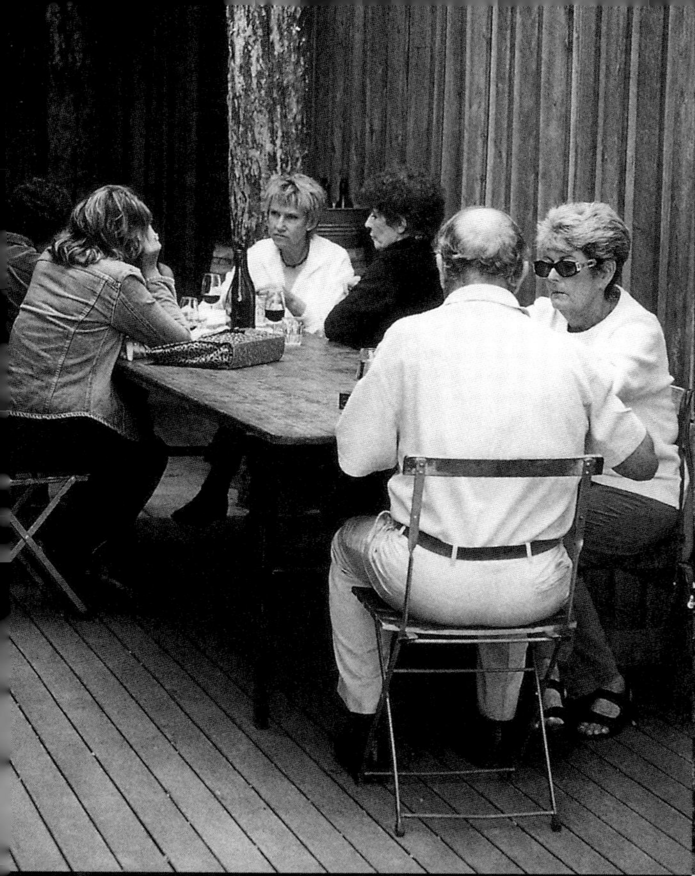
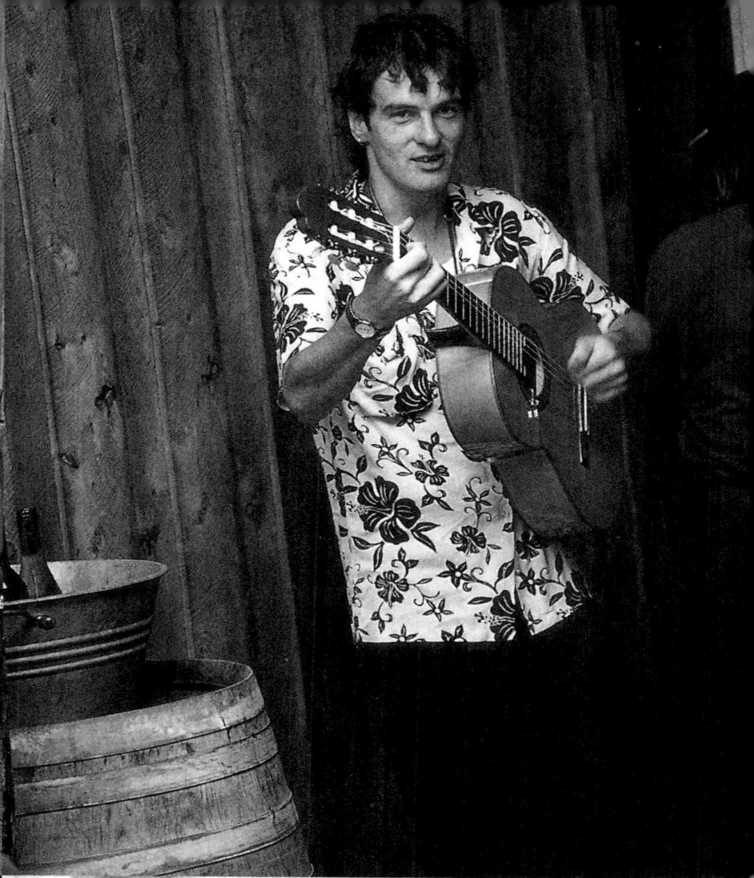
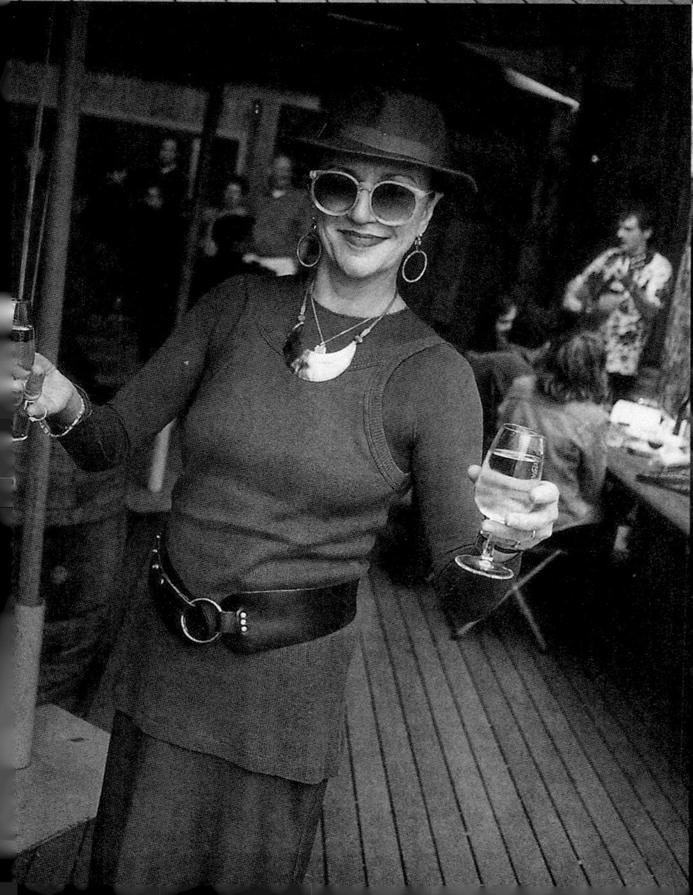
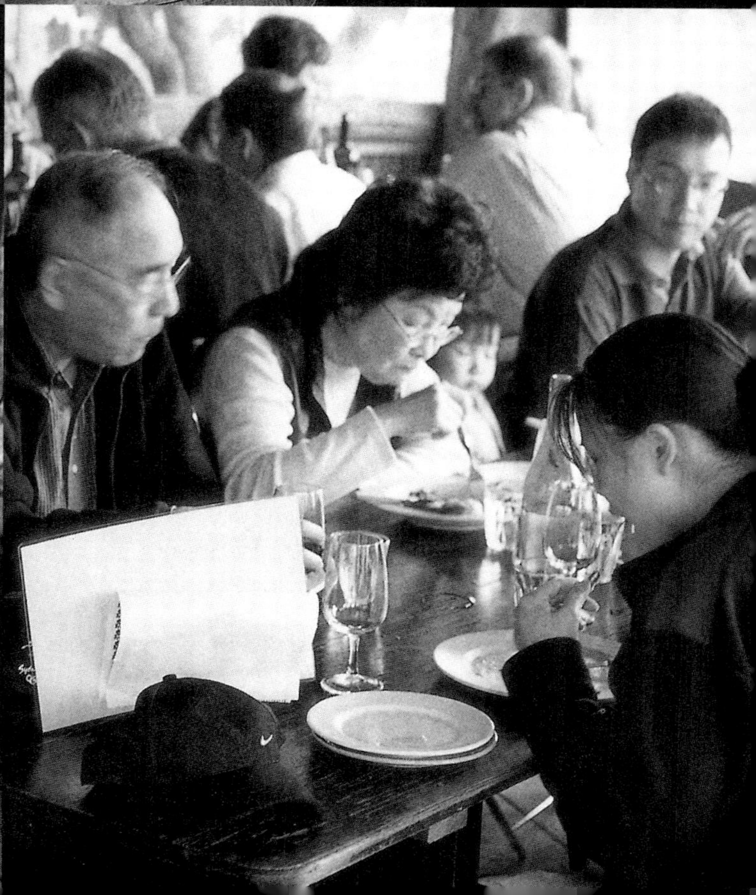

quite like drinking wine that comes from grapes grown right outside the door.

It's hard not to like La Baracca at the T'Gallant winery, which sticks two fingers up at contemporary design, and offers instead rustic Italian fare in an old shed. At the weekends the place is packed with visitors who come to taste the renowned T'Gallant wines and stay for pizza from the wood-fired oven in the courtyard, or a more languorous dining experience in the trattoria.

The food is designed by well-known Melbourne caterer-turned-country-girl Louise Lechte. Like many other Melburnians, she was so charmed by the loveliness of the peninsula that she made the seaside weekender a permanent home. A firm believer that wine should be tasted with delicious things to eat, after a visit to the winery back in 1997, Louise approached T'Gallant owners, Kathleen Quealy and Kevin McCarthy, with some food ideas. The three quickly discovered that they shared the same informal – even irreverent – approach to life, and by the end of the following year La Baracca opened, with a menu of unpretentious rustic Italian fare and a singing waiter for entertainment value.

Virtually from the week it opened, visitors have been seduced by the quirkiness of La Baracca, and delighted in the stunning flavour combinations of the dishes. Louise likes to use local produce wherever possible, including Flinders tomatoes, Red Hill cheese, local seafood, strawberries from Sunny Ridge Farm and figs plucked from the tree outside the restaurant. Drawing inspiration from the Italian-style wines (pinot gris and pinot grigio) for which T'Gallant has become renowned, Louise prepares simple Italian classics, including sensational antipasto platters, homemade pastas and risottos and dishes from the chargrill.

The winery at T'Gallant is equally individualistic in its approach. Husband and wife team Kevin and Kathleen came to the peninsula in the late 1980s, determined to make wines that truly reflected the region, rather than imitative versions of wines from other parts of the world. Their first decision, which flew in the face of conventional wisdom at the time, was that their chardonnay would be unwooded.

'I can't bear wines that taste of oak,' says Kathleen bluntly. 'I like my chardonnay to taste of the soil it's grown in. In cool climates like this, the fruit has longer to ripen, which gives it plenty of complex flavours. It really doesn't need the wood.' And the T'Gallant chardonnays prove her right. The 1999 vintage, for instance, has heaps of pear flavours, with a complex underlying smokiness. The 2000 vintage is crisper, but still full of bright apple-like freshness.

Kevin and Kathleen's next big decision was to introduce pinot gris to the region. It was a bold move at the time, but today pinot gris and its twin, pinot grigio, are the hippest varieties being grown on the peninsula.

'It was inevitable, really,' explained Kathleen. 'We realised that the Mornington Peninsula is the only place in Australia – possibly the world – where you can grow both pinot noir and pinot gris successfully. In Burgundy they don't grow pinot gris, and in Alsace they don't grow pinot noir. Their climates are continental and are more marginal, whereas here on the Mornington Peninsula, the climate is not just cool, but also strongly maritime. Both varieties thrive here.'

Pinot gris and pinot grigio are the same grape variety, which is itself a mutation of pinot noir. They have the same heart of honey fruit, but are capable of making two very different styles of wine, depending on where they are grown. At T'Gallant, Kevin and Kathleen plant pinot grigio on the eastern-facing slopes on lower vineyards, closer to sea level.

'We pick the grapes earlier because they

tend to be warmer sites, and the soil in these areas tends to be lighter and more friable. It doesn't sustain the grapes so well, so they just have to be picked earlier.'

To Kathleen, the pinot grigio has salty, sea-breeze smells. It's a lighter wine: smoky, savoury and briny. As Kathleen says, 'You just know it comes from an area near the sea.'

Pinot gris is the more elegant older sister. It's planted on the north and west-facing slopes, the soils tend to be deeper and richer, and the grapes make bigger, fatter wines. 'Because the vineyards are usually higher, we pick the grapes a full month later. They need that extra sun, which gives them higher sugar levels and makes for a more serious wine.'

Aficionados describe their pinot gris as voluptuous, heady and full of rich honey flavours. If you taste the T'Gallant 1999 Tribute Pinot Gris, you cannot help but admire its warmth, depth and an almost oily complexity.

T'Gallant make a large range of wines, for themselves and others. Besides their flagship Tribute Pinot Gris, there's also the Imogen Pinot Gris – a sweet young thing with hints of pear and honey. There's an elegant dark pinot noir, a white pinot, a pinot blanc de noir and a botrytis version – Io – which is all treacly fruit with deliciously herbal undertones.

Whether you go to eat La Baracca's delicious food, or to sample the outstanding wines, you can't help but be impressed by the stamp of freshness and originality that is the T'Gallant philosophy.

EATING OUT

You get the full gamut of eating experiences on the Mornington Peninsula, in keeping with its position as Melbourne's leading summer playground. And this is both good and bad news for the food lover.

The bad news is that all too often the food options in the busy, tourist-thronged beach resorts are of the greasy, fast-food variety, or are restricted to that ubiquitous double act: pizza and pasta. Even in chic, moneyed resorts such as Sorrento, much of what is available is drab and unimaginative. Even worse, in my opinion, is the 'don't give a damn' attitude that prevails at some of the trendier new places – usually located in prime spots – where the view and hip décor are meant to make up for dull food and woeful service.

That's the bad news. Thankfully, things are getting better all the time. There is a definite sense that things are changing, as increasing numbers of people make the lifestyle decision to move away from the city, and the peninsula is close enough and gorgeous enough to be the perfect spot. As more people make the move to permanent residency, so the demand for better quality and consistency in food increases.

But let's not forget that holidays and tourism are a very large part of what makes the Mornington Peninsula tick. Weekend visitors are still a key contributor to the region's economy. And every month it seems as if yet another new golf course is built on the peninsula's gently rolling hills, bringing still more crowds. As the tastes and demands of these visitors become more sophisticated, so, too, are the food choices on offer.

There are a number of well-established posh hotel resorts in the region, such as the spectacular Delgany at Portsea. At Red Hill there is Lindenderry, a luxurious hotel and conference centre and a favourite spot for wedding parties.

Restaurants such as Arthur's and Opus offer superb fine-dining experiences. Then there are old favourites like the delightfully rustic Bittern Cottage and interesting new spots like safi buluu, an innovative seafood restaurant at Flinders.

The Mornington Peninsula is also blessed with a number of terrific winery restaurants. There's Max's at Red Hill, Jill's at Moorooduc Estate and the excellent restaurant at Paringa Estate, all of which offer superb fine-dining experiences. Then there's more rustic French-style food at Hanns Creek, Margaret Crittenden's simple, rustic fare at Dromana Estate, and the charmingly individualistic La Baracca at T'Gallant.

There is also an increased demand for simpler eating out options, which is one reason why the Portsea and Sorrento hotels are packed to the rafters over the summer and holiday weekends. It's also why fun, family-oriented places like the Smokehouse pizza restaurant in Sorrento does a busy trade most nights.

Simple or fancy, the selection of places I offer here has one thing in common: they are run by people who are absolutely passionate about what they are doing. Some are well-established favourites, others are newer, but all are well worth visiting on your next trip to the peninsula.

Jill's at Moorooduc Estate

It was a blazing hot summer's day as I hurtled through the countryside on my way to lunch. I was running late and I was hungry. It had been a long dry summer, and all around me the fields crackled hot and yellow in the midday heat. All of a sudden, through the glare of the sun, I saw the turn-off to Moorooduc Estate along a long, dusty dirt track. I slowed the car and turned, and through the window came the hot stink of eucalyptus.

A few minutes later I pulled into the forecourt of the Moorooduc Estate winery. The nets were on the vines to protect the precious grapes from the birds, and vintage was only a week or so off. I passed quickly by the winery cellar door, and at long last entered the blissful quiet and coolness of the restaurant to meet Jill McIntyre.

The new winery at Moorooduc Estate is a dramatic, modern, rammed-earth building, designed by renowned architect Greg Burgess (best known for the Uluru Aboriginal Cultural Centre in the Northern Territory and the Brambuk Living Culture building at Halls Gap in the Grampians). It's an expansion and development of the first winery Jill and Richard McIntyre built on the land, back in the early 1980s. That first building was a simple, multifunctional rammed-earth construction, but the McIntyres loved it so much that they wanted to recreate the atmosphere, but on a larger, grander and more comfortable scale.

The new winery was also to house elegant and comfortable guest accommodation, and private quarters for the McIntyres. They also added a small dining room so that Jill could fulfil her dream of running her own restaurant. We passed through the deceptively simple space of the dining room, stopping to admire the gently undulating ceiling – a clever reference, perhaps, to the vaulting arch of a barrel cellar? – and out onto the veranda for lunch.

Jill poured me a taste sensation to get the ball, and the conversation, rolling. It was a ruby-red froth of chilled grape juice, pressed from the new vintage pinot noir grapes that very morning so that Richard could test the baume levels. We sat contentedly, sipping the sweet fruity drink, gazing out over the vineyard. I asked her how it all began.

'We bought the land back in 1982,' began Jill. 'Garry Crittenden had just bought a parcel of land down the road, and he called Richard to tell him about this block. When we came down to see what we had bought, there was nothing on it at all. Absolutely nothing.'

She paused to cut me a piece of homemade duck terrine, and to break off a hunk of crusty Baker Boys ciabatta. 'We planted our first vines in 1982, and had our first vintage in 1986. Of course we were just part-timers then. Richard was working at Monash (he's a gastro-enterology surgeon) and we used to come down with the kids to do the weekend winemaker thing. But we always knew we'd move down here permanently sooner or later.'

Over the years, Richard's wines under the Moorooduc Estate and Devil's Bend labels earned more and more accolades. The land is sandier and the climate warmer up here than in the cool volcanic soils around Red Hill, so he is able to grow later-ripening shiraz and cabernet sauvignon grapes as well as the more traditional Mornington Peninsula varieties of chardonnay and pinot noir.

The McIntyres finally made the decision to move to their winery permanently in 1998. They were keen to get on with the business of running the winery full-time, so Richard relocated his surgery practice to nearby Frankston, and cut down his hours. After eighteen months' intensive planning with Greg Burgess, building began in February 1999, and the structure was completed just in time for a big dinner in the restaurant over the Queen's Birthday weekend in 2000.

By now, Jill and I had moved on from the grape juice to a glass of Richard's smooth, honeyed chardonnay. As we nibbled on silky marinated peppers, caramelised onions and Jill's own home-cured olives I perused the menu. It reflected her passion for fresh, locally grown produce (from her own garden, and organic wherever possible). On the menu that week, for instance, in addition to the tasty antipasto items, was a simple but tasty gazpacho, grilled free-range lemon chicken with organic new potatoes, a delectable rose-scented geranium pannacotta and a selection of cheeses from the local Red Hill cheesery.

Like so many other passionate cooks, Jill attributes her initial interest and subsequent inspiration to Elizabeth David. Jill's own food epiphany happened while she and Richard were living in England in the mid-1970s. They had arrived in the middle of a miserable winter, with two toddlers and a third child on the way. Jill knew absolutely no one, and the children kept her house-bound. It was only the discovery of some Elizabeth David books that kept her sane during those days.

Today she has a vast collection of cookery books and is an avid reader. But her approach is more than just intellectual. She experiments constantly, and now that she has a large winery garden to play around in, is busy growing her own organic herbs, vegetables and fruit trees.

I followed Jill into her airy, well-equipped kitchen and helped her clear the plates. I gazed out the window at the orderly rows of pinot and chardonnay stretching down towards the dam. A clucking brood of Jill's chooks were busying themselves in the garden beds beneath the window, and in the distance, I could just make out the shimmer of the bay waters. For a moment I felt a little frisson of envy here, in this perfect confluence of food, wine, architecture and nature.

Arthur's Restaurant

If ever there was a view to die for, then it's to be found here, up on the mountain-top at Arthur's Seat near Red Hill. It's been attracting visitors since the late 1800s, when the first European settlers in the area enjoyed it as a Sunday picnic spot.

These days, its attractions are many. Busloads of visitors come all year round to

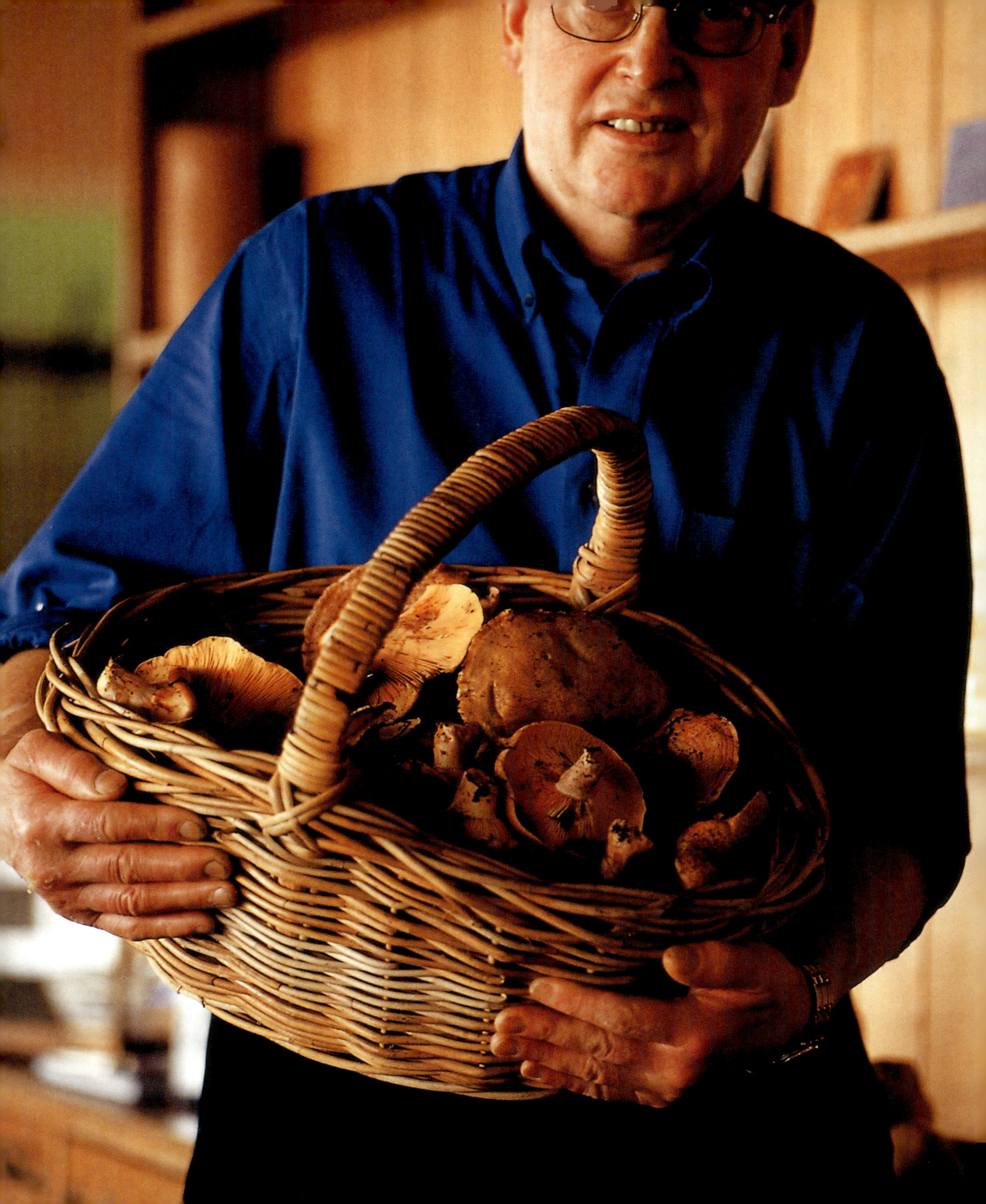

ride through the treetops by chair lift to the summit, while the old viewing tower (83 steps and 16 metres high) offers spectacular views of land, beach and ocean. The energetically inclined can enjoy walks in the unspoilt bushland of the Arthur's Seat State Park, while the rest of us can take advantage of the facilities at the nearby picnic area.

There is also another excellent reason to drive up the steep, winding road from Dromana to the summit. And that is to enjoy a meal at Arthur's Restaurant, which is owned and run by restaurateur legends, Hermann and Faye Schneider. For nearly half a century the Schneiders have been building an enviable reputation and a devoted following for their dedication to the restaurant scene. Many Melburnians remember them from their days at the acclaimed Two Faces restaurant. And now, they have turned their skills to Arthur's, in their beloved Mornington Peninsula.

I went there for dinner one Friday evening in late autumn. The sky was turning as I belted down the road; a silvery harvest moon loomed large between the pine trees and the horizon was tinged with pink. I arrived at Arthur's in a bit of a dither, and collapsed gratefully in a chair by the window to enjoy the last of the daylight. This is what I'd been rushing for: to watch as the landscape below vanished into night, and the lights of Mt Martha and Mornington came twinkling into view.

Inside, the dining room was warm and comfortable, and despite its top-notch tourist location, the décor had the self-assured feel of a well-established and rather formal European restaurant, which aims for substance rather than style.

To eat at Arthur's is to experience the skills of two consummate professionals. Faye Schneider supervises the dining room, and waiter service is exemplary. In the kitchen, Hermann Schneider is behind the stoves, doing what he has done so superbly well for nearly fifty years. His menu is produce driven (local when possible, and changing frequently) and everything is cooked with care. The result is a sense of harmony in each dish, and a refinement, so that even the most complicated dishes have deceptively clear and simple flavours.

On offer for starters was a creamy fish soup scented with dill, served with mussels and clams. There was a kind of glorified prawn and avocado salad, with a mango and ginger-scented mayonnaise. There were agnolotti with a sand crab farce in a light crustacean sauce. But finally I plumped for tea-smoked quail on a rocket salad with prosciutto, fresh figs and goat's cheese curd, a sublime composition of colours, textures and flavours.

Not everything is as traditional as one might expect. There are flashes of modernity – in an oven-baked loin of lamb with a chermoula crust, for instance, or a rare-roasted kangaroo with honey and mirin-glazed quince slices. I ate pink-roasted fillets of duck breast with sour cherries in a vintage port wine sauce, which was cooked to perfection.

As you would expect from two people with such an extensive and renowned knowledge of wine, the list at Arthur's is exceptionally well constructed, offering a thoughtful selection of some of the best wines from the peninsula, as well as outstanding vintages from elsewhere in Australia and from overseas.

All too often, it seems, view equals dollars (often lots of them) on the bill. But despite its touristy location, Arthur's is exceptionally reasonably priced. It also offers an alternative to the fine-dining fare of the restaurant in the form of the Vinoteque Bar , where you can enjoy simpler fare along with a glass of Mornington Peninsula wine.

Left: Hermann Schneider, with fresh-picked local mushrooms.

Poffs'

It might have been the vodka I'd consumed, or it might have been the sheer joy of a warm sunny day after a week of squally rain, but the Saturday afternoon I spent sitting on the terrace at Poffs' was the closest thing to perfection I'd experienced in a long time.

Poffs' is perched up high on Red Hill, and I was looking out over delightful landscaped cottage gardens to a valley scene of almost idyllic loveliness. Butterflies fluttered in the hot afternoon sun and stretched out before me were vineyards and rolling hills and great towering pine trees. And there, off in the distance, were Western Port Bay and French Island. I drifted off into a happy daydream. In the background was the contented hum of happy diners, the clink of glassware and muted notes from a jazz track on the speakers.

Poffs' is little short of charming, with its high wooden eaves, wide veranda and a riot of geraniums in window boxes. There are some nice old-fashioned touches, too, like the teeny-tiny posies of flowers on each table, the immaculate curls of chilled butter on icy silver dishes, and heavy-duty, properly bound menus. And don't let the vodka thing fool you – Poffs' also has a perfectly respectable wine list of Mornington Peninsula wines, and a small 'old and interesting' cellar of vintage wines from further afield.

Just for the record, the vodka had come icy-cold with the Siberian pelmeni, little lamb dumplings that are the house speciality. As I sat chatting with chef–owner Sasha Esipoff later that afternoon, he told me a bit about the dish and his Russian heritage. 'You find dumplings like this all around Russia, with variations depending on how far west or east you are. In the western parts they come in vinegar with a dollop of sour cream, but further east you find them with the more oriental influence of soy sauce.'

Sasha's pelmeni seemed to combine the best of both these worlds. They were plump little morsels in a savoury soy-based sauce, flavoured with just a touch of garlic and chilli, and topped with sour cream and parsley. I idly wondered just how many pelmeni he'd made during his lifetime. He laughed. 'Sometimes I make them in my dreams too,' he said. They are pretty labour-intensive to make, so it's usually done with a group of friends and a couple of bottles of vodka to speed things along. (Ah, that's where the vodka comes into it!)

Sasha also likes to offer other dishes that reflect his heritage. So, besides the pelmeni, you might find starters like 'A True Russian Beginning' of marinated herring and hot potatoes with dill cucumbers and apple mayonnaise. Or a 'Quartet of Smoked Fish', which includes a fabulous tuna and gravlax that he cold-smokes himself. But Sasha's menu is seasonal and wide-ranging, with favourites like Hunter's Pie, a rich winey pie using seasonal venison, or duckling with a wild rice pilaf and sour cherry sauce, or, for an Australian touch, kangaroo fillets and bush-tomato relish.

After polishing off my meal I followed the example of some fellow diners and went for a wander in the charming garden. In the field next door a couple of goats frolicked under the pine trees and by the time I returned to my table for a cup of excellent coffee I was quite ready to sell the inner-city pad and move down to Red Hill for good.

Gennaro's Table at Villa Primavera

One of my favourite spots in the Mornington Peninsula, Villa Primavera, is also one of the least pretentious. It's not big and fancy, but it does what it does extremely well. It's one of those places that make you feel very smug to have discovered, but then you start talking to people, and learn that it's one of the worst kept secrets on the peninsula.

Gennaro Mazzella runs Villa Primavera as a

Right: Sasha Esipoff of Poffs' Restaurant.

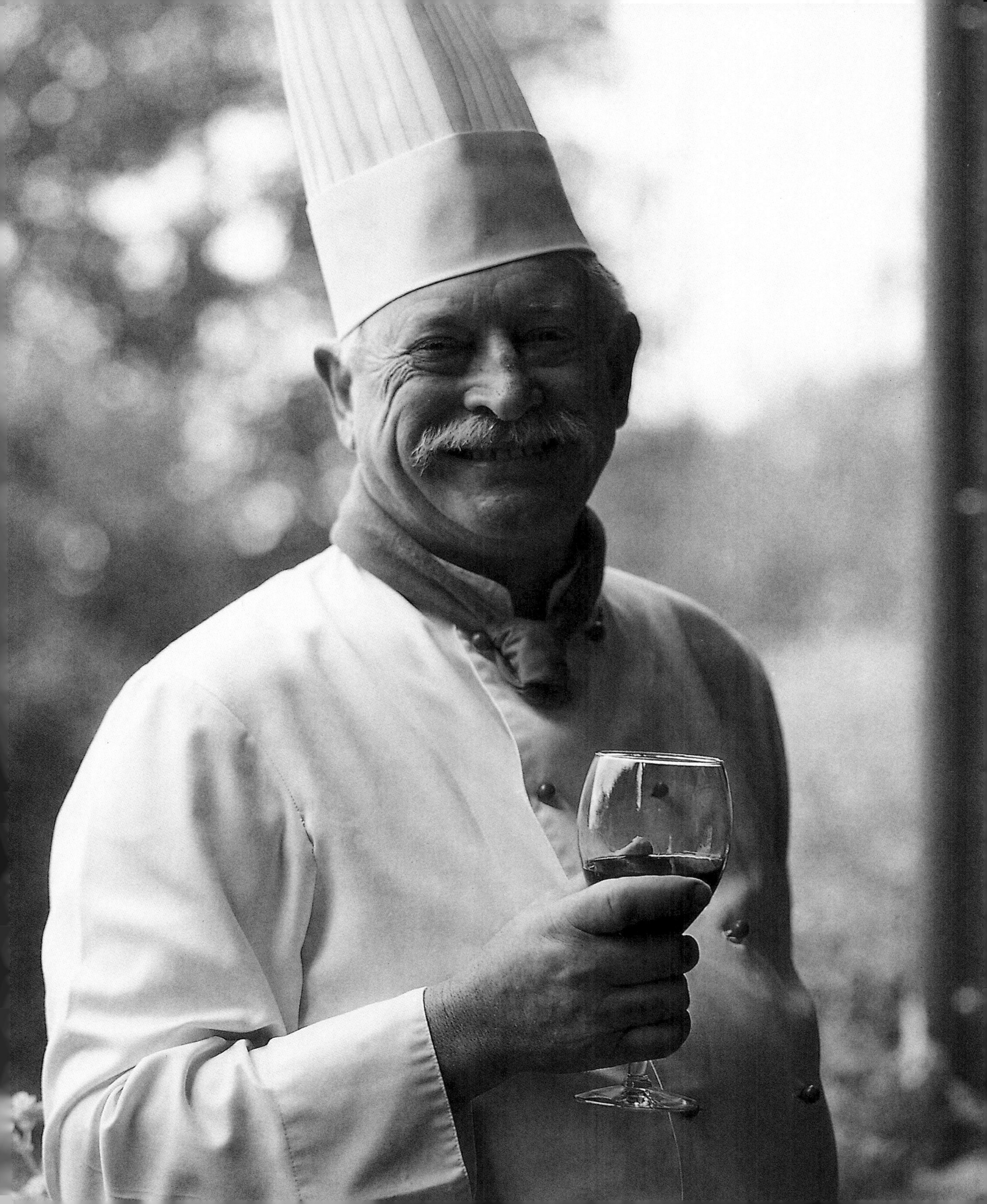

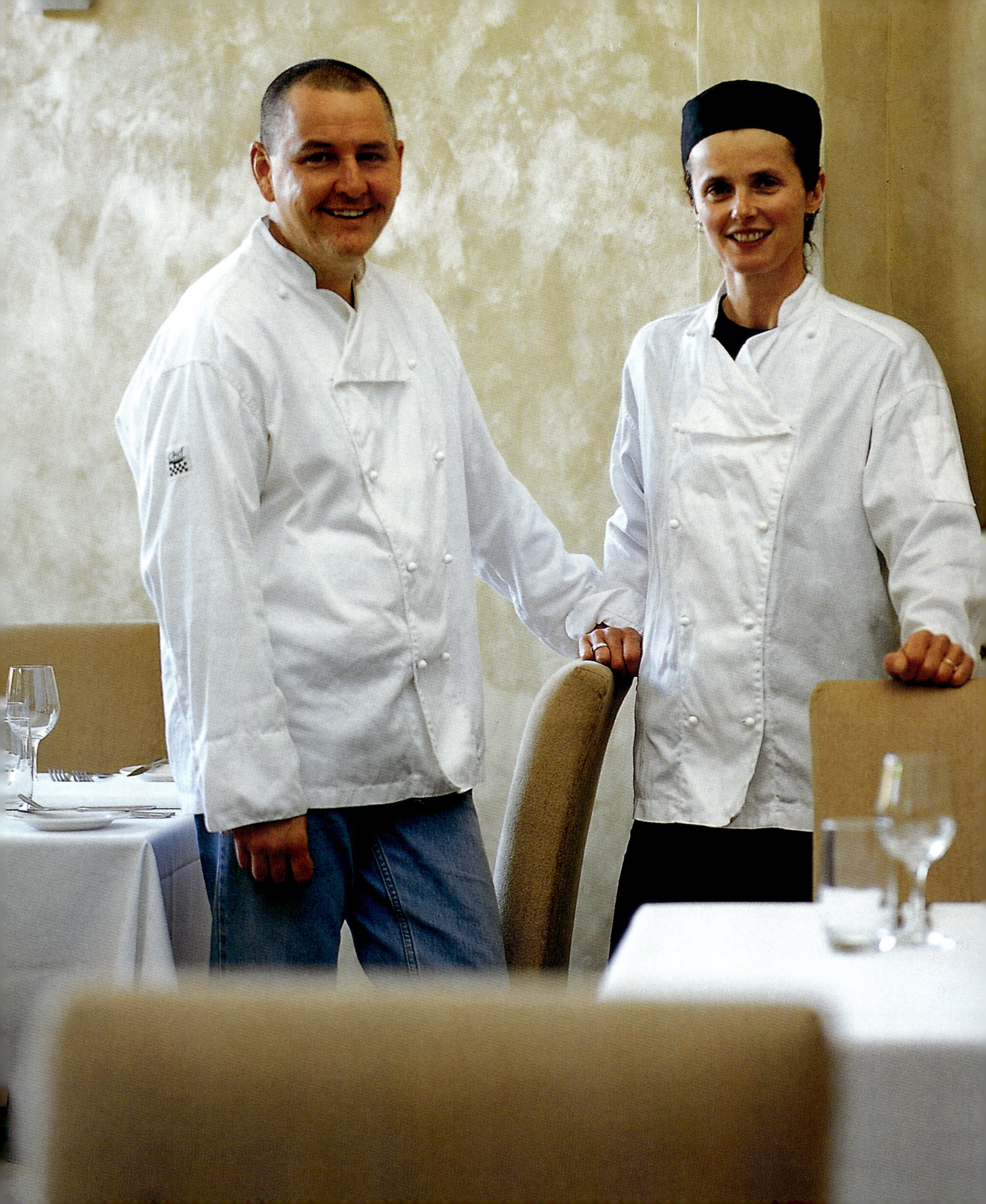

winery, a restaurant, a cooking school and a place to create delicious Italian food products for his shop at Melbourne's Queen Victoria Market. That makes it sound like something of an empire, but nothing could be further from the truth. Gennaro just believes in using the products and facilities at hand to their optimum capacity. So, although the restaurant only operates limited hours (Friday evening and weekends) the kitchen runs at full tilt during the rest of the week, making all kinds of delicious preserves and jams, biscotti and cakes and his legendary chocolate panforte.

Things did start out on a much smaller scale. Gennaro moved to the peninsula in 1986 to satisfy his growing interest in wines – in particular for the cool-climate wines that were beginning to take root around Red Hill. So he bought his plot of land on a slope overlooking a beautiful valley near Main Ridge and planted some vines. Fifteen years down the track his vineyards provide the grapes that go to making wine for the restaurant. And with new plantings of pinot noir and pinot grigio they will continue to make good-quality lively young wines that perfectly match his rustic home-style cooking.

When I met Gennaro I asked him if he'd ever harboured any ambition to make wine himself.

'I make good vinegar,' he replied frankly. 'I leave the winemaking up to the experts!' But he did have ambition to produce excellent food – both in the restaurant and for the shop. He started out with a range of preserved goods – olives, artichokes, eggplant and sardines– which he sold at first at the Red Hill Market, and also used in dishes for the restaurant.

Over the years, the range expanded to meet the demands of diners, customers and students at his cooking classes so that the larder at Villa Primavera is usually stocked with produce reflecting the seasons. In the winter, for instance, he makes his own smallgoods. Gennaro pointed out a row of hooks high up in the eaves. 'We make our own sausages, salamis and prosciutto. I've found a really good Italian butcher for my pork.' Gennaro's smallgoods are the real thing: dark and intensely flavoured, with none of the nitrates and nitrites you find in most commercially available products.

Homemade pasta and breads are also important at Villa Primavera. In fact for Gennaro, bread is the most important thing of all. 'I think it's a cultural thing,' he explained. 'You know, we Italians have to have bread with every meal.' The restaurant itself is cosy and inviting – an attractive wooden building with doors that open out completely in the summer, when tables and chairs, too, spill out onto the terrace overlooking the vineyard. Dining at Gennaro's table is casual; there is one long communal refectory-style table in the centre of the room that makes for lively chatter between groups of diners.

Gennaro's seasonal menus offer simple home-style fare, all of it superbly cooked and presented. On a recent visit a friend and I enjoyed an excellent antipasto platter, which featured goodies from the Villa Primavera larder, such as olives, preserved artichokes and sardines and home-cured prosciutto. We scoffed it down with Gennaro's famous crusty bread and tasty olive paste. Also on the menu that evening was a stunning small baby chicken braised in the estate chardonnay and served with baby vegetables. My friend's homemade pasta with Flinders mussels and flavourful local tomatoes was equally simple, but delicious.

Before leaving, we stocked up on some of Gennaro's spiced chocolate panforte and a bottle of limoncello, and went home content.

Opus

Some restaurants seemingly have all the advantages: spectacular outlook, heaps of passing trade, stylish architecture, fabulous

Left: Chef/owners of Opus, Tony Ryan and Deb Ongarello.

contemporary interior design. Some, on the other hand, have none of these benefits, yet still manage to excel, thanks to the passion and dedication of their owners and the exceptional quality of the food they serve.

Opus falls well and truly into the second category. In fact, when it comes to location, you'd be hard put to find a worse one in buzzy Sorrento. It's not on the gorgeous beach front, it's not even on the main drag, but instead, is tucked away in the backstreets in a semi-industrial part of town, so there's no passing trade to be had either. But you definitely have to seek this place out.

Since opening in 1999, Opus has earned a reputation for serving up some of the finest food on the Mornington Peninsula, something that chef–owners Tony Ryan and Deb Ongarello have worked for.

'We didn't have the money to spend on a fancy fit-out,' said Tony. 'So we've kept it simple and hope that the food speaks for itself.' The interior may be simple, but it has a calming and comfortable feel, and creates a serene backdrop to the superbly crafted contemporary food.

I was chatting with Tony after enjoying one of the best meals I'd had in a long time. His food is inventive and expertly cooked. Each dish is a superb balance of flavours – time-consuming to put on the plate, but it all comes together in an effortless balance. That night I'd enjoyed a sublime starter of prawns, served with apple and chive salsa, shredded cos lettuce, a parmesan wafer stuck jauntily in a parmesan mousse and the whole dressed with a tangy apple vinegar and parmesan oil vinaigrette. It was quite simply stunning.

Next course was a rack of lamb on a nice buttery braise of du Puy lentils and red cabbage, with a crisp potato roesti cake, and a Sauternes sauce. My dining companion enjoyed half a roasted duck that came on wilted spinach, studded with little pieces of dried fig and pancetta. There was a little mound of herb spatzle on one side, sauced with a late-picked semillon jus. Sauces are one of Tony's great strengths. They are intense and concentrated, revealing the time and care that have gone into their preparation.

Although not trained as a chef, Deb is, according to Tony, a perfectionist, and everything that comes from her section is exquisite. Pudding that evening attested to that fact. We shared a tangy passionfruit tart, which came with a scoop of silkily smooth, sweet mango sorbet and a rich orange caramel sauce.

This was cooking at its most sensuous and refined, with innovative and personal touches, too. Deb and Tony are wholeheartedly committed to putting the very best produce onto our plates, and I, for one, will be eating as much of it as I possibly can. They deserve our support.

Right: Among the barrels at the Stonier Winery.

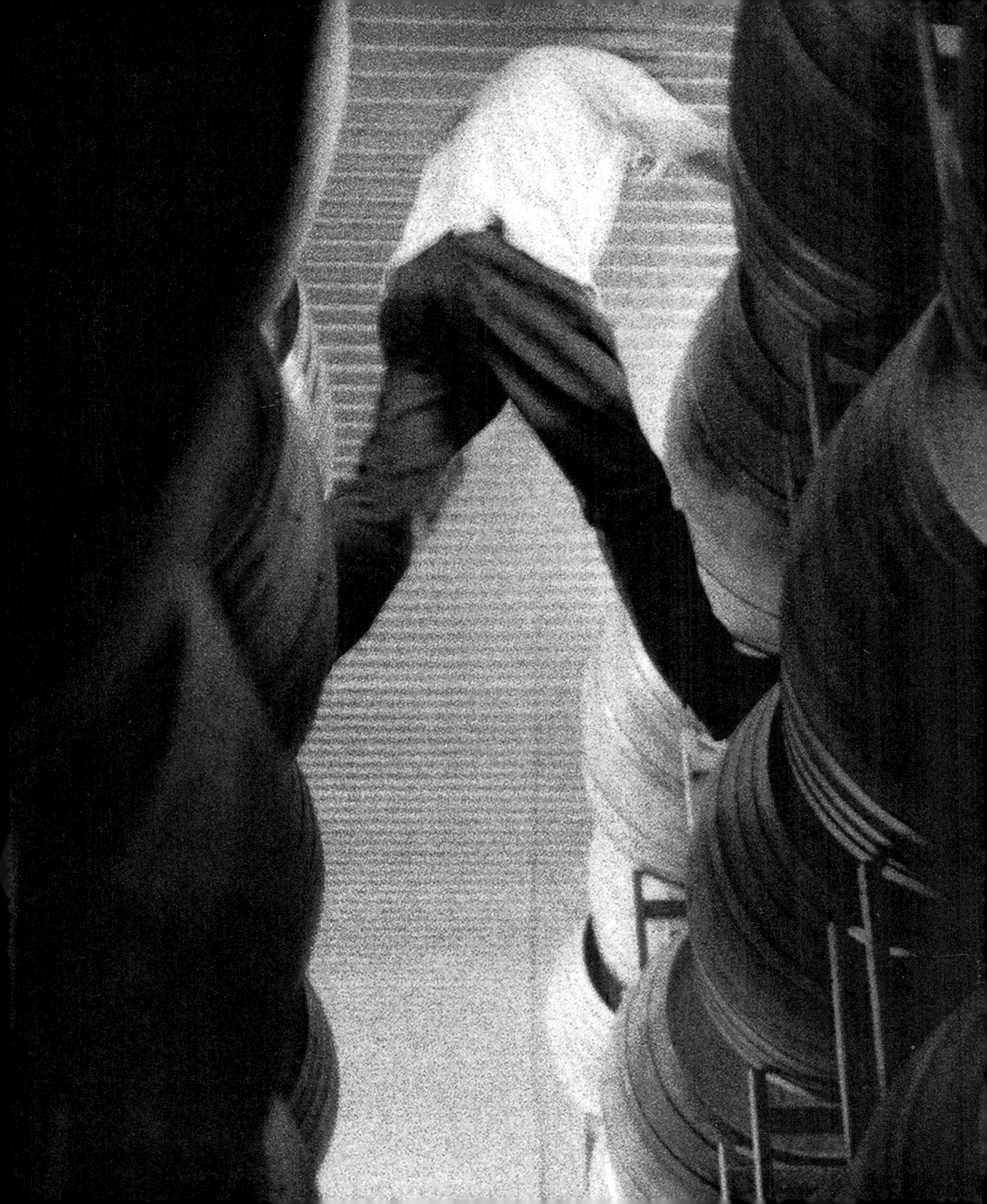

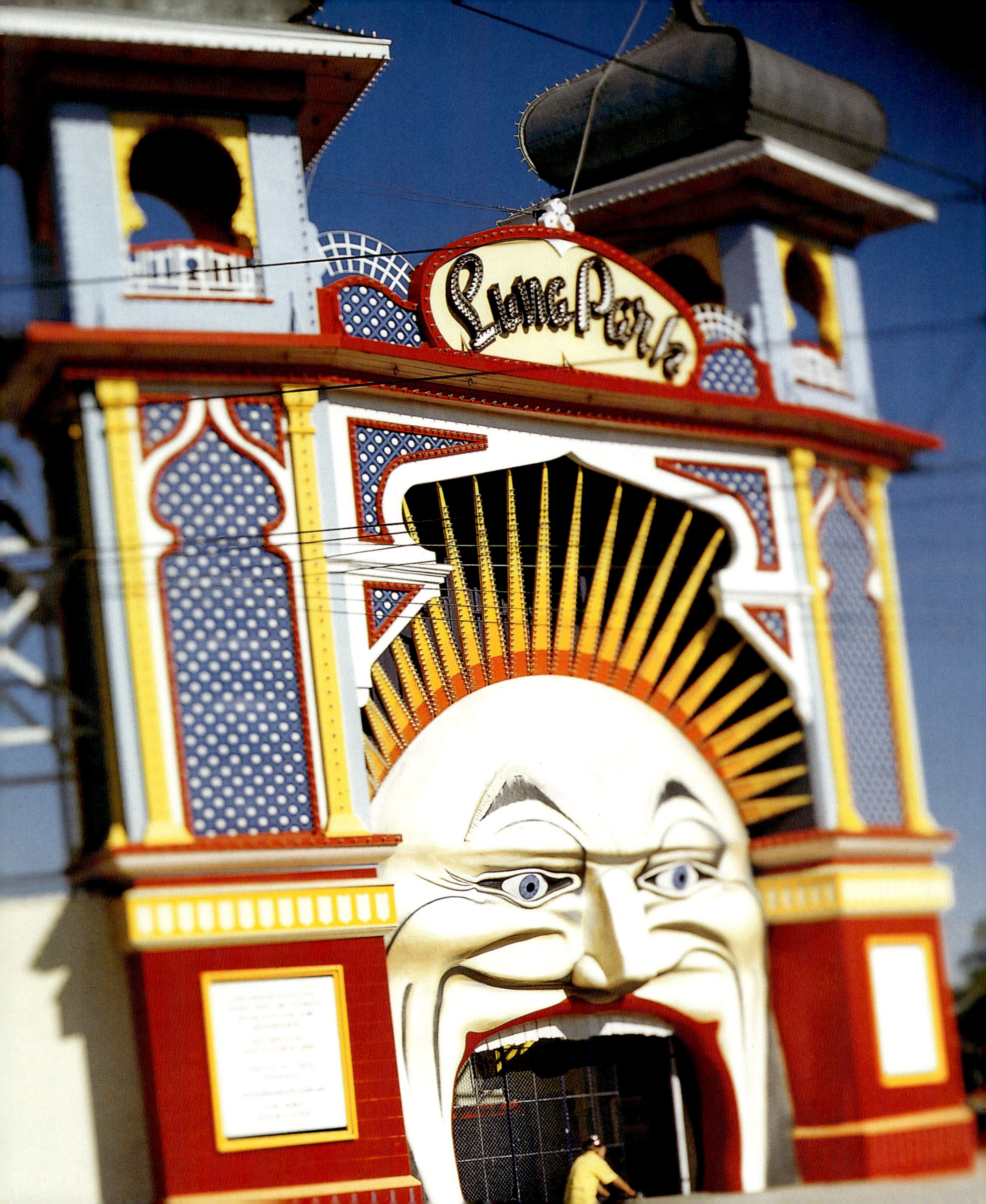
Luna Park

TOP OF THE BAY

Call me biased, but despite all claims to the contrary from my Sydney friends, I firmly believe that Melbourne is the food capital of Australia. There are umpteen books and guides devoted to cataloguing its restaurants, bars and cafés, so the last thing I want to do is go over the same ground.

Instead, what I have done is taken a tour around the bay suburbs and written about the places I like the best. What follows is a personal selection of restaurants, markets and delis that have inspired and delighted me in the twelve years I've lived in this wonderful city.

WILLIAMSTOWN

Officially a bayside suburb of Melbourne, Williamstown has the feel of being a small town in its own right, a condition that is emphasised by its position on the other side of the Yarra River, set well apart from the rest of Melbourne.

This quaint historic seaport has been a watery playground for well-heeled Melburnians since the turn of the last century. It was where steam-trains and steam-ships disgorged their passengers by the hundreds for a day out at the seaside. Little seems to have changed. In the summer Williamstown's waters are crowded with all manner of gleaming pleasure-craft, and on most weekends the open-air cafés and sandy beaches are full of happy families and camera-clicking tourists. But what good things are there for the food and wine lover to discover?

Given its waterside location, one might have thought that, at the very least, Williamstown would be a sea-food lover's paradise. Sadly, Williamstown has never really been about fishing. Even back in the very early days, the first settlers were more likely to have dined on boiled mutton, potatoes and beer. The harsh reality was that early Williamstown was dirty, smelly and awash with sly grog from illegal shanties and pubs, with enticing names such as the 'Bucket of Blood'.

Even in the early 1900s, the local newspaper, *The Advertiser*, bemoaned the lack of decent eateries for visitors to the place who might hanker after a refreshment saloon that would be 'cool and airy . . . with a tiled floor, marble tables for strawberries and cream . . . counters for the sale of soda and milk, lemon squash and cordials . . . a nice clean sweet-looking building'.

Sad to say, the visitor is still likely to be a little disappointed when it comes to the hunt for good food. Despite Williamstown's relatively recent gentrification, you get the feeling that people struggle to eat well here. Sure, there are the usual fashionably crowded waterfront spots, where the decibel count often borders on intolerable, and busy Nelson Place is packed to the gills with all manner of cafés, tea-rooms and ice-creameries, but on the whole there is little to excite the palate.

There are a few exceptions, however. For a posh meal out, Benbrook at Lalor House is probably the best bet for contemporary and imaginative food, albeit in slightly fussy surroundings. The restaurant at Sirens, a smart Art Deco building set right on the sands on the Williamstown esplanade is also a pleasant spot to spend a Sunday afternoon over a bottle of wine or two.

For simpler fare such as good old fish and chips, there are a couple of options, as you would expect in a seaside resort. Mussels Fish & Chippery on Nelson Parade, and Top of the Bay both have customers queuing down the streets over the summer – but for my money, the daggy old fish and chip shop on the Old Melbourne Road does the best fish in town – and most of the locals agree.

Lever & Kowalyk

Luckily, there is one true beacon of foodie excellence to be found in Williamstown. It's not in a prime waterfront location, nor is it on the tourist-thronged main promenade, Nelson Place. To find Lever & Kowalyk, one of my favourites of Melbourne's bright new food spots, you have to head to where the locals do their shopping in busy Ferguson Street. L&K is one of those impeccably modern cross-breeds – a café/restaurant and produce store combined – which offers a range of ultra-desirable foodstuffs and really top-notch meals in smart surroundings.

The inspiration for L&K came after co-owner and chef, Rohan Lever, visited Jones the Grocer and bills on a trip to Sydney. He had known Mark and Helen Kowalyk for twenty-odd years, and the three of them had always talked about opening up a café together (albeit in a half-joking way). When they finally took the plunge, they had a clear vision of what they wanted to create: a stylish and welcoming environment where locals (and visitors) could enjoy the same kind of excellent food and friendly, efficient service that they might find in the Big Smoke on the other side of the West Gate. And this is exactly what they have achieved at L&K.

While it's often said that two's company and three's a crowd, in this case the

Left: The marina at Williamstown, with Melbourne in the distance.

arrangement works splendidly. Between them, Rohan, Mark and Helen run their business with seamless efficiency. One of them is always on-site, but at the same time, they each have the flexibility to balance the rigours of the restaurant with the varying demands of new babies, teenagers and other domestic duties. Things work so well, they believe, because they each have their roles to play – Rohan creates the menus and manages the kitchen with head chef Matthew Fegan; Mark and Helen run front-of-house – and because they share the same vision and commitment to the place.

Which isn't to say that things haven't evolved in the three years they've been operating. At first, there was a strong emphasis on take-home food – homemade soups, casseroles and risottos were made daily to fill the take-home fridge. And the stuff just walked out the door – the locals just couldn't get enough of it. But the restaurant, too, just kept getting busier and busier, and with the limited size of the kitchen, it became much harder to keep the take-away fridge stocked. Finally, some simple economics dictated that it made more sense to use the fridge space for a couple of extra tables. While the three still firmly believe that there is a large demand for their kind of easy-to-cook ready-prepared meals, they have regretfully decided to put that side of the business on hold for the moment.

So for now, if you want to eat L&K's delicious food, you have to eat in, and that's no real hardship! The décor manages to achieve that happy balance of chic and comfort. One side of the smallish dining room is taken up with smart wooden display shelves stocked with a small range of designer comestibles and sparkling bottles of imported water. There are feature walls in a smart royal blue, banquettes of soft white leather, and funky white plastic bucket chairs. And then there is the central table piled high with cookery books, magazines and the daily newspapers in front of a cosy log fire.

In the beginning, apparently, there was quite a lot of apprehension about that central table. But these days folk seem to have no such qualms. On a recent visit for Sunday brunch, the table was crowded with a group of serious-looking young professionals engaged in lively political debate over strong lattés and autumn fruit compote. Other tables were full of young families happily dunking toast soldiers in their 'googies' or wolfing down the delectable ricotta hotcakes with maple syrup and grilled bananas (L&K is very child-friendly). Elsewhere, middle-aged couples sat reading the newspapers over a bottle of wine, while waiting for their Yarra Valley venison sausages with quince relish and chermoula-marinated snapper on smoky eggplant couscous.

The menu swings effortlessly through the

Above: Helen Kowalyk and Rohan Lever.

encourages its customers to do the same, so you can bring your bottles back for refilling. The wine itself is selected from around the country, and they also sell a small selection of preservative-free and biodynamic wines.

Back where we started, we stopped in front of the Chinese dumpling stall, where a group of noisy Chinese women were busy stuffing tray upon tray of tiny shiu mai, har gau and shui gau. Greg pointed out two more of his favourite stalls. 'Judy's Rabbits has been there forever. It's one of the only places in Melbourne where you can get wild rabbits and hares. I often used to pop down here to get them if my suppliers let me down. And while I was at it, I used to visit that stall over there,' he said sheepishly, pointing out the Market Pie Shop. 'I couldn't possibly have gone back to work without morning tea for the kitchen staff!'

The Vital Ingredient

My first port of call on a food-shopping expedition to South Melbourne is invariably The Vital Ingredient. It's the place to go for inspiration and is undoubtedly your best bet when on the hunt for unusual or hard-to-find ingredients. Many of Melbourne's top chefs think so too, with much of The Vital Ingredient's business being done through its wholesale arm. Every day of the week its vans are out on the road, delivering goodies to the best restaurants, hotels, department stores and delis around Victoria.

This is the kind of glorious place where I can easily kill a couple of hours, wandering around in a happy daze, picking up a jar of white truffle cream here, or a slab of macadamia nut nougat there. Every now and then I play a little game with myself, and try to think of some outrageous item they might not stock. The Vital Ingredient nearly always manages to show up my limited imagination and stun me with the extent and quality of

Chinese Five-spiced Duck Breast on Warm Potato and Porcini Salad

LEVER & KOWALYK

Brush the duck breasts with oil then dust with five-spice powder. Heat a frying pan and sauté the duck breasts over a low heat for 8–10 minutes, until they are cooked medium rare. Turn them from time to time so they cook evenly. Remove from the pan, cover and keep warm. To make the salad, wipe out the pan, then melt the butter and add the onion and potatoes and sauté for 5 minutes or so, until soft and lightly coloured.
Remove the mushrooms from their soaking water and squeeze dry. Add to the pan with the tomatoes and spinach and sauté for a further 2 minutes.
To make the sauce, melt the butter and sauté the onion and garlic until soft. Add the honey, then deglaze the pan with the muscat. Add the veal jus and bring to a gentle boil. Lower the heat and simmer until the sauce is reduced by a third. Season with salt and pepper to taste and strain.
To serve, heap a spoonful of salad onto each plate. Slice each duck breast into 6 and fan out on top of the salad. Spoon the sauce around the salad and serve straight away.
Serves 4

INGREDIENTS

4 LARGE DUCK BREASTS

50 ML OLIVE OIL

1 TEASPOON CHINESE FIVE-SPICE POWDER

SALAD

1 TEASPOON BUTTER

1/2 SPANISH ONION, FINELY CHOPPED

4 POTATOES, PEELED AND DICED INTO 1 CM CUBES AND BLANCHED

2 TABLESPOONS PORCINI MUSHROOMS, SOAKED IN WATER

2 TOMATOES, CUT INTO STRIPS

A HANDFUL OF SHREDDED BABY SPINACH LEAVES

SAUCE

1 TEASPOON BUTTER

1/4 ONION, DICED

1/4 CLOVE GARLIC, CHOPPED

2 TEASPOONS LEATHERWOOD HONEY

50 ML MUSCAT

200 ML VEAL JUS

SALT AND PEPPER

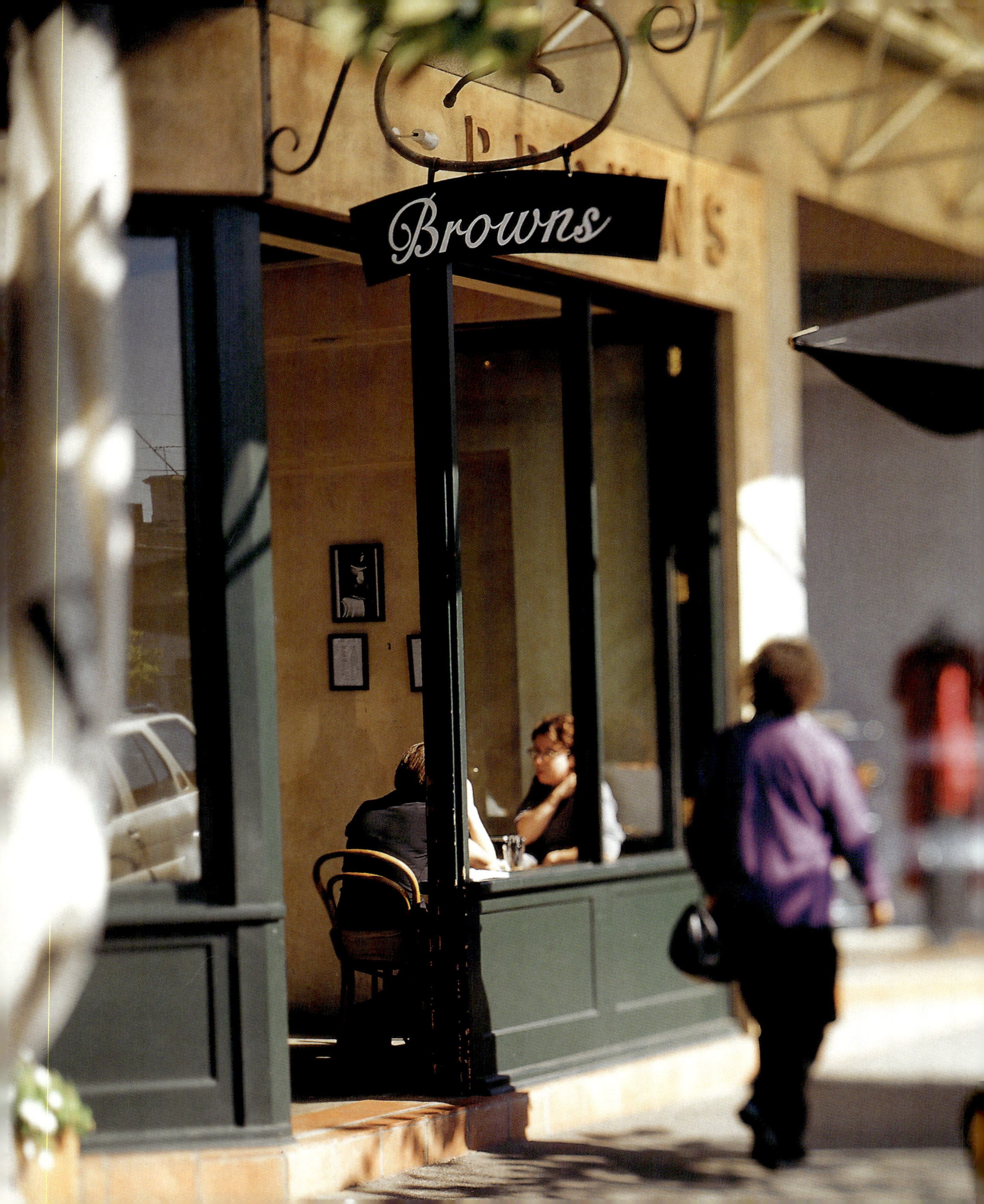
Browns

their range. (Who would ever have thought of looking for sugar from Swaziland or of making oil from cucumbers?)

Whole bins are devoted entirely to exotic dried mushrooms, salts (French, English, Sicilian – take your pick) and mustards. Shelves groan with bottles of the best local and imported olive oils and vinegars. There are vast selections of rice, pasta and flour, and row upon row of exquisitely packaged and gleaming jars of jams, chutneys and preserves. You can buy blocks of Swiss chocolate and jars of homemade chocolate sauce. For the antipasto platter there are preserved capsicums, artichokes, eggplant and tomatoes. If you fancy bush-tucker, then take your pick from alpine bush tomatoes, native peppermint or alpine pepper – and wash it all down with a glass of rainforest lime splash.

At the other end of the airy barn-like space is an enormous refectory table: the perfect spot to sit with a coffee and reflect upon all this bounty, or to browse through the store's vast range of cookery books. Wander upstairs and inspect their range of kitchenware, or check out the newsletter and book into a cookery class conducted by some of Australia's best chefs. Or just give in to temptation and load up the shopping basket with all manner of foodie goodies and go home to cook up a storm.

ALBERT PARK

I have friends who live in this most respectable and family-friendly of Melbourne's bayside suburbs, and if truth be told, I have always been a tad envious. Not just for the closeness of the wide, tree-lined streets to the sand and waters of Port Phillip Bay, nor for the rocketing value of the real-estate here, but because the main streets of Albert Park have become something of a mecca for food lovers in recent years.

In Albert Park, the food scene centres around Bridport Street and its continuation, Victoria Avenue, which leads down to the wide foreshore. My friend Caroline, local resident and mother of two, had always told me that it was the best place in Melbourne to live as far as food and lifestyle were concerned.

In terms of the variety and sheer quality in a concentrated area she is not wrong.

There are butchers and bakers, pastry shops, fishmongers, delis and health food shops, and a plethora of cosy cafés and bright modern eateries. A great favourite is the Fruit Palace, one of Melbourne's best greengrocers, which is tucked in next to the post office. It's a pleasure to visit this bright well-organised shop, which sells only the best quality seasonal produce and hard-to-find ingredients, as well as fresh farm eggs, dried fruit and nuts and an abundance of gorgeous flowers that spill onto the pavement outside.

Above: Browsing at The Vital Ingredient.

A little further down is Brown's Bakery, with its superb range of breads and French-style cakes and pastries. The legendary Greg Brown, who is well known in Melbourne's food scene as a top chef as well as baker, now owns an empire of bread shops which are scattered around the suburbs. Favourites are the tangy, chewy San Francisco sourdough, the rich and dark walnut and raisin loaf as well as his first-class baguettes, brioches, croissants and savoury tarts. A few yards away, he has a rival in Laurent Boulangerie and Patisserie, whose owner Laurent Boillon started up his shops after working in the world-famous Le Nôtre bakery in Paris. Here too, there are a large range of superb traditional breads and mouth-watering pastries and cakes. Pick up a filled ciabatta for lunch, and pass over, if you can, the legendary chocolate-filled doughnuts!

There is good quality fish at Bottom of the Harbour, freshly made juices (any fruit or vegie combo you like) at Feeling Fruity, and top-class meat at Polkinghorne's, a new 'designer butcher', where you can even get a cup of coffee and a meal.

Albert Park is exceptionally well served with cafés and delis too. There is the popular, family-run Albert Park Deli, which offers a terrific selection of hearty take-home meals, such as moussaka, Italian and Moroccan chicken and beef stroganoff. A couple of shops away is Dundas Place Café, where George and Julie make one of the best toasted sandwiches around. At the weekends the pavement tables on this part of the street are crowded with groovy couples with dogs, and young families with toddlers.

Stroll a little further down and you hit Victoria Avenue, and the Japanese home-style restaurant, Misuzu's, one of my favourite restaurants on the street. Once tiny, in recent years Misuzu's has expanded into neighbouring space, so you no longer run the risk of being disappointed if you turn up late on a busy night.

ST KILDA

St Kilda is a place of contrasts and extremes: it is seedy and stylish, dissolute and designer-clad. It's the place where musicians and artists hang out, and tourists and day-trippers come to gawk. Visit on a sunny weekend over the summer and you could almost imagine yourself in California. The foreshore is a heaving mass of humanity: rollerbladers jostle for space with joggers and cyclists, and the beach is packed with happy sunbakers. Back on the esplanade, crowds come to rummage through the stalls of the weekly craft market, the pubs rock, and the roller-coaster at nearby Luna Park rattles around to a background of excited screams.

It is also extraordinarily well served when it comes to food and drink. Down on the foreshore there are the fabulous Stokehouse and Donovans, and if fine dining is your thing, you could do worse than to head for Fitzroy Street. Among all the grunge and the building works lurk some of Melbourne's finest restaurants: there's Di Stasio's for stylish Italian food, Circa at the Prince for a taste of opulence, and further down towards Albert Park, the superb Melbourne Wine Room.

Acland Street

While the inexorable march of progress continues in the world of food as relentlessly as anywhere else, some things, thank goodness, remain constant. Scheherezade in busy Acland Street is one such place. While many surrounding businesses have been touched with the style brush, or bought out by chain-stores, Scheherezade remains

Right: Acland Street, St Kilda.

ST KILDA BEACH 96
2094
PICK ME UP

EDELWEIS
St Kilda's Deli

Chakra

CAKE SHOP

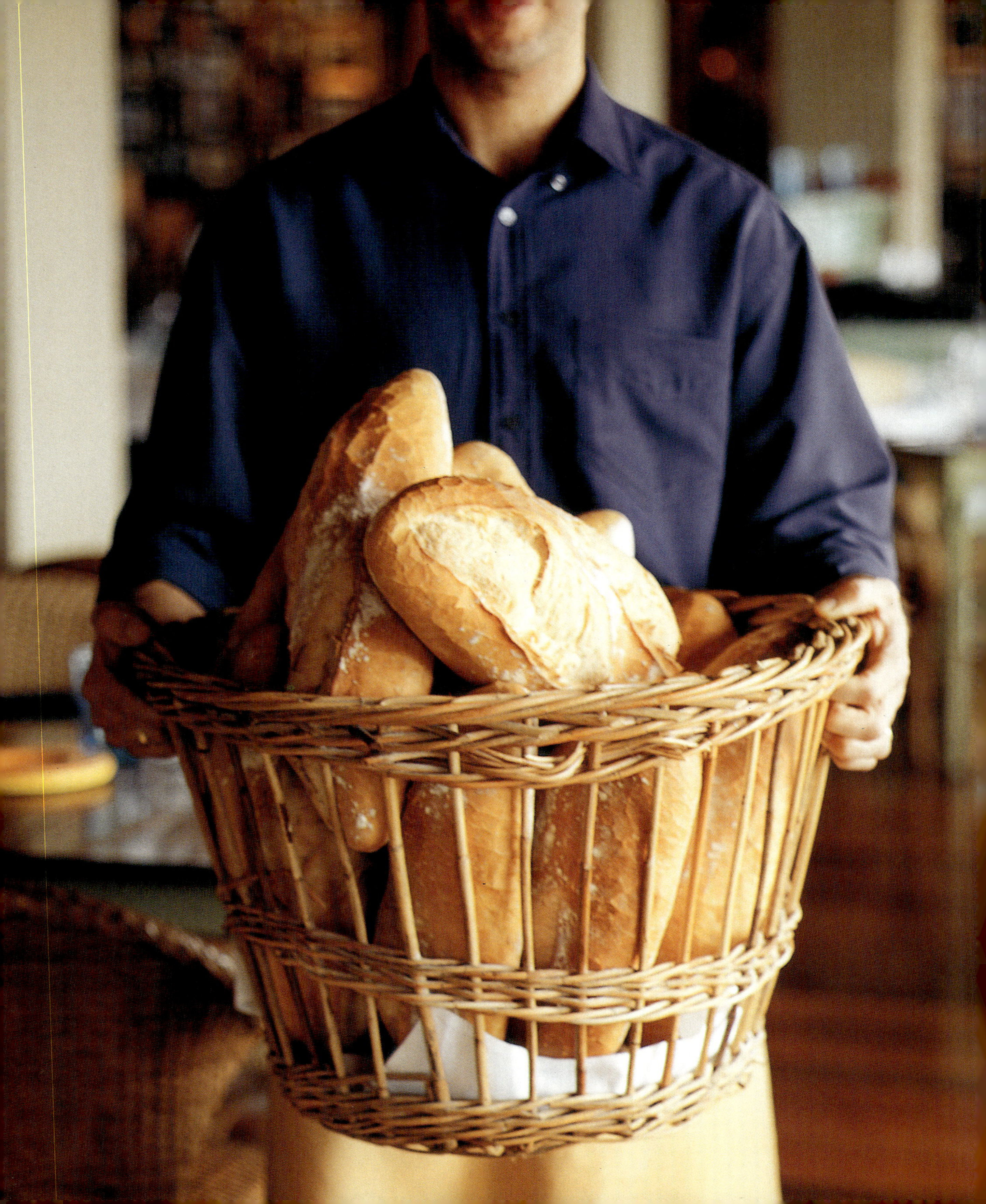

true to its Eastern European roots. The décor is unapologetically daggy, with its original gold floral wallpaper and laminated tables, and the menu never changes. It sees a daily stream of regulars lining up for traditional Eastern European favourites such as borscht, potato latkes, cabbage rolls and the legendary schnitzel.

Back in the late 1950s, when Scheherezade first opened its doors, St Kilda was a very different place. The first home to a large influx of Eastern European and Jewish immigrants, Acland Street then was full of continental delicatessens and cake shops. Today, although food outlets still rule the roost, Scheherezade's neighbours represent a much more diverse ethnic mix, including Malaysian, Chinese, Indian, Middle Eastern, Italian and Modern Australian.

But despite the many changes, Acland Street is still a top spot for food lovers. You can breakfast in any one of a number of groovy cafes: try 189 Espresso Bar, Café Vibe or Big Mouth for fashionable breakfast fare such as poached winter fruits with mascarpone, fluffy buttermilk pancakes, eggs Benedict or Florentine, or avocado on thick sourdough toast. If a major cholesterol hit is more your style on a Sunday morning, then at Greasy Joe's you can load up on a more traditional big breakfast or one of their famous monster burgers.

Acland Street is also the bustling busy home of Chinta Ria Soul, where people come in their droves for the terrific curry laksa and a dose of jazz, and the Red Rock Noodle Bar, which is more determinedly minimalist, with a menu that crosses many oriental boundaries.

If you have a sweet tooth, then Acland Street is certainly the place for you. While many of the original continental cake shops have disappeared, a few legends remain, such as Monarch Cakes, Acland Continental Cakes and European Cakes. Their windows are stacked high with a mind-boggling selection of traditional goodies, such as kugelhopf, baked cheesecakes, black forest cakes, vanilla slices, macaroon sandwiches, chocolate Florentines, plum cake and all sorts of fruit flans. Pass them by if you can.

Although most of the original delis have disappeared, a few terrific successors carry on the business of providing top-quality specialist foods to the neighbourhood.

Opposite: Bread especially made for Donovans Restaurant.
Left: Chef Robert Castellani at Donovans Restaurant.
Right: Kitchen utensils used as decoration at Donovans Restaurant.

Edelweiss is my favourite, with a mouth-watering window display of interesting salads, dips and sweet treats. It offers a good range of smallgoods and cheeses, and on a sunny day you could do worse than order a freshly made gourmet sandwich (on Phillippa's bread) and juice and take them down to the foreshore for an impromptu picnic.

More leisurely or upmarket dining is also an option in Acland Street, albeit of a funky and often noisy kind. Cicciolina is one of my favourites – cosy and snug in winter, and open to the streets in summer, its exuberant bold modern Mediterranean food and sassy, energetic pace are a joy. But be warned, there is a no-booking policy, and on hot summer nights or busy weekends you will almost certainly have to queue unless you get there unfashionably early.

Veludo is another favourite. It, too, is determinedly cool, with its downstairs devoted to bar-flies and smokers. But climb the industrial steel staircase to the upper level and you enter an airy, light-filled and pleasing modern dining space. The food is decidedly modern – of the 'Asian spiced duck with a red wine-poached pear' and 'beetroot-crusted lamb and roasted quince' variety – but here the mix-and-match approach works beautifully.

Donovans

For me, Donovans is the restaurant that best sums up the spirit and charm of St Kilda. It's a million miles away from the current trend for chilly, soulless over-designed places, where everything is blond wood and stainless steel. Instead, the restaurant completely reflects the extraordinary imagination and flair of its owners, Gail and Kevin Donovan. As Gail says, 'I had a nutty idea that I wanted to have a restaurant that felt like a home.' And that is exactly what the Donovans have created.

Everywhere you look there are things to delight the eye: surfaces are crowded with cosy family photos; a collection of willow pattern china adorns an old marble dresser; at the entrance a collection of brightly coloured Wellington boots are neatly lined up next to an old wooden wheelbarrow. Deep squishy sofas, piled high with cushions, are arranged for cosy

Left: Vanilla slice with candied chestnuts (see page 85).
Right: Gail and Kevin Donovan.

Vanilla Slice with Candied Chestnuts
DONOVANS

Preheat oven to 190°C.

Cut pastry in half and roll each piece out until it is about 5 mm thick. Cut each piece of rolled out pastry in half again, and place between two heavy oiled baking sheets. Cook in a pre-heated oven for approximately 15 minutes or until golden brown. Remove from oven and allow the pastry to cool completely before slicing each piece into three rectangles, each about 6 cm x 10 cm. This makes a total of twelve rectangles.

To make the pastry cream, bring the milk to a boil with the vanilla pod, half the sugar and the lemon zest, then turn off heat and allow to infuse. Place the remaining sugar in a mixing bowl with the eggs and egg yolks and whisk well until light and creamy. Fold in the cornflour and custard powder. Pour the hot milk into the egg mixture and whisk until combined, then return to a clean saucepan and cook over a medium heat until the custard thickens. Strain into a clean container and lay a sheet of Gladwrap over the top to prevent a skin from forming. Chill until ready to use.

To make the chestnut cream, fold the pastry cream and whipped cream into the chestnut purée.

To assemble, place a rectangle of puff pastry in the middle of each plate.

Fill two piping bags – one with plain pastry cream and one with chestnut cream.

Pipe alternating strips, widthways onto each pastry rectangle – aim for five strips altogether. Top with a second pastry rectangle and repeat the piping process with more pastry cream and chestnut cream. Top with a third pastry rectangle and dust with icing sugar. Serve garnished with candied chestnuts (marrons glacés – obtainable from specialist food stores).

Serves 4

INGREDIENTS

500 G GOOD QUALITY PUFF PASTRY (OR MAKE YOUR OWN), CHILLED

PASTRY CREAM

1 LITRE MILK

1 VANILLA POD

250 G SUGAR

ZEST OF 1 LEMON

2 EGGS

4 EGG YOLKS

75 G CORNFLOUR

2 TABLESPOONS CUSTARD POWDER

CHESTNUT CREAM

1 TIN (375 G) SWEETENED CHESTNUT PURÉE

1 CUP PASTRY CREAM (SEE ABOVE)

1 CUP WHIPPED CREAM

groupings next to the central fireplace and the coffee table is stacked with cookery books and magazines.

And if all that sounds a bit twee, rest assured it most certainly is not. The real success of Donovans is that nothing feels contrived – instead all is colour and comfort – you can't fail to be charmed. And while things look laid-back, the place runs like a well-oiled machine. All this quirkiness just wouldn't work without a team of dedicated and highly professional staff to keep things spick and span (it came as only a small surprise to learn that there are nearly 80 staff at Donovans).

The home-style approach extends to the kitchen too. Talented chef Robert Castellani, who earned his stripes as head chef at Stephanie's restaurant before joining Donovans, has created a menu of imaginative but accessible dishes. As you might expect, there is a nod to his Italian heritage in the homemade pastas and risottos: there might be a ravioli of baby eggplant and mint with parmesan, or a risotto of lemon and leeks with tiger prawns. Heartier dishes might include a home-style fish stew for two, or braised oxtail and pudding with caramelised vegetables. Robert is also big on barbecues – organic pork chops with Italian sausage and garlic butter are as popular with diners as Bermagui swordfish with a dried tomato and lemon dressing.

At Donovans it's well nigh impossible to resist the desserts – there might be a muscat wine trifle with pears and champagne custard, or lemon gelato with a slosh of grappa. And then there's the Donovans' signature dessert: good old-fashioned bombe Alaska, an astounding construction of hazelnut and chocolate ice-cream smothered with meringue.

Thought and attention have gone into the extensive wine list, too. Up front, you will find Kevin's choice of wines by the glass. The rest of the list is sensibly divided into wines from the 'Old' and 'New' worlds, and for a big night out, there is an impressive selection of cellar reserves and museum bottles.

Like the view outside the windows, things inside the restaurant are always changing. Gail and Kevin are firm believers in implementing fresh and inventive ideas so that neither staff nor customers become jaded. So twice a year the restaurant gets a makeover and a new wardrobe. The menus, too, change with the seasons, to showcase the best available produce. But what remains constant is the obvious dedication and sheer professionalism of this dynamic duo and the entire Donovans team. And somehow, all that energy is infectious: whenever I visit, I go away feeling not just well fed and watered, but inspired and uplifted. You can't ask for more than that from a dining experience.

Above: Owner Lisa Hodgson outside the Brighton Food Store.

BRIGHTON & BEYOND

Take the beach road out of Melbourne one day and you'll get a real feel for Port Phillip Bay and the city's bayside suburbs. Once you leave the crowded St Kilda Esplanade, with its rollerbladers and Sunday strollers, you pass leafy Elwood with its foreshore parklands and busy marina. The road then heads inland, away from the sea, taking you through the wide streets of wealthy Brighton where the money is older and so is the population. It's home, too, to those famous beach bathing boxes, in their poster-paint colours, as well as a number of gentle sandy beaches. But as you continue your beachside journey the suburbs seem to spread themselves out a little, and the broad expanse of the bay itself seems to impinge more and more on your sightlines. I have to confess to loving it most on cold winter's days, when the water stretches out like a great flat sheet of steel, disturbed only by the odd monster cargo ship lumbering across the horizon.

Brighton and Hampton are both very well served by cafés, restaurants and food shops. Chic Church Street, for instance, seemingly has everything for the discerning food-shopper or diner. You might spot an immaculately coiffed Brighton mum on her way home clutching a Brown's box filled with millefeuilles or a sensational lemon tart. There is homemade gourmet pasta to be found at Donnini's, excellent coffee from The Beanery and an outstanding selection of Japanese fare at O Mu Ro.

I've never been quite sure where the boundaries lie between Brighton, East Brighton and Hampton, or whether they exist only in the mind of real-estate agents, but one thing I know for certain is that people who live near Hampton Street are very lucky when it comes to food.

To begin with, there is Devola's, the legendary fruit and vegetable shop that offers an outstanding range of the best quality produce. There are a couple of excellent delicatessens and food stores (Lafayette Fine Foods is probably my favourite) and Vintage Cellars – a large airy wine shop that is big on service, and offers regular tastings and helpful advice.

Head for the bay and you pass two very diverse bakeries. At one end of the spectrum is Brown's (to satisfy your need for batard, pain rustique and escargots), and at the other is Marmaris, a tiny Turkish restaurant much frequented by locals who pop in to stock up on dips and savoury pastries. But Marmaris also makes some of the best Turkish pide bread around, and throughout the day you'll find a seemingly endless stream of enormous fluffy loaves emerging from the oven, filling the space with exotic yeasty aromas.

Brighton Food Store

In New Street you find the Brighton Food Store, one of my favourite spots for take-home fare. If I were absolutely forced to pick one reason for loving this place it would have to be the amazing raspberry and white chocolate muffins. But there are many other good reasons to visit this lovely little shop, whether you live locally or are just passing through.

Despite its small size, the Brighton Food Store actually stocks a huge range of house-made goodies. It is aimed firmly at the take-home market, although for most of the day the pavement tables and window seats are packed with happy eaters, munching on a freshly made gourmet sandwich or enjoying an Illy coffee and sweet pastry.

Although it has been serving the neighbourhood for ten years or so, the Brighton Food Store has recently changed hands and undergone a bit of a face-lift. Everything, from the outside awning to the labels on the produce, now sports the smart burnt orange and black colour scheme. But new owner Lisa Hodgson has kept on all the favourite dishes, and even added a few new goodies of her own to the range.

Sweet offerings might include their mouth-watering pear and raspberry almond tarts, New York cheesecakes, jaffa cakes, the ever-popular lumberjack cake or squidgy moist chocolate brownies, all stylishly displayed. There's a different casserole and soup made everyday, as well as the perennial favourites: salmon patties, couscous, Asian noodle stir-fries or simple roasted vegetables jostle for space with honey-soy drumsticks, tandoori chicken and an imaginative range of savoury tarts.

The freezer, too, is stocked full of take-home stocks, soups and sauces, as well as casseroles, curries and their legendary dhal. On the shelves there are 'crispies' to go with the dips and a selection of homemade cookies and jams. One trip here and you need never worry about what to have for dinner!

Ricketts Point Fine Foods

If there is a better ice-cream in the world than Val Gaskell's Lemon Delicious, I have yet to taste it. And I am not the only person who thinks so: in 2001 it was named champion at the Australian Dairy Industry 'Oscars', one more in a long history of Val's awards. The walls of the funny little corner shop on busy Bluff Road are jam-packed with certificates and medals, garnered over the past twelve years or so, since the business began.

One autumn evening, I braved the rush-hour traffic and drove down to Black Rock to see Val. As I walked into the shop, a warm fug of marmalade smells hit my nostrils. Unless I was very much mistaken there was a batch of cumquat and brandy ice-cream in the offing! A few moments later, Val arrived.

'Sorry to keep you waiting,' she puffed. 'I've just had to drive ten boxes of lemons and six boxes of limes over to the new factory, and get my son onto the job of squeezing!'

As she showed me round the premises, it seemed hardly believable that until then all those exquisite ice-creams had been churned out of the tiny kitchen behind the shop. But things were about to change. 'I've finally bitten the bullet and decided to move into bigger premises,' Val said. 'We make ice-cream for hotels like Sofitel and the Novotel, and restaurants like the Flower Drum and Italy 1, so having proper commercial space will make life so much easier.'

My eye roamed greedily around the shop. Two freezer cabinets were stocked with ice-cream and sorbet, and on the wall behind the counter was a board outlining the flavours on offer that day. Although Lemon Delicious is the flavour that everyone seems to have heard of, there are others which are fast becoming legends in their own right. That day I could have tucked into Treacle Nut Brittle, Botrytis Supreme or Chocolate Bourbon, among others. At Christmas, Val makes thousands of litres of her famous Plum Pudding ice-cream, to go with the more traditional hot pud.

I wondered out loud what had set the whole ice-cream thing in motion. 'Well, I've always thought that it's the last thing people eat at a meal that they remember the best,' said Val with a smile. 'And I guess I inherited a sweet tooth from my mother. I started making ice-cream at home – lemon was always a bit of a favourite – and it got to the stage when friends came over for a meal that they'd say "we don't care what you cook, as long as you give us that delicious lemon ice-cream!" Things just kind of happened from there.'

Val worked for twenty-odd years as a home economics teacher before setting up her ice-cream business. From the very early days she was determined to make flavours

Right: Ice-cream at Ricketts Point.

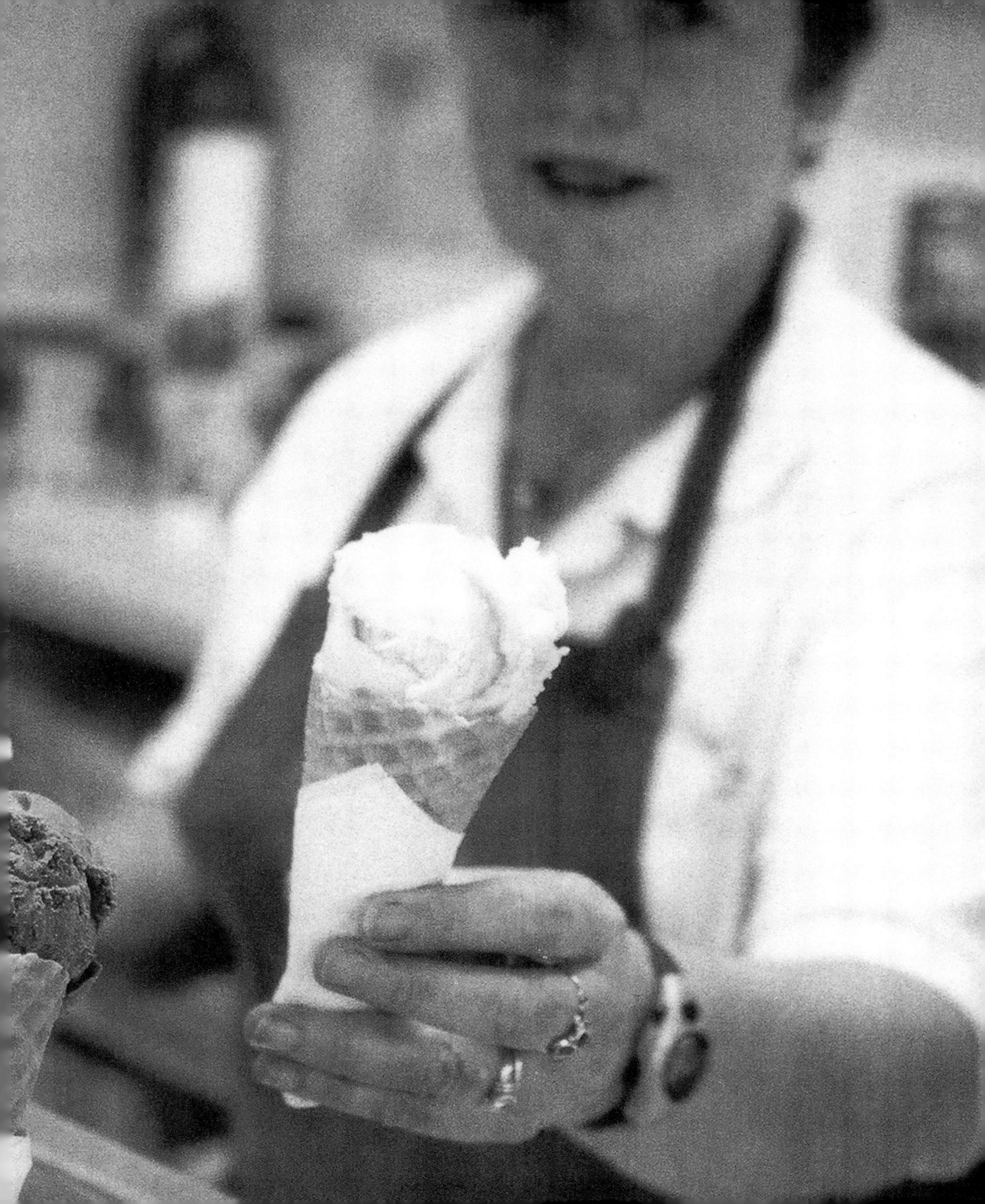

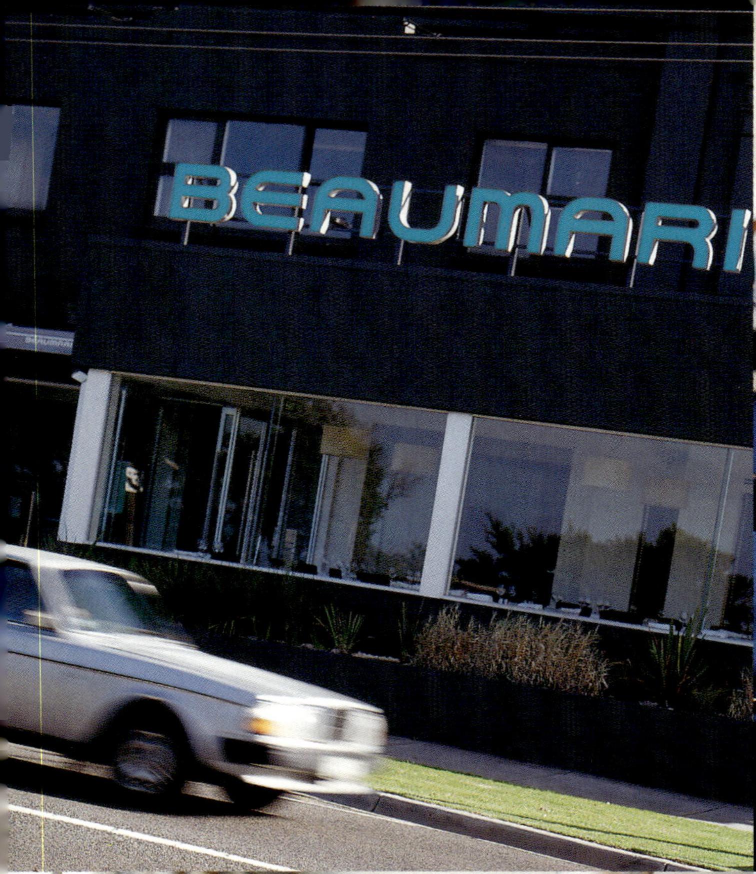
BEAUMARI

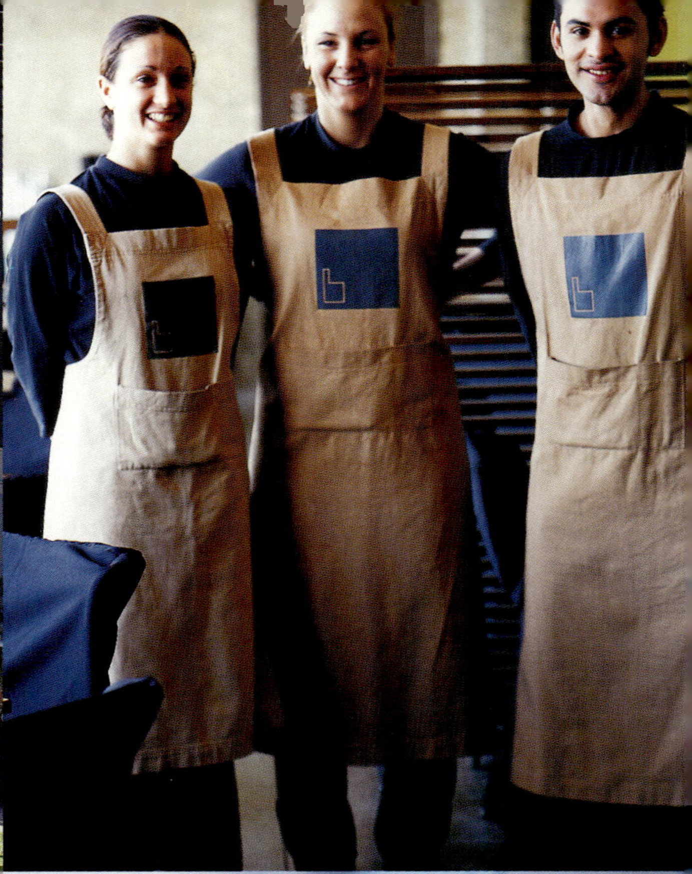

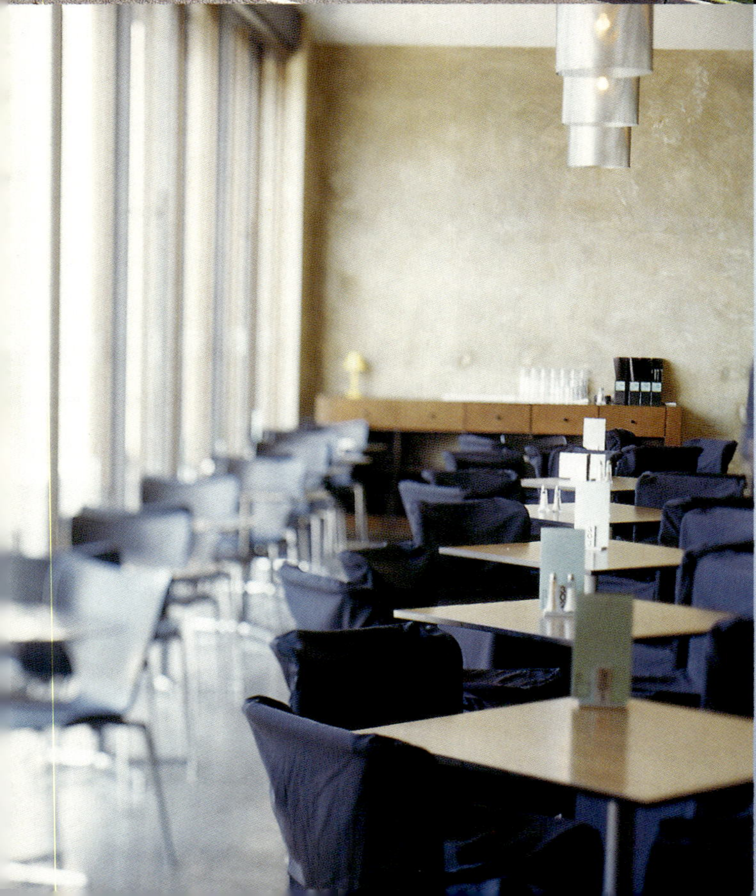

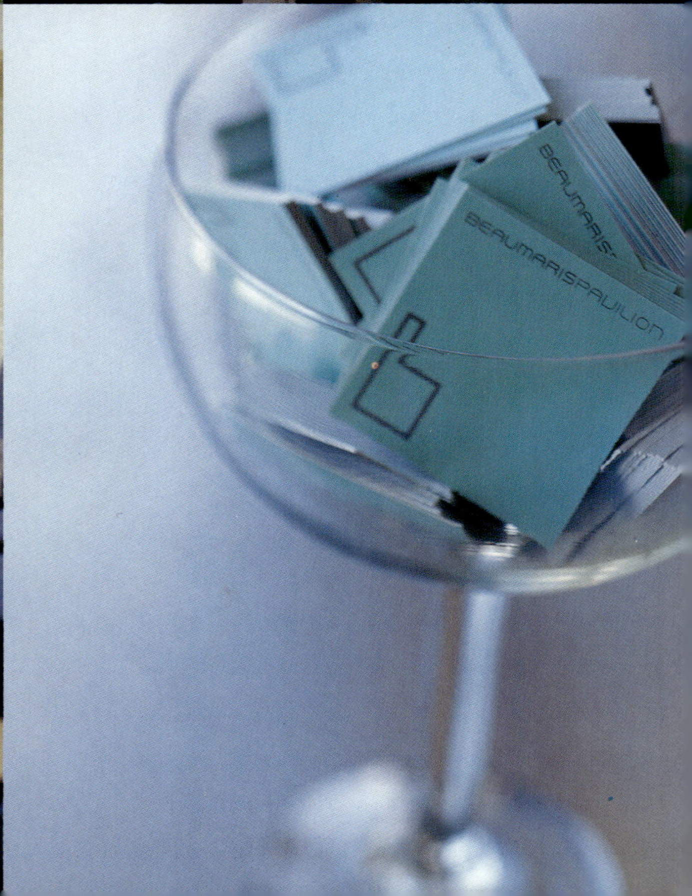
BEAUMARISPAVILION
BEAUMARIS

that differed from other commercially made stuff. Twelve years on, she is just as passionate about her product, and is constantly thinking up new and delicious flavour combinations.

All through the summer, and most weekends, people line up for Val's ice-cream. Although you can find Ricketts Point ice-cream at selected food outlets around Melbourne, I can think of no better way to conclude a day trip to the beach than a stop off at Val's shop to stock up on my favourite flavours.

Beaumaris Pavilion

When you think of Beaumaris, words like 'design' and 'fine dining' don't exactly spring to mind. But after a visit to the swishly remodelled Beaumaris Pavilion, you may just have to adjust your way of thinking. There is no denying that the new Pavilion is an imaginatively conceived and beautifully appointed addition to Melbourne's dining scene, all the more remarkable when you consider that it is not located in the swinging heart of the city, but on the outskirts of a conservative bayside suburb.

The old 'Beauie' Hotel, with its gaming rooms and counter meals, has disappeared forever. Where once there were fishing nets suspended from the ceiling and pictures of the Cutty Sark, now there is an intimate lounge area and a stylish modern bar. Where once there were tiny brown windows, too high and dingy to see through, now there is a spacious dining room with vast panes of glass looking straight out onto the crescent sweep of the bay. And where once there were 'pokie' machines and fish 'n' chips, now there is a chic new café, with tables spilling out onto the terrace.

In fact, this is just the sort of place that would normally send an anxious shiver down my spine. The city of Melbourne is groaning with far too many expensively designed restaurants, where the 'in your face' architecture and aggressively modern décor vie for your attention. All too often the service is arrogant (or completely lacking), and menus follow the same drearily contemporary lines.

But the minute you approach the smart new façade at the Pavilion, you sense that things are different. Straightaway there is that soothing sensation that the staff know what they are doing, and from the first glance at the snappy green acrylic menu, you just know that the food is going to be a serious proposition.

And when you learn that the executive chef is Ian Curley, then the sense of excitement about the whole proposition increases. Once upon a time, Ian was known as a member of the talented and ambitious 'Brit Pack' who came to Australia in search of adventure and better prospects than they might hope for in cut-throat London. Ian has been in Melbourne for nearly twelve years, and the city has, to all intents and purposes, claimed him as its own. I had eaten and enjoyed Ian's food all around Melbourne: from the early days at Rhubarbs in grungy Fitzroy, to a mellower and more refined menu at The Point in Albert Park. So it was with a great sense of anticipation that a friend and I took the coastal road to Beaumaris for lunch one autumn's day.

We decided to begin proceedings with a 'starter' while we examined the menu. A few moments later, a shot glass appeared, sprouting fine shreds of green mango, papaya and daikon. Underneath nestled a plump Pacific oyster on an icy bed of vodka and lime granita. It was a nice way to prepare the palate for the delights ahead.

When the first course arrived, we fell into a reverential silence. My friend had chosen a chicken and shiitake mushroom terrine, which came as a succulent slab of buff and

Left: The Beaumaris Pavilion and welcoming staff.

black on a chunky pool of brilliant yellow piccalilli. This looked like hearty fare, but a first bite revealed the subtleties of its composition. And as I chewed, savouring the delicate tastes and textures, the unmistakable sexy flavour of truffle oil spread through my mouth.

With a wrench, I turned my attention to my own meal. On my plate was an impressively constructed tower. Two fat pink discs of Sichuan-spiced tuna sandwiched thin slices of avocado and tomato, and a tian of more chopped tuna, bound in a light mayonnaise. Around the tower were thin shreds of intensely green seaweed, and bright red blobs of a sweet tomato purée.

Ian Curley is quite keen on compositions on the same basic flavour theme, and they pop up from time to time in his menus. My main course (a quartet of duck) was another example. A tiny cup of intense consommé sat next to a flaky pithivier of shredded duck, while further along the plate was a perky green 'chipolata' – a tiny duck-stuffed cabbage roll – perched on top of two discs of duck sausage. Taking up the largest part of the plate was a fan of perfect pink slices of duck breast and some sweetly caramelised witlof. To cut through all this richness and intensity, the dish came with a lively rocket and mint salad, speckled with segments of ruby grapefruit.

My friend's whole snapper was simpler, but no less brilliant. It came perfectly cooked, with a minimum of fuss, and drizzled with an intense lemon-infused oil. To one side was a timbale of ratatouille. So far, all was very good.

Desserts continued to impress. We could have tried Ian's legendary toffee crunch bar cake with chocolate caramel sauce and honeycomb ice-cream, or a wicked sounding double-layered Valrhona manjari chocolate tart. But in deference to the chilly weather outside I plumped for a steamed orange pudding with cumquats and Grand Marnier ice-cream.

A short while later, the thin afternoon sun came flooding through the windows. I carefully scraped the last skerrick of jammy cumquat from my plate and looked around the light-filled room. Around us were scattered tables of similarly contented-looking fellow diners. It was a Thursday lunchtime, and the Pavilion was about a twenty-minute drive from Melbourne's CBD, making it definitely a 'destination' restaurant. But the others looked as glad they had made the trip as we were.

Right: Outside The Stokehouse on the beach at St Kilda.

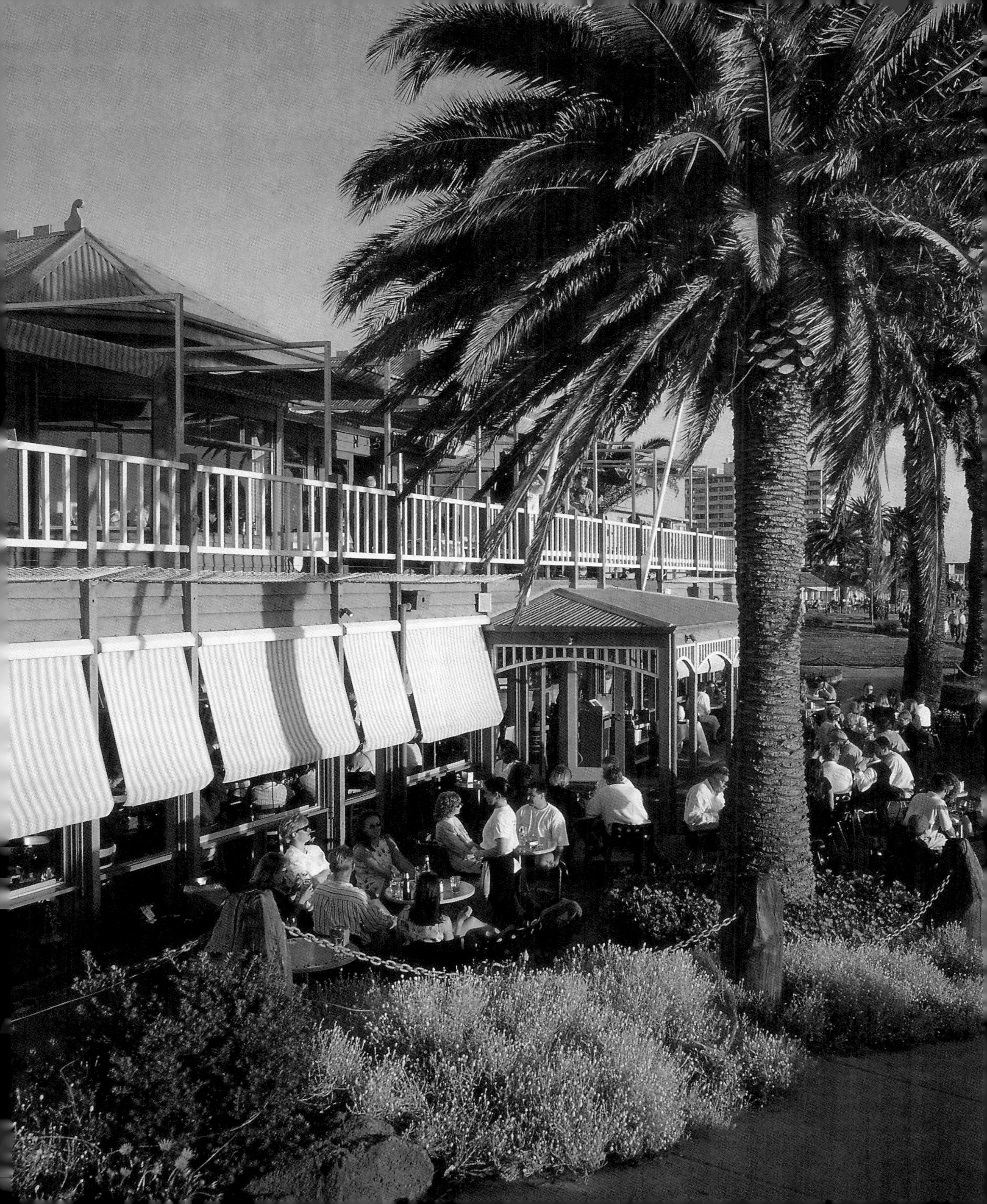

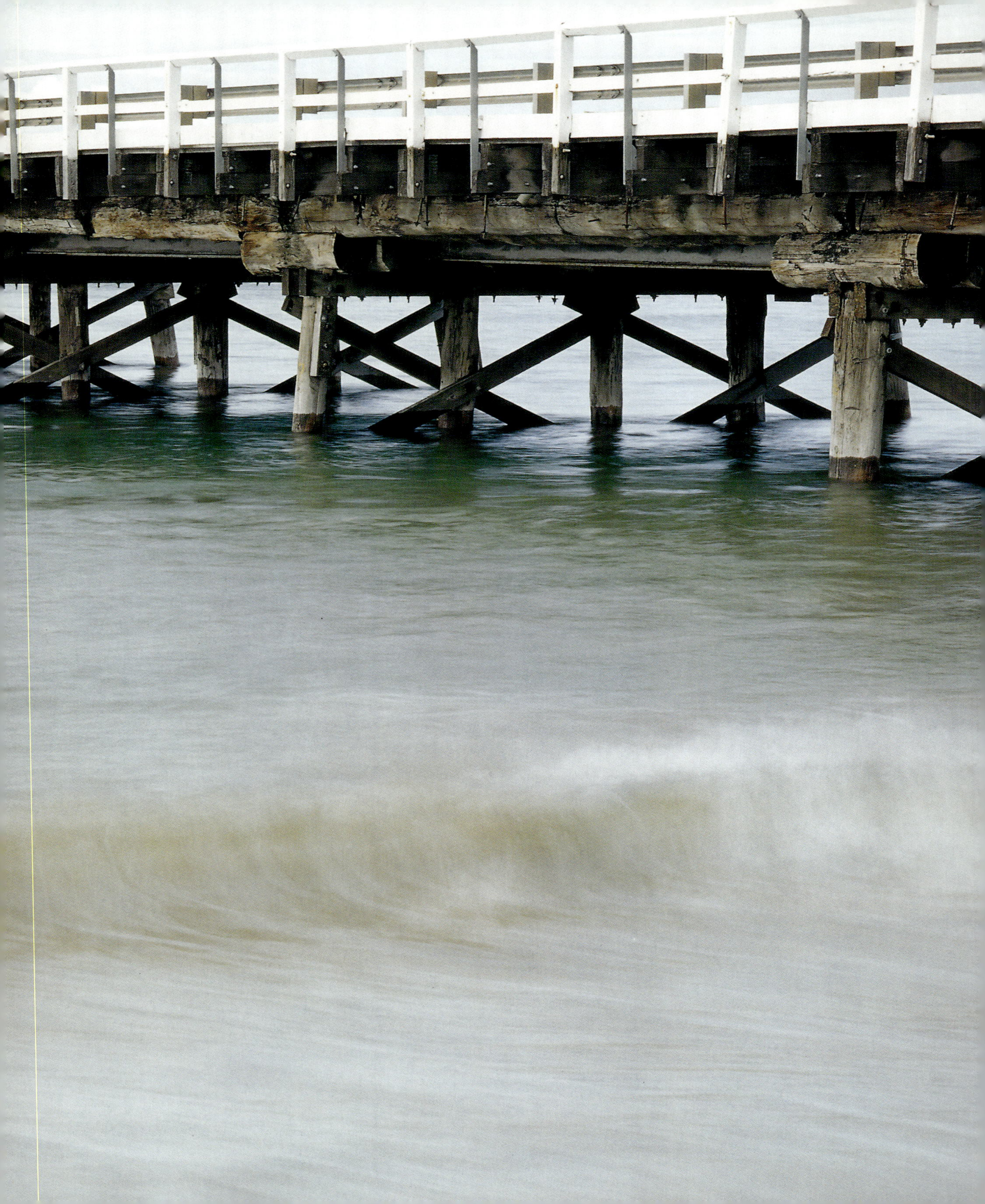

BELLARINE PENINSULA AND GEELONG

I must confess to having something of a soft spot for Geelong and the Bellarine Peninsula. This might have something to do with family connections (my father grew up in Geelong), but is also due to that great Australian tradition of supporting the underdog. Let's face it, there are plenty of 'Aussie battlers' in this part of the world. Over the centuries, the region has seen its substantial winemaking reputation cut off at the knees by the phylloxera blight, it's suffered a century of dusty droughts that have hit as hard at farmers as vignerons, and Geelong itself has had to fight back from the grim reality of economic recessions that seem to have been its lot in recent decades.

And yet, every time I hit the Melbourne–Geelong Road, a road I know very well from my childhood, I feel a sense of excitement. As children, my brother and I spent endless Friday nights squabbling in the backseat of the car on the way to our grandparents' beach house at Point Lonsdale. It was only the promise of our favourite gelati at Werribee (chocolate and lemon for me), and dim sims from the fish and chip shop at Queenscliff that kept us from killing each other.

I'm happy to say that my gastronomic needs these days are a little more sophisticated. I'm even happier that these needs are being very satisfactorily met in this part of the world. Geelong is slowly shaking off its reputation as a provincial food desert, and today, there is even a sense of – dare I say it – trendiness around the place. In once forlorn city lanes groovy bars and cafés are springing up, with chic little restaurants like Sempre setting enviable standards in style and culinary know-how. Enterprising youngsters are starting super-cool bars like Tonic, or busy modern pubs like The Barking Dog in Pakington Street. Even old local favourites, such as the Sawyers Arms in Newtown, have been handed on to the next generation of smart young operators, although its former owner, the inimitable Mrs 'Clat' still pops in to chat with regulars of an evening!

The revamping of the city's waterfront into a vibrant and elegant foreshore precinct has also worked wonders in helping to restore a sense of pride to locals. Today, visitors to the city on a sunny day can only be impressed by the beauty of the sparkling, wide-crescent sweep of Corio Bay, fringed by long green promenades and lovely gardens. Down by the pier, the hungry can choose to eat at a growing range of eateries: from posh and expensive to humbler family-style eateries and fish-and-chipperies.

Point the car seawards away from Geelong, take a left turn into the Bellarine Peninsula, and the scenery changes. There's a 'blasted heath' quality about the countryside; it's wide and flat under an enormous sky. But there's a sense of space and light, even on grey days, and you always feel that the sea is not far away. Take the coastal road from Portarlington through Indented Head to St Leonards and be charmed by the sleepy, almost old-fashioned, flavour of these seaside resorts. There's still a lingering feeling that this peaceful corner of the peninsula is something of a hidden jewel, and it's hard to fathom why the area has been passed over by the great stampeding exodus of Melburnians who descend every summer upon the more fashionable Great Ocean Road.

But there is also a strong sense that change is in the air, due in no small part to the *SeaChange* phenomenon. Indeed, much of the ABC television show was filmed in and around St Leonards and Barwon Heads, and there are signs from the prices in real estate windows, and from the number of cafés and restaurants popping up, that this area won't be sleepy or remain forgotten

Page 94: Pier at Barwon Heads.

for much longer. Portarlington, for instance, now boasts several new terrific restaurants, the original bakehouse has re-opened, and the old family pub has been reborn as The ol' Duke.

Further around the peninsula are Queenscliff, Point Lonsdale and Barwon Heads, long popular seaside resorts for city folk. In the summer they are choc-a-bloc with happy families. Over the years, the repertoire of eating options has expanded from milk-bar hamburgers or fish and chips, which used to be the holidaymaker's lot. In Queenscliff there is Harry's down by the pier for excellent seafood, and the fish and chip shop really is legendary. For more upmarket dining (and wining) there are hotels such as Mietta's, The Ozone and the Vue Grand to choose from.

For the wine lover, too, there is an abundance of wineries to visit around Geelong and the Bellarine Peninsula. The region might not be as well promoted or as organised as the Mornington Peninsula, but things are certainly changing.

FOOD SHOPS AND PRODUCERS

I think I can see myself living in Geelong. I would live in one of those charming Victorian houses in Newtown, complete with a wrought-iron veranda and pretty landscaped garden, and I would do nearly all my food shopping in Pakington Street, which is starting to get a name as Geelong's food strip.

At the top end is Vince & Rosa's, one of my all-time favourite greengrocers. Further along you can stock up on seafood from Lorne Fisheries, free-range local chickens at Warren & Hutch, and get your cheeses and other smallgoods from Mondo Deli. For your drinking needs, Bannockburn Cellars have one of the widest ranging selections of Australian and imported wines you could wish for, and if you're stuck, the staff are

Above: Health and pleasure trips around Port Phillip Bay on the Weeroona, Hygeia and Ozone, circa 1910.

½ Celery 95¢ each $12.99 kg
Fennel Bulb $1.95 each
Baby Fennel $16.00 kg

Celeriac $2.90 each

always full of informative advice. Another plus in my book is that they seem to be as happy to sell you a bottle of a local cleanskin as one of their pricier, older vintages.

Up the other 'river' end of Pako, there are a number of good cafés to eat at. Two of my favourites are The River End Café and Figaro's Deli and Coffee Shop, where you can pick from over twenty blends of coffee (and almost as many teas) as well as a tempting range of top-notch chocolates. At Paritz Bakery over the road, you can stock up on tasty quiches, cakes and the best custard-filled cannoli in town.

Good produce in Geelong is not confined to Pakington Street. In the CBD there is an outstanding delicatessen called Mr Deli; there's the Original Mediterranean Bakery for Turkish pide bread and savoury spinach and cheese pastries; and just back from the foreshore is Catos, where in-the-know locals shop for the best and freshest fish.

Within twenty minutes or so of Geelong are the beach resorts, which are no longer the badlands when it comes to food shopping. The people who have set up business in these small towns with their more transient and seasonal populations have taken something of a leap of faith, and it is heart-warming to see their businesses taking root. When you pass their way I urge you to drop in and sample their wares – you'll be glad you did.

V&R Fruit and Vegetable Market

Of all the reasons I can think of to live in Geelong, Vince & Rosa's (as it's known to locals) is one of the most compelling. Started over twenty years ago by Vince and Rosa Gangemi, today it is much, much more than a mere greengrocer.

For the past few years, Vince and Rosa have handed over most of the day-to-day running of the business to their daughter Connie and her husband Joe, and since then the product range has expanded dramatically. These days, V&R's is something of a one-stop shopping experience. Besides super-fresh fruit and vegetables of exceptional quality, you can also choose from a comprehensive range of deli items.

V&R's stocks a large number of upmarket imported goods. If Iranian fairy floss is your fancy, then this is the place you'll find it. There is crème fraîche from France, Cypriot haloumi, Spanish saffron, salt from England and endless shelves of the best Italian Arborio rice, dried pasta, olive oil and balsamic vinegar.

Top-notch local ingredients also find shelf space here. You'll find wafer biscuits from The Biscuit Tin, the Screaming Seeds spice range, smoked goods from the Cobden Smokehouse, olive bread from the Original Mediterranean Bakery, and a delicious range of sourdough breads from Irrewarra near Colac. And in the fridges you'll find a wide variety of Victorian dairy produce: Meredith and Timboon cheeses, buffalo milk yoghurt from Shaw River and Kirks cultured butter, to name but a few.

The fruit and vegies are fantastic too, with everything neatly arranged in a tempting and bountiful display. There are piles of pumpkins and potatoes, crinkly cabbages and shiny capsicums in all colours of the rainbow, mounds of opulent purple eggplant and celery and rhubarb lined up like soldiers. At various times of the year you will find newly picked mushrooms, fresh pistachios, sweetly perfumed lychees still clinging to their branch, as well as peaches (yellow and white), nectarines and pomegranate, nashi, starfruit and fresh coconuts and an acre of summer berries. There are great rustling mounds of salad leaves and, at the end of one aisle, little tubs sprout great fragrant bunches of fresh herbs.

V&R's is the perfect place to stock up on

Left: V&R Fruit and Vegetable Market in Pakington Street, Geelong.

Greek Vegetable Soup
STARFISH BAKERY

INGREDIENTS

2 TABLESPOONS OLIVE OIL

1 LARGE ONION, DICED

4 CLOVES GARLIC, MINCED

2 MEDIUM-SIZED CARROTS, PEELED AND DICED

3 CELERY STALKS, DICED

2 TABLESPOONS FRESH THYME OR 1 TEASPOON DRIED THYME

2 TABLESPOONS FRESH OREGANO OR 1 TEASPOON DRIED OREGANO

1 X 400 G TIN CHICKPEAS, WELL RINSED AND DRAINED

4 POTATOES, PEELED AND DICED

1 FENNEL BULB, FINELY SLICED

1 RED CAPSICUM, DICED

2 LITRES VEGETABLE OR CHICKEN STOCK

2 X 400 G TINS PEELED, CHOPPED TOMATOES

1 TABLESPOON TOMATO PASTE

GARNISH

100 G FETTA (A NICE CREAMY ONE LIKE SOUTHCAPE)

2 TABLESPOONS EXTRA-VIRGIN OLIVE OIL

2 TABLESPOONS CHOPPED PARSLEY

Heat the olive oil in a large pan and sauté the onion and garlic until soft. Add the carrots, celery and herbs and cook over a low heat for a further couple of minutes.

Add the remaining ingredients to the pan and slowly bring to the boil. Then lower the heat and simmer gently for 40 minutes.

To make the garnish, in a separate bowl, mix the fetta with the olive oil and parsley until well combined. When ready to serve, ladle the hot soup into serving bowls and top with a blob of the cheese mixture.

goodies for a picnic or on your way down to the beach house. On a recent visit I stopped to buy a slab of creamy Meredith goat's cheese, a crusty loaf of sourdough and a couple of locally grown tomatoes. I completed my feast with a perfect peach and headed for the foreshore at Geelong's Western Beach. It was just the place to spend a lazy afternoon, gazing out over the bay at the brightly coloured spinnakers, and the joggers running along the esplanade.

Warren and Hutch

When I first walked into Jane Gray and Sarah Nelson's smart poultry shop they were laughing hysterically.

'We opened ten days ago,' Sarah explained. 'You know how it is . . . we've been waiting and waiting for deliveries of just about everything, and it all seems to be arriving today!'

I looked around the spotlessly clean and tidy shop for signs of chaos. Apart from a young man fiddling around with a screwdriver everything looked to be exceptionally well organised. Behind the glass display cabinet was a fine-looking array of poultry and game birds. I noticed my favourite Milawa free-range chickens, and yes! there were also rabbits, which seem to be harder and harder to come by these days.

With its elegant dark-green and gold awning and handsome window display, Warren and Hutch reminded me of some of the better-class butchers and poultry shops you find in smart English country towns. Inside, the air of old-fashioned elegance continues. Sarah and Jane were pretty well-turned out themselves, in calf-length black skirts, crisp white blouses and not a grey hair out of place. The two met over thirty years ago and have an easy good-humoured way with each other and with their customers. Between them they have a rich and varied experience in businesses of one kind or another, ranging from catering, flower selling, raising cashmere goats and importing sheep embryos. They joined forces in the 1990s to start a small business raising rabbits.

Jane said with a self-deprecating laugh, 'I saw a picture of a rabbit on the cover of a local newspaper and thought it would be the perfect business for a couple of old ladies!' The reality proved to be back-breakingly labour-intensive (imagine cleaning out 500 rabbit hutches every couple of days), so twelve months later they sold out and decided to put their considerable energy and charm into marketing the rabbits instead of rearing them.

And so Warren and Hutch, Provenders was born. Sarah and Jane headed for town with a few bunnies in an esky, and started knocking on restaurant doors.

'We were so naïve,' laughed Sarah. But the two were amazed to discover how quickly top Melbourne chefs pounced on the produce. Rabbit meat is fashionably lean and has become very popular in recent years. And because wild rabbits are a big no-no, farmed rabbits are in greater and greater demand.

Top restaurants such as Pomme and Stephanie's (since closed) were eager for the bunnies, and before long they were asking Sarah and Jane to source hare, squab, guinea fowl and suckling lamb and piglets. In a couple of years, their provendering business had grown beyond their wildest expectations. 'We never even had a business plan,' they laugh. 'In fact, we still don't. These days we don't even have time to worry about one.' They supply restaurants around Melbourne, the Bellarine Peninsula and the Mornington Peninsula across the bay.

It seemed only natural for these two inimitable ladies to make the move into retailing. When a chook shop in trendy Pakington Street became available, they took a deep breath and signed the lease. They have big plans for Warren and Hutch, intending it to be a general 'provender' store rather than just a humble chicken shop. But for the moment it is the chickens their customers are queuing up for. While they stock the usual range of pre-prepared pieces, Sarah and Jane's big aim is to build up the free-range side of the business.

'It's very gratifying,' said Jane 'Our orders of free-range birds (from Milawa, Glenloth, the Barossa Valley and a local bird from Freshwater Creek) are doubling every week.'

One of the very nicest things about Sarah and Jane is their belief that life – including business – should be fun. And they appear to apply this philosophy to everything they do, whether it be handling the tricky demands of Victoria's top chefs, dealing with suppliers and their various problems, or simply chatting happily to customers in the shop. As I was leaving, the shop had filled up with the afternoon rush of customers, a delivery man was knocking on the back door and the phone began to ring. As I turned to wave goodbye I was delighted to see that they were both still laughing.

Starfish Bakery

It wasn't that long ago that Barwon Heads was a sleepy little holiday place with a pub, a fancy golf course and a caravan park. The population swelled with the summer seasons, but let's be honest: the average age of its permanent residents was definitely in the third age!

Over the past couple of years things have changed dramatically, for which we have Diver Dan and the *SeaChange* phenomenon to thank – in part at least. Drive out the back of Barwon Heads today, and instead of ramshackle little weatherboard weekenders you find smart new housing and lots of young families looking for a slower, better way of life in a place where the air is cleaner, the people are friendlier and the beach is only a hop, skip and jump away.

Dinah Karklins and her husband Paul Fox made the decision to move out of Melbourne several years ago to find more space for the four of their five daughters who were still living at home. It took them two years of hunting within a one-and-a-half-hour drive from Melbourne before they landed in Barwon Heads.

They loved the place immediately and, before they knew it, found themselves with new premises and a plan to start up a bakery. 'It was a bit of a leap of faith,' said Dinah. 'When we moved here, eleven of the fourteen shops in the street were up for sale. But when we saw this place we just couldn't resist the challenge.'

It must be said that neither of them is exactly a stranger to this kind of operation – Dinah's parents own the Natural Tucker Bakery in East Brunswick, and Paul had spent the past ten years baking there and managing the business. At the time of their move, though, there was simply no decent bread being baked on the peninsula, and they just had a feeling that changes were afoot in sleepy Barwon Heads.

So they built a bakehouse out the back and spruced up the front with funky colours – all hot pinks, turquoise and purple. There is some cunning tilework around the windows and inlaid into the table-tops – among other things, Paul is a dab hand at tiling, and I learnt that his Irish grandfather had done a lot of the tiling on the *Titanic*! Although Hitchcock Avenue, the Barwon Heads shopping strip, is a block away from the water, their shop had a nice little sheltered courtyard out the front, where they put tables and chairs for hot sunny days.

On the day I went to visit though, it was rainy and cold, and I was in the mood for hot chocolate and breakfast. In a rare attempt at being health-conscious, I decided to forego scrambled 'green' eggs and ham and a selection of fabulous-looking pastries, and opted instead for a bowl of Starfish toasted granola, which came with cinnamon-spiced apple and apricot compote and a dollop of creamy yoghurt. (And before anyone starts to tell me that the toasted stuff is full of fat, let me assure you that Dinah has perfected a delicious version that is wholly fat-free.)

Although still in its infancy, Starfish has already established its popularity with local residents. As I munched my granola, a steady stream of raincoats came dripping into the bakery looking for takeaway coffee, homemade sausage rolls, muffins and focacce as well as their daily bread.

'We learnt a lot in our first summer of trading,' said Dinah. 'Lots of people run up from the beach for a sandwich, and even those who want to sit down and eat are in a hurry to get back to their sun-baking. So we have deliberately kept the menu small, and everything has to be quick to prepare.' Small the menu might be, but the food is imaginative and very tasty.

And then there are the breads and pastries. Dinah and Paul have been gradually weaning the more conservative customers away from the traditional white tin loaf to their fantastic sourdough range, and are delighted to say that most people become eager converts to this better-tasting style of loaf. At the weekend the range expands to include more exotic items, such as a pumpkin, polenta and almond bread, and a fruit loaf scented with orange-blossom water. They employ a French baker to work with Paul, so the cakes and pastries are superb too.

On the way out I nibbled a bit of almond Toscana cake – moist almond with a

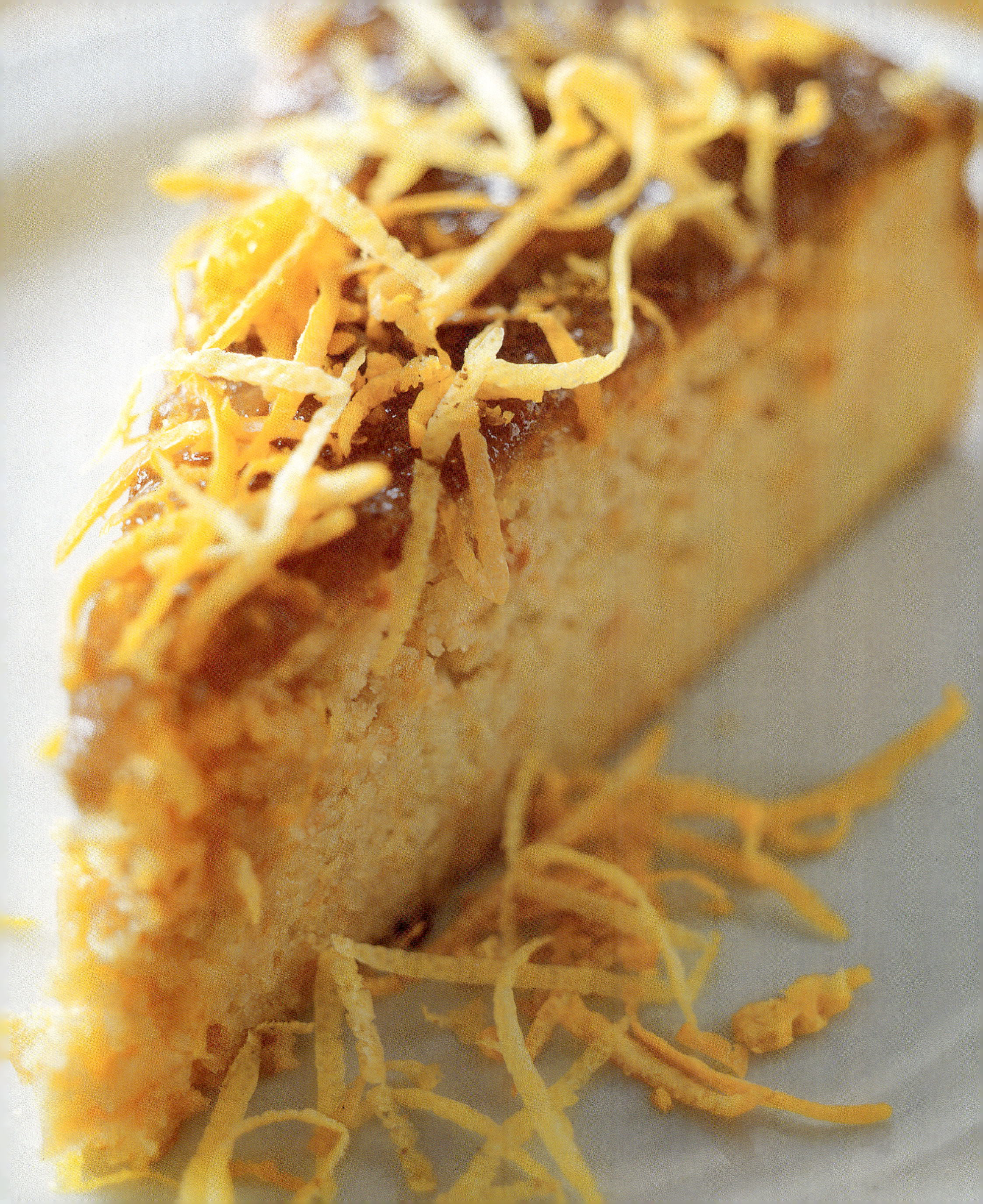

caramel-almond topping. It was out of this world. I asked Dinah if she and Paul were happy with the move they had made. She grinned. 'I always wanted to live by the beach. And now, even in the winter, I get to pack a picnic and get down there with the kids after school. I have to say that things really are just as good, if not better than I could ever have imagined!'

Peppercorn Foods

A little further along Hitchcock Avenue, on the other side of the road from Starfish, is Peppercorn Foods. Heather McCarthy, who runs the place, has attained almost iconic status among locals and holidaymakers for her wonderful home-cooked tucker. Friends of mine who live part-time in Barwon Heads swear by the lasagna, which they pick up late in the afternoon when they arrive tired and cranky, kids in tow. It never fails to please.

I popped in to see Heather just before lunchtime. The weather was dismal, but inside the shop it was warm and cosy, and the windows were pleasantly fogged up with delicious savoury smells. Heather was finishing scraping chocolate curls for a twenty-first birthday cake, so I sat in the window with a piping-hot cup of tea. It came in one of those no-nonsense, stainless steel pots, was made from tea leaves rather than a bag, and was quite the best cuppa I'd had in a long time.

Actually, everything about Peppercorns seemed pretty no-nonsense. The blackboard menu above the counter offered wonderful old-fashioned favourites such as lemon slice and hedgehog, as well as sausage rolls, beef stroganoff and a range of quiches and pies. And I was quite charmed to see that if the fancy took me, I could even have a cup of instant coffee!

Gourmet food this certainly wasn't, but it all felt as reassuring and homely as my granny's kitchen. Even though I'd just finished breakfast, I gazed around and wondered idly about lunch. Would it be a home-cooked pie? The cheese and cauliflower sounded good, and so did chicken and mushroom, and beef and burgundy.

Heather joined me and filled me in on her background. She moved to Barwon Heads around fourteen years ago, but only opened up the shop in 1998 after parting ways with the Education Department, her employer of thirty-two years. One might have thought that she'd be ready for a rest after that feat, but instead, she decided to put her considerable cooking and organisational skills into running a business. In fact, she already had many years' experience catering part-time, so taking over commercial premises made things much easier.

Over the years Heather and her food have become an integral part of the community. Providing take-home food for holidaymakers is one thing, but more valuable are the other

Above: Heather McCarthy of Peppercorn Foods.

services she provides: Heather and her staff make school lunches every day for the local primary school and frequently provide lunches for local council and business meetings. Her home-cooked meals have always been particularly popular with the older folk, and Heather herself likes to do the deliveries, particularly on Sunday and Tuesday, which are 'roast nights', so that she can stop and have a bit of a chat. But she is pleased to note that as the demography of Barwon Heads changes she is seeing more and more young mums popping in for a family-sized pie, or a sweet beef curry on the way home from the school run. And that's just got to be better for the kids than fast food.

The Portarlington Bakehouse

The original Portarlington Bakehouse has been brought back to life. Dormant since 1952, the old wood-fired oven was re-lit in November 2000, and has been baking bread every day since.

When Terry Christofi agreed to take on the challenge of running the place, things were looking a bit grim. The original shop-cum-residence was in a state of total disrepair, and the bakehouse out the back didn't look much better. As it turned out, the only thing that required virtually no work at all to fix up was the oven itself.

Terry hired Jarred and Warren, two young bakers from Tasmania who'd trained in the highly specialised art of baking wood-fired bread. They arrived, gave the oven a good sweep-out, then lit a fire and allowed the old oven to heat up slowly over eight days or so. It was as easy as that. They made things to last back in 1882!

The oven itself is lit every night at about 1 a.m. The fire blazes intensely for a couple of hours, then is put out, and the oven floor and walls are swabbed with a damp mop. The dome shape ensures that the remaining heat is distributed evenly, and the considerable insulation (over 27,000 bricks and two feet of sand) means that they can keep baking throughout the day.

The bakery produces a rustic style of bread known as pasta dura, which is hard and crusty on the outside with a soft, fluffy crumb inside. As it emerges from the cavernous depths of the oven, crisp and golden, you can't help but think 'this is what bread should be like!'– all knobbly and irregular in shape. It's a delightful change from the squishy stuff that passes for bread in so many places these days and tastes little better than blotting paper. Here is bread with real flavour and texture – toasty and crunchy on the outside, and tangy and chewy on the inside.

As well as the pasta dura loaves, which come in all shapes and sizes, the Portarlington Bakery also makes more traditional white and wholemeal loves, a cornbread (very popular with the Greek customers, apparently), a flat Turkish bread and on most days, a vegie bread.

One of the bakers, Warren, spent some time working with legendary French baker Louis Vaussenat at Il Fornaio in St Kilda, and his influence shows in the light-as-air éclairs, choux pastries and sweet tarts on offer in the front display cabinet. And that's not all. Rita, Terry's mum, is responsible for a nice line in Greek sweets. She comes down on a Friday afternoon and is immediately put to work out the back, making sticky baklava, moist semolina cake, kourambiethes (Greek shortbread) and koulourakia (aniseed and sesame cookies).

The Portarlington bakery is one of that new breed of bakeries that offer far more than just bread. It is also a café, with good coffee and a fine line in simple home-cooked food. There is freshly made soup, toasted focacce, interesting salads, as well as Greek-style goodies such as stuffed tomatoes, peppers, cabbage rolls and dips. Terry is also developing a range of home-packs, which are proving very popular with holidaymakers. In one corner, there is an immense old wooden mixing trough, which serves as a display counter for a small selection of fresh fruit and vegetables.

It might have been a long time coming, but with so much good stuff on offer, holidaymakers and locals alike can be very glad that the Bakehouse has re-opened its doors.

Portarlington Mussels

Here's a question for foodie fans: who knows where most of Australia's mussels come from? If you guessed Victoria, then you'd be right on the money. In fewer than ten years, since the first major mussel farms were established in and around Port Phillip Bay, our very own Portarlington has become the mussel capital of Australia.

I am a big fan of these sweet native blue mussels and have eaten them all around the Mornington and Bellarine peninsulas, fresh from the sheltered waters of Port Phillip Bay. In the past I have made many a happy trip down to the ramshackle old wooden jetty at Beaumaris to stock up on Keefer's mussels, and been charmed by the sparkling blue waters, diving cormorants and greedy pelicans.

But the day I visited Portarlington, things were not quite so rosy. Southern Victoria had experienced its worst rains in a quarter of a century, and there were no mussels to be had. Mussels are filter feeders, and the regulations controlling when they may be harvested are stringent. After heavy rains, farmers must wait at least 48 hours before they can head back out to the ropes.

That morning, I met up with Sheryl Raines, sales manager for a cooperative of local mussel farmers, for a coffee and a lesson in aquaculture. Although the deluge had finally stopped, the weather remained unsettled. Little squalls of wind billowed through the dark cypress trees opposite the café where we sat, and every now and then, watery sunshine pierced the clay-coloured sky.

'It's like any other kind of farming,' said Sheryl, peering out a little glumly, 'we're totally at the mercy of the weather.' And if it's not the weather, there's the risk of algae blooms, which drift into the bay from the cold waters of the Antarctic during the winter months. And then there's the damage caused by recent invaders of Australian waters, such as the lethal Japanese starfish, which are turning up on the mussel ropes in alarming numbers.

'But it's worth all the hassle because they're such a fantastic product,' Sheryl continued. And indeed they are. Victorian blue mussels are plump, tender and sweet, and according to Sheryl are frequently judged among the best in the world. The largest and most productive sites are at Clifton Springs ('just about anything grows there') and Grassy Point, around the corner from Portarlington on the west coast of Port Phillip Bay. Smaller fields are located at Beaumaris and Mornington on the eastern side of the bay, and at Flinders in the colder, faster moving waters of Westernport Bay.

'We are still only producing around 1000 tonnes of mussels a year,' said Sheryl. 'They go all around Victoria, up the east coast as far north as Cairns, and we can't keep up with the demand.' There is beginning to be signs of interest from overseas as well. Asia is the obvious market for Victorian mussels, as they are already familiar with the excellent quality of our seafood. But Europe and the US are also keen potential customers, although distances mean that this would be a processed rather than fresh product.

Clockwise from top left: Morning coffee in Portarlington; Fishing from the pier; The Portarlington Bakehouse; Mussel boats at Portarlington.

Wood fire baking since 1880
Phone 5259 2274

The Portarlington Bakehouse
WOOD-FIRED OVEN
HOME-MADE FOODS
BREAKFAST / LUNCH
(ALL DAY)
TAKE HOME FOOD
FRESH CAKES + PASTRIES
PIES/PASTIES/SAUSAGE ROLLS
WOOD-FIRED BREADS
FRESH FRUIT + VEG
OPEN-FIRE

The good news is that the state government has just allocated an additional 1000 hectares of water near Pinnace Channel at the southern end of the bay, which will give operators the chance to expand their output to meet growing national and international demand.

I learnt lots of other interesting facts about mussels that day. Like the startling information that it is their gonads which make them sweet! This is one of the reasons why they are thin and bitter during the late winter spawning season from July to September. I learnt, too, that after spawning, Port Phillip Bay is flooded with the wriggling larvae of miniature mussels, swimming free for the only time in their lives, until the inevitable day comes when they stumble upon a rope, dangling enticingly in a peaceful part of the bay. And there they settle to pass their quiet lives, rocked gently by the rise and fall of the tides. The final inevitable stage in their otherwise uneventful lives comes when a mussel farmer, knife in hand, comes to wrench them from their watery home. Before they know it, they will have been thrown into a pot to meet a steamy end, then served up to hungry diners like you and me.

WINERIES

When it comes to winemaking, Geelong and the Bellarine Peninsula have been born again. It might come as a surprise to learn that this area was actually one of the very first parts of Victoria to be planted with vines, and that in its heyday, it was one of the largest and most important grape-growing areas in Australia.

The story began in 1842, when the first tiny vineyards were planted by Swiss and German settlers in the Barrabool Hills close to Geelong. By 1869 there were more than 400 acres of vines in the area – more even than there are today – and Geelong itself was quite a centre for wine-related activity. A thriving export trade sprang up, and the principal grape varieties of the day, shiraz and pinot, began to earn a name for themselves around Europe.

Sadly, all this burgeoning activity came grinding to a halt while the industry was still in its infancy. The Gold Rush drained labour away from the area and then there was an economic depression. But the real killer was the arrival of the phylloxera vine aphid, brought into Australia on vine cuttings from Europe. Phylloxera had already ravaged vineyards across Europe, and in 1875 it was discovered for the first time on vines at Fyansford near Geelong. The government of the day reacted by panicking, and ordered the total eradication of vines from the Geelong region. Within a decade, grape growing and winemaking in the area were but a distant memory.

For the first half of the twentieth century, most Australians were only interested in drinking beer, and any wines which were consumed were imported from France and Germany. It wasn't until the 1960s that a few enlightened souls had the bright idea of growing grapes and making wine locally again.

The man who is widely credited with getting the ball rolling again was Daryl Sefton, a great-grandson of one of the original Swiss settlers in the region. He and his wife Nini established their Idyll Vineyard in the hills and dales of Moorabool Valley, and began to plant vines and make wine. Over the next thirty years the Seftons' wines achieved great success and acclaim, both nationally and abroad.

In the late 1960s and early 1970s other wine enthusiasts followed the Seftons' lead, and new vineyards were established at Mt Anakie north of Geelong and at Mt Duneed. In 1973 local businessman and wine lover Stuart Hooper planted what has become one of the area's most respected vineyards at Bannockburn, recruiting Gary Farr to be his winemaker.

Under Stuart Hooper's management (until his death in 1997) and Farr's skilful winemaking, Bannockburn has consistently produced exceptional and strongly individualistic wines. The best known are undoubtedly the standard cool-climate varieties – pinot noir and chardonnay – but Bannockburn also produces a nicely spicy shiraz, a sauvignon blanc and a refreshing pink wine called saignée.

The cool climate means that things take longer to develop; Bannockburn wines tend to be held back for a couple of years before release so that all the characters can settle in the bottle to their full potential. At their best, this potential is realised in Bannockburn's exceptionally fine and elegant chardonnay and in its dense, intensely rich pinot noir.

The small Prince Albert vineyard, established at Waurn Ponds by Bruce Hyett in 1975, is also renowned for its pinot noir – in fact this is the only wine made there. It's

The saignée was something Farr learnt to make on one of his many visits to Burgundy, and this French influence is clearly visible in other aspects of his winemaking. So, the pinot grapes at Bannockburn are densely planted to produce concentrated fruit; he favours wild, natural yeasts rather than cultures from a packet; and he likes to barrel-ferment his chardonnay for finer oak flavours.

the perfect position for growing pinot grapes: a north-facing suntrap of a vineyard, planted in red soil on a limestone base. And the result, in a good year, is sensational: an elegantly rounded wine, with strawberry depths and a long, silky smoothness in the mouth.

The 1980s and 1990s saw a steady but slow consolidation of winemaking activity around Geelong and the Bellarine Peninsula.

Left: Wine stored in barrels at Scotchmans Hill.
Right: Scotchmans Hill Chardonnay.

the food and wine lover's guide to Melbourne's Bays and Peninsulas

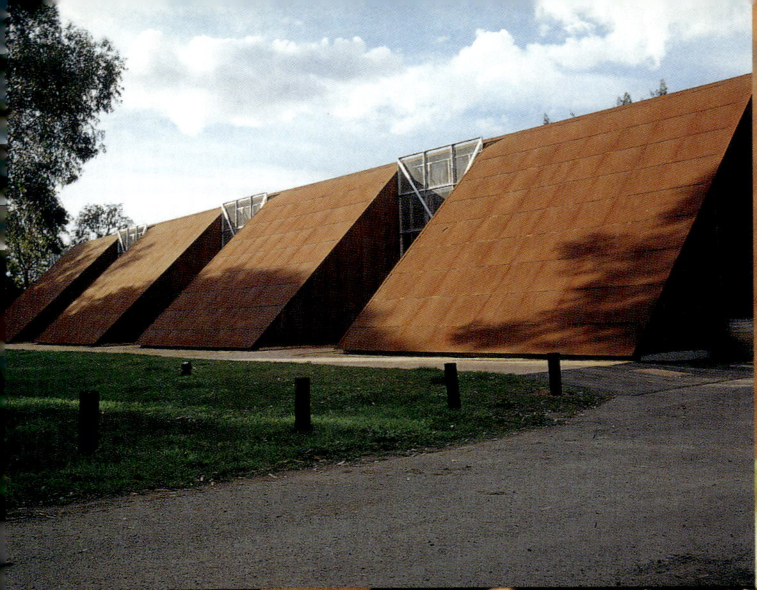
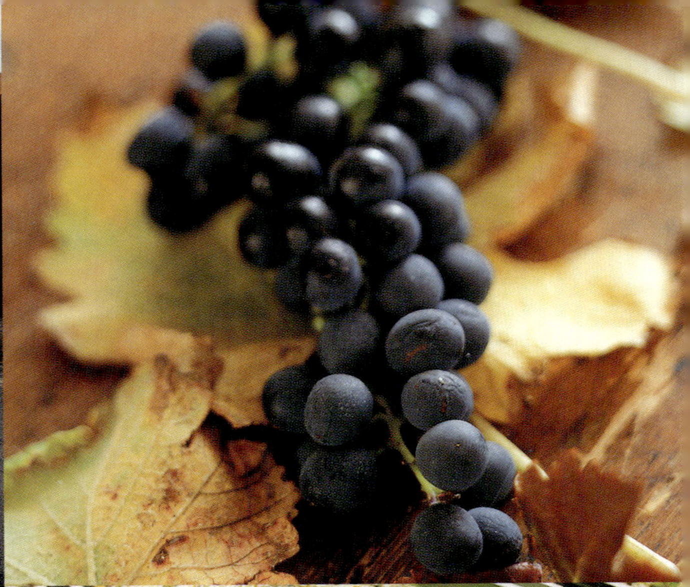
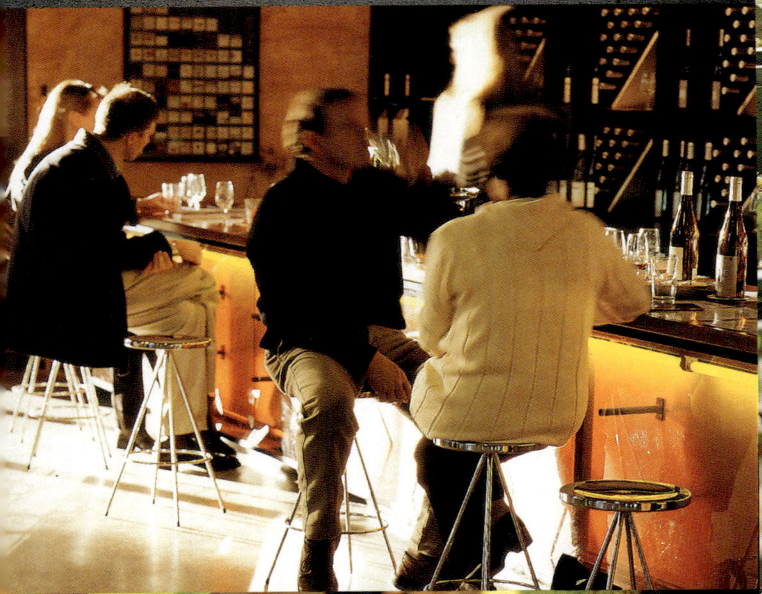
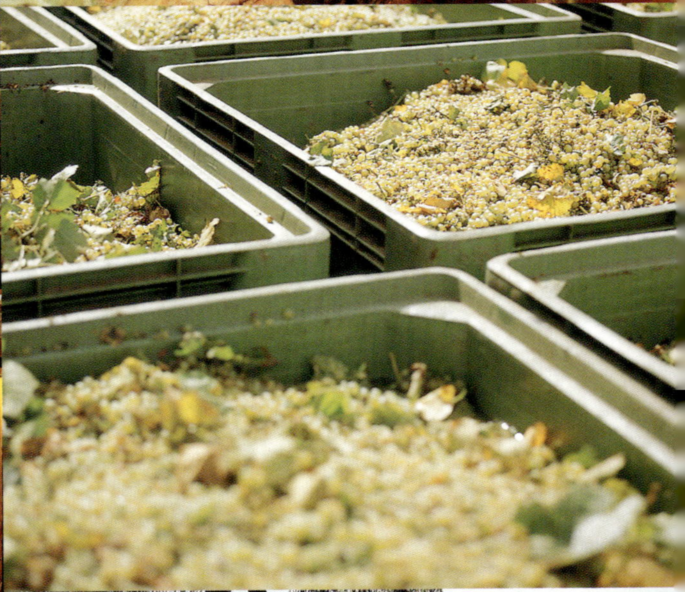
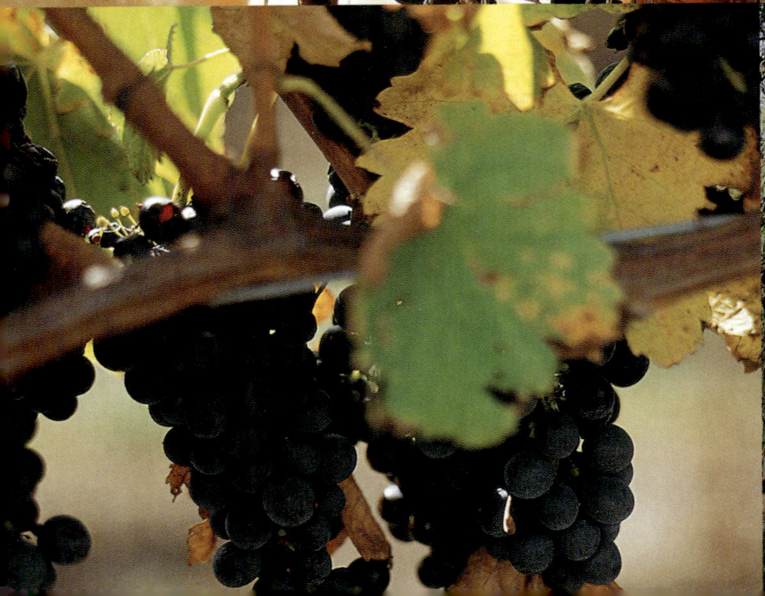
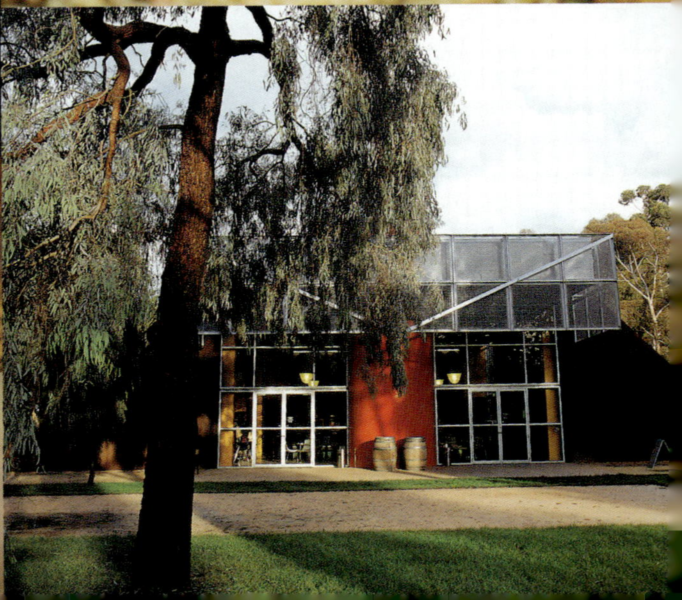

There are now interesting vineyards to be found at Innisfail, Kilgour Estate and the Bellarine Estate, to name a few. And in the late 1990s the very impressive Scotchmans Hill Group expanded their operations in the Bellarine Peninsula with the purchase of the historic property at Spray Farm, where they planted extensive new vineyards.

But unlike the Mornington Peninsula, on the other side of Port Phillip Bay, where you stumble across a vineyard or winery every few hundred metres, winemaking around Geelong and the Bellarine Peninsula remains a much more fragmented and less well-developed affair.

It is not easy to explain why this should be so. One suggestion is that wineries in the region have been less proactive at marketing their products. There are a few notable exceptions, of course. The Seftons, in their day, were tireless promoters of the Geelong district, and more recently Bannockburn and Scotchmans Hill have worked hard to raise the profile of their wines to national and international acclaim.

There are economic factors at play too, perhaps. The region is still one of the coolest maritime climates in mainland Australia and is not an easy place to grow grapes. Prospective grape growers have to contend with spring frosts, blistering winds and brutal hail, and the harsh reality of dismal rainfall more often than not. All of which means frighteningly low yields. It's also a sad fact that, unlike the Mornington Peninsula, people do not as yet view Geelong or the Bellarine Peninsula as serious wine destinations in their own right. All too often they whiz straight past them on their way down to the beaches of the Great Ocean Road.

Attitudes are slowly changing over time. There is no doubt that the region produces some outstanding wines, and increasing recognition of its excellence can only help to attract more interest and visitors to the area.

A couple of bright new players have emerged on the scene, who fly the region's flag with enthusiasm. One of these is the exciting new Shadowfax winery at Werribee Park, which has received a terrific reception since opening at the end of 2000.

Another new place to keep an eye on is the Pettavel winery restaurant at Waurn Ponds, due to open its cellar door by Christmas 2001. It's an ambitious enterprise, the brainchild of Mike and Sandi Fitzpatrick who have been growing grapes in the district for nearly fifteen years. They've hired a well-travelled and energetic young winemaker, and – a real coup – have persuaded the wonderful George Biron to come and set up the dining facilities in the bold new building. Food and wine lovers alike will be eagerly awaiting its opening.

Scotchmans Hill & Spray Farm

On the day I first visited the historic Spray Farm homestead they were gearing up for that evening's performance by legendary pianist, David Helfgott. The sun was shining on the shimmering blue waters of Corio Bay, and it was a perfect day for an outdoor concert.

The series of intimate courtyard recitals and operatic spectaculars in the open-air amphitheatre that make up the Spray Farm Summer Festival have become an essential activity for many Victorians since they first began in 1999. Every summer, on a few perfect evenings, thousands of eager concert goers descend upon this idyllic spot on the Bellarine Peninsula. They come by car and coach from Melbourne and Geelong, they cross the water by ferry or in their own private yacht and some even come puffing through the countryside on a specially commissioned steam train – the Sauvignon Express from Queenscliff.

From these beginnings, the evening only

Clockwise from top left: The winery at Shadowfax; scenes from 2001 vintage; wine tasting at the Shadowfax cellar door.

gets better. Just imagine yourself sitting on a picnic rug among the gum trees, with a glass of excellent Scotchmans Hill chardonnay in hand, and goodies from a gourmet hamper to nibble on. As twilight descends upon this magical part of the peninsula, the excited chatter around you seems to fade away and then, suddenly, sublime notes of music begin to drift through the air.

If all this sounds romantic, be assured – it is. And summer concerts are just one part of the Spray Farm experience. If you visit during the day, as I did, then you can while away several happy hours wandering through the magnificently restored homestead and gardens, or indulge in a spot of wine tasting at the cellar door.

The property itself was built in the 1850s and although grand in its day, had been allowed to fall into a state of disrepair for most of the past fifty years. In 1994, it was purchased by the Browne family who own the Scotchmans Hill vineyard a few hundred metres away on the other side of the road. They began a major restoration project to bring the place back to its former splendour, and today the beautifully proportioned rooms are home to small art showings, and the venue for private dinner parties. A wine bar and café has been set up in the historic stables, and in the summer, tables and chairs spill out onto the sheltered courtyard among terracotta pots of perfumed lavender.

If you prefer, you can sit on the front veranda to eat, while you take in breathtaking views across the vineyards to the You Yangs and the Melbourne skyline gleaming in the distance. The food at Spray Farm is appropriately elegant. Chef Greg Heath uses local produce wherever he can: mussels from Portarlington, King George whiting from the bay, goat's cheese from Meredith and bread from the Starfish bakery in Barwon Heads. Although the menu has been designed to complement the excellent wines from their own vineyards, the wine list also offers a truly extraordinary range of Australian and international vintages. If the budget allows, you might like to taste a 1969 Grange or to sip reverentially at a 1934 Chateaux Margaux.

Wine is the other major reason for visiting Spray Farm, with its cellar door offering wines from the Spray Farm estate and from the nearby Scotchmans Hill vineyard. The Browne family, who own the Scotchmans Hill Group, have put an enormous amount of time, money and effort into their superbly run vineyards and winery. Although the business remains family-owned, it is run on a large and very commercially successful scale. Consider this: for the 2001 vintage, their well-equipped winery crushed nearly 1000 tonnes of grapes, and will make around 65,000 cases of wine for distribution around Australia, and overseas.

Rather confusingly, Spray Farm wines are now bottled under the Swan Bay label – apparently because the European market baulked at the word 'Spray' on a wine label. Swan Bay wines have been designed by winemaker Robin Brockett to complement and extend the Scotchmans Hill range. They include grapes from the relatively new vines planted at Spray Farm, and from other growers in the region. Swan Bay wines, like the 2000 chardonnay and pinot noir, are typically fresh, youthful and fruit driven, intended for earlier drinking than their cousins from Scotchmans Hill.

And what of the Scotchmans Hill range? They are unquestionably some of the most admired wines from the region – and some of the best known. The Scotchmans Hill label is now seen on restaurant wine lists in places as varied as Japan, Hong Kong, the United Arab Emirates, Switzerland and Canada. Obviously, there is an emphasis on traditional cool-climate varieties, but there are other successes, too, such as a sauvignon blanc and cabernet merlot.

The sauvignon blanc is one of Scotchman's big sellers – whether it be the dry, minerally 1998 version, or the intense, citrussy 2000 vintage. Other favourites are the delectably smoky, golden-hued chardonnays and its best selling pinots. Scotchmans Hill is one of the largest producers of pinot noir in Australia. Although they are well priced and popular wines, they are far from being mere early-drinking queffing wines. Older vintages are evolving into deep, densely fruity wines, and even the more recent vintages show signs of elegant berry characteristics.

But the true achievement of the Scotchmans Hill winery is that its commercial success has not been gained at the expense of the quality of the wines it produces. Robin Brockett's wines superbly reflect the local soils and cool sea-influenced climate, and perform consistently well in all the major wine shows. And there seems little doubt that the success story is set to keep on unfolding.

Shadowfax

Think for a moment about the great wine-growing areas of the world: there is something magical about the way humble grapevines seem to transform their surroundings. Think of how a blaze of scarlet vines stripe the countryside around Bordeaux or Tuscany in the autumn. Think, too, about the inspired architecture that seems to go hand in hand with all that natural beauty. For centuries, the great vineyards of Europe have been linked with magnificent chateaux, but what about the vineyards of the New World, and in particular Australia?

It looks as if local operators are increasingly embracing the idea of beauty as well as functionality in their vineyards. As the Australian wine industry matures and gains greater confidence in the quality of its product, more and more vignerons seem to want to operate in surroundings that reflect the excellence.

Of course, the public is taking a greater interest in wine and its making too. These days wineries are increasingly becoming a destination in their own right, and canny operators know that if they want to attract visitors to the cellar door, it is worth making the trip special in as many ways as possible. The days of traipsing through a muddy field to taste superb boutique wines in a ramshackle old tin shed are gone for ever. The trend is towards inspired contemporary architecture that superbly complements the landscape and affirms a new pride in the product. In Victoria, we are lucky to have many wonderful examples of this brave new world of winemaking. Think of the witty corrugated-iron barn that serves as the cellar door at the Stonier winery in the Mornington Peninsula, or the dramatic sweep of brick at Yering Station in the Yarra Valley.

And then there is Shadowfax, the bold new winemaking venture hidden among the gum trees in the grounds of Werribee Park. Four immense plates of sloping, rust-coloured steel rise out of the ground like great mounds of the surrounding red earth. And inside is just as dramatic. The vaulted space is filled with light and a vibrant palette of colours – purple, lime green, acid yellow and red – form large geometric panes of glass, reaching high up into the ceiling. At one end of the room, a striking orange tube houses the circular stairway down to the low, gently arched cellar below.

One wall of the winery is given over to displaying gourmet food produce (cellar door manager Victoria Wilson previously worked at The Vital Ingredient in Melbourne).

Opposite, a long tasting counter stretches the length of the room, and behind it, display shelves are crammed full of neatly stacked rows of Shadowfax wines.

It's a big leap from the first few weeks of operation, back in July 2000, when there was only one wine on offer. 'For eight long weeks, all we had to offer people was the 1999 riesling,' laughs Victoria. Thankfully, with a couple of vintages now under their belt, the range is expanding. There are now around eight terrific and distinctive wines on offer, including a lively sauvignon blanc–semillon 2000, a creamy chardonnay 1999, a savoury, spicy pinot gris 2000, and my favourite, the McLaren Vale shiraz 1999. This was the first red to be bottled at the winery, and it is a delectably fleshy wine, full of sweet berry fruit and a generous, smooth finish.

Everything about Shadowfax speaks of the enthusiasm and passion of the owners and operators. The investors in the venture, which include the neighbouring Mansion Hotel Group and Stewart Langton of the well-respected wine auction house, have dug deep into their pockets to finance the project. And the trio they've put in charge of operating the place are champing at the bit to live up to the brilliant dream.

As mentioned, Victoria Wilson is the enthusiastic cellar-door manager, whose aim in life is to inspire and educate the winery's visitors. She is also in charge of developing a small, seasonal menu of locally sourced produce to complement the wines on offer. Unsurprisingly, the winery space is already proving to be a popular venue for corporate functions (often in tandem with the Mansion Hotel), and there are plans to extend the food operations next summer to include Sunday barbecues and concerts.

The vineyard operations are run by viticulturalist Andrew Tedder, and the winemaker is Matt Harrop, a talented young New Zealander who came from the Nautilus winery in Marlborough. The two have a refreshingly no-nonsense, laid-back approach to winemaking, which comes through in the finished wines.

Shadowfax is not your traditional estate winery, but one of the new modern breeds. You can't actually make wine if you don't have any grapes, so Andrew and Matt are enthusiastically sourcing grapes from regions as diverse as nearby Geelong, McLaren Vale, the Adelaide Hills, Tallarook (near the Goulburn Valley) and a premium site at the old Zuber Estate at Heathcote. They have also begun picking from the newly planted vines next to the winery, and obviously this will increase over time.

And the result of this diverse range of age and region? A series of distinctive varietal wines that are ready for early drinking. With all that dedication and passion behind them, things are destined only to get better and better.

EATING OUT

Good things are slowly starting to happen in the Geelong dining scene and around the Bellarine Peninsula. I began to get a feel for a growing interest in things gastronomic at the Pako Street Festa – Geelong's annual fundraiser for its diverse ethnic communities. Festa is intended to be a celebration of each participating culture, and naturally enough, much of the celebrating revolves around the tummy. For an entire weekend Pakington Street is full of local families happily munching their way around the world on a plate, with food stalls offering everything from Bosnian pide breads and Spanish chorizo sausages to Filipino satays and Dutch apple fritters.

Sadly, this exciting vision of gastro-multiculturalism is not yet really reflected in Geelong's restaurant scene, although things

Right: The 'Pako Street Festa.'

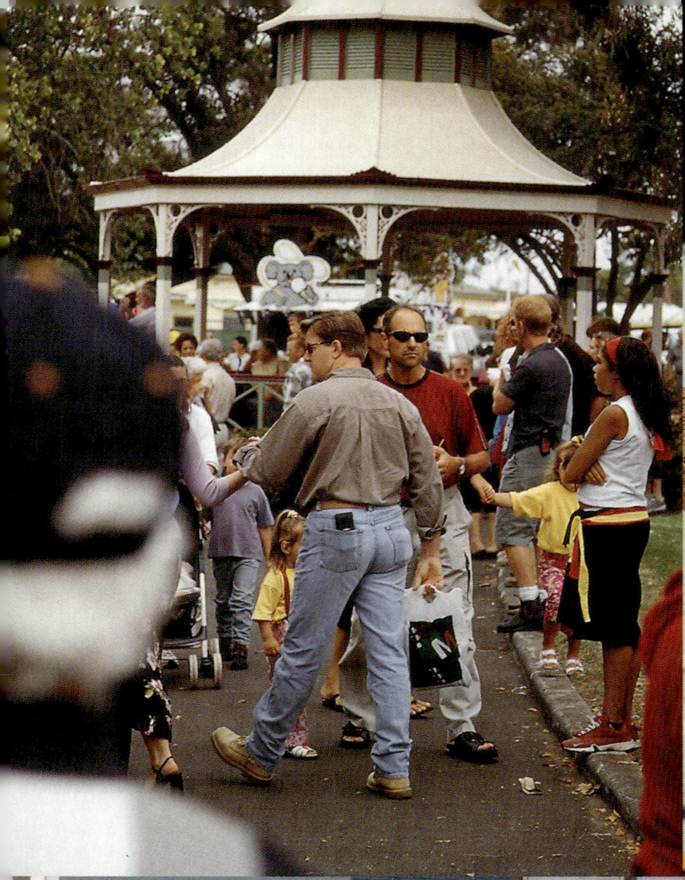
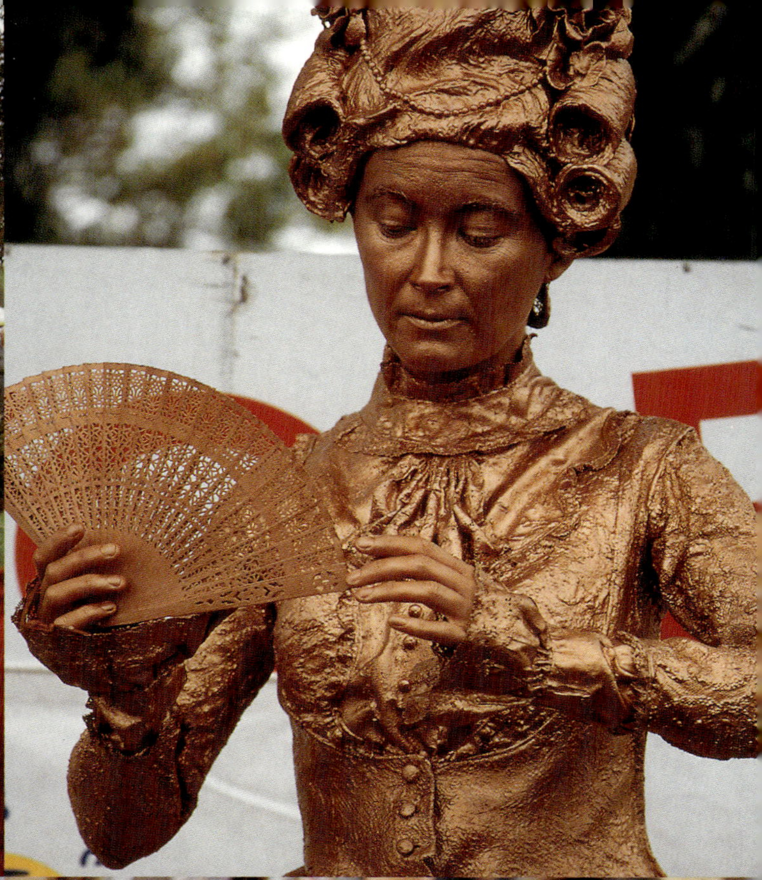
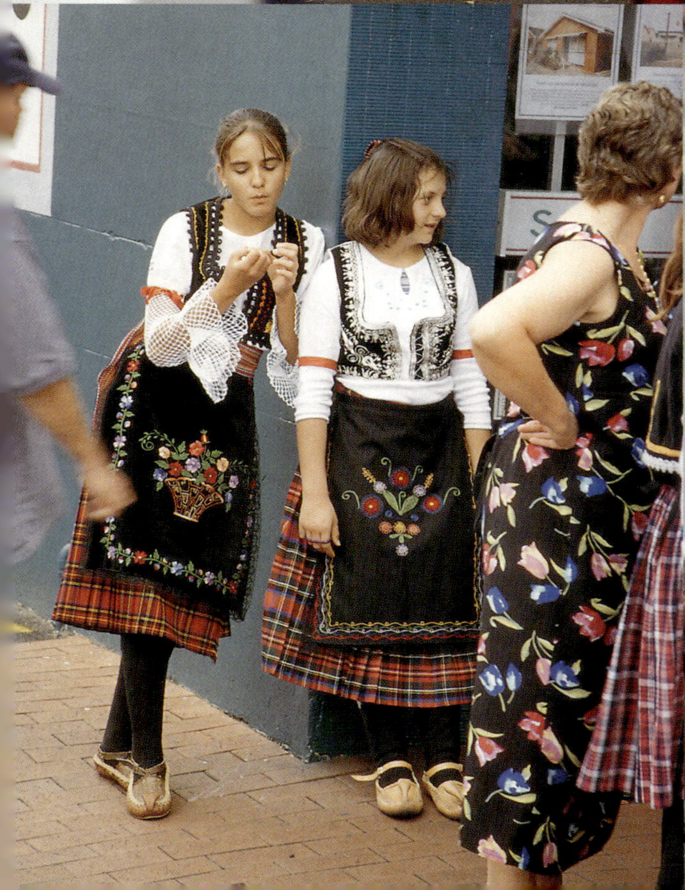
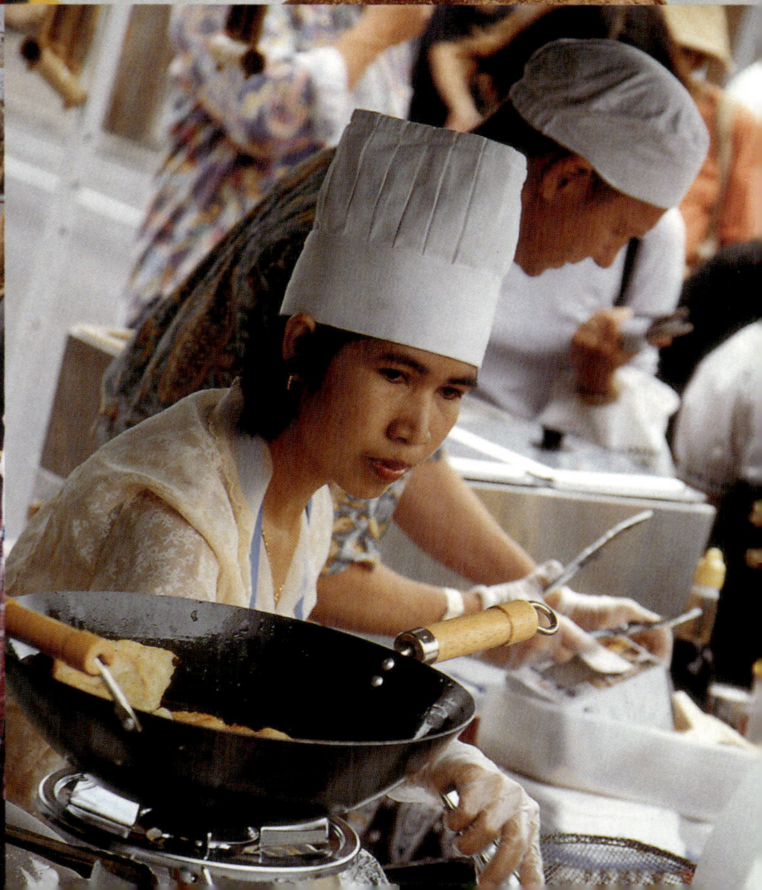

Amaretti Chocolate Torte
BAZILS

INGREDIENTS

100 G BEST-QUALITY DARK CHOCOLATE, CHILLED

110 G AMARETTI BISCUITS

250 G SOFTENED, UNSALTED BUTTER

250 G CASTER SUGAR

5 EGGS, SEPARATED

100 G PLAIN FLOUR

ICING SUGAR FOR DUSTING

Preheat the oven to 180°C.

Roughly chop the chocolate and put it in a food processor with the amaretti. Blitz to a fine powder.

Cream the butter with 150 g of the caster sugar until light and fluffy. Add the egg yolks, one at a time, until well incorporated, then gently mix in the flour.

In a separate bowl, add the remaining sugar to the egg whites and whisk until stiff.

Fold a spoonful of the egg whites into the chocolate mixture to loosen the mixture, then gently fold in the remainder.

Butter and line a 25 cm springform cake tin. Pour the mixture into the tin and bake for an hour or until a skewer comes out clean. Allow the torte to cool in the pan for 15 minutes before carefully turning out and peeling away the paper.

To serve, dust the torte with icing sugar and accompany with thick country cream and fresh or poached fruit.

Serves 4

are slowly improving. There are some reliable stalwarts such as Le Parisien, Fisherman's Pier, the Empire Grill and Café Botticelli and a good Japanese restaurant called Koaki in Rippleside Park. And then there is Sempre Caffe e Paninoteca, one of the newest and best Geelong restaurants offering some of the most interesting and sophisticated Italian food in the city centre.

With the exception of Queenscliff, where there have been a number of terrific eating-out options for quite a few years now, most of the Bellarine Peninsula has been something of a foodie wasteland. Until recently that is, for things are definitely changing in this part of the world. Most of the towns around the peninsula are beach resorts, and suffer from seasonal swings in their population. But there is a growing realisation among food operators that these visitors (and, indeed, the locals too) are no longer satisfied with the limited range of toasted sandwiches and greasy snacks that have been the main food options up until now.

It is quite heart warming to see these places smartening themselves up in the food department. In the main, the new era of good eating around the peninsula has come about due to the efforts of enthusiastic young people. So the new eateries are not necessarily smart and upmarket (in the main, they are anything but), but what they do have in spades is an absolute commitment to providing good quality, delicious food.

I've enjoyed wonderful meals – some quite straightforward and simple, some superbly complex – at each of the places I have chosen to profile. I have included Joseph's restaurant at the Mansion Hotel in Werribee, even though it is not on the peninsula at all. But to me, it doesn't feel a part of Melbourne either, given that it is well and truly on the way to Geelong.

Naturally, my list of eating-out suggestions in Geelong and the Bellarine Peninsula is far from comprehensive, and I urge you to refer to Max Allen's *Food Lover's Guide to the Great Ocean Road*, which details more wonderful places to seek out.

Bazils

One of my favourite Geelong restaurants is Bazils. It's the kind of place you could happily eat at night after night (and in fact many regulars do just that). Neither fancy nor pretentious, the place has a cosy, relaxed feel, with its bright scatter cushions on comfy cane armchairs, piles of magazines and modern artwork on saffron yellow walls.

Owner and chef Marilyn Osborne is far from casual when it comes to food, however. I went to meet her early one Friday morning, before she began cooking for a large wedding she was catering the next day. A small forceful lady, with her grey hair scraped back into a tight little ponytail, she fairly bristled with determination. Indeed, she must have a backbone of steel to keep going through the dramas that besieged her during the first eighteen months of trading.

As she said ruefully, 'It was a drama from go to whoa.' First of all, council renovations to the street outside kept the restaurant closed for over a quarter of the year. A far greater personal tragedy, though, was the loss of her husband Bryan to cancer just before Christmas 2000. A woman with lesser fortitude might have given up, but Marilyn kept going.

She certainly knows her food, and knew what she wanted to achieve with Bazils. 'I like food that is simple and not tricked up. I like dishes to be uncomplicated and I try hard to use only the best fresh local ingredients.' And Marilyn's dedication to her beliefs comes through in her Mediterranean-inspired food: her menu features goodies such as Spanish jamon and chorizo sausages from local

Chilli Mussels
PORT PIER CAFÉ

To make the chilli sauce, heat the oil in a large cooking pot. Add the onions and sauté over a low heat for a few minutes until softened. Then add the garlic and wine and simmer for about 5 minutes. Add the tomatoes, oregano, chilli, salt and pepper and simmer for a further 15 minutes, until the sauce is nice and thick.

Scrub the mussels clean of any sand and dirt and pull away the beards (throw away any that refuse to open after a brisk tap).

Heat the oil in a large cooking pot, and add the onion and garlic. Stir around over a medium heat for a few minutes, tip in the mussels and shake the pan to move them around over the heat. Pour in the wine, cover the pan, turn up the heat and steam for about 6–8 minutes, or until all have opened. Shake the pan vigorously from time to time. Now take the pan off the heat and discard any mussels that haven't opened. Strain some of the cooking liquor into the chilli sauce, taking care to leave any gritty bits of sand in the pot. To serve, divide the mussels between 4 large bowls and spoon over the chilli sauce.

Serves 8

INGREDIENTS

CHILLI SAUCE

2 TABLESPOONS OLIVE OIL

2 LARGE ONIONS, FINELY DICED

1 CLOVE GARLIC, FINELY DICED

250 ML WHITE WINE

1 X 400 G TIN CRUSHED TOMATOES

1 TABLESPOON FRESH OREGANO

1 FRESH CHILLI, FINELY CHOPPED

SALT AND PEPPER

3 KG MUSSELS

2 TABLESPOONS OLIVE OIL

1 ONION, FINELY DICED

2 CLOVES GARLIC, FINELY DICED

250 ML WHITE WINE

smallgoods producer Angel Cardoso; free-range chickens from nearby Freshwater Creek; and sensational fresh fruit and vegetables from V&R in Pakington Street. And then there are her tomatoes – 'I've found the best tomatoes on the peninsula,' she says with pride. I make a mental note to try the vine-ripened tomatoes with basil on toast for breakfast on my next visit.

Before starting Bazils, Marilyn worked for twelve years as a cooking teacher and ran a very successful catering company. She is an inveterate reader of cookery books and over the years she has also travelled extensively through Italy and France, which she credits as the source of much of her inspiration.

'Holidays give you time to think and reflect,' she muses. 'I think I've become less of a purist about food, too. For instance, after sampling twenty different bouillabaisse in the South of France one year I realised that each was slightly different! It taught me to be more relaxed about dishes and to rely less on the cookery books and more on my own gut-feel about dishes.'

As we talked about bouillabaisse (her version is a gutsy, flavoursome interpretation, full of the best and freshest local seafood) I remembered some other terrific dishes I had eaten at Bazils at previous dinners: a simple but delicious starter of grilled Meredith goat's cheese, and a particularly fine cassoulet, full of hearty white beans, meaty sausages and a fine confit of duck.

I felt myself getting hungry and started to cast my eye, as casually as possible, over the menu. That day for lunch I could choose from good, straightforward dishes such as a steak open sandwich made with toasted sourdough, onion jam and homemade relish; a vegetarian frittata made with free-range eggs; or homemade spinach and ricotta gnocchi baked in a creamy tomato sauce. It all sounded very tempting, but there was only one small problem: it was still only 10 a.m.!

Top: The courtyard at Bazils Café.
Bottom: Portarlington mussels at Katialo Restaurant.

Port Pier Café

Urban culinary trends have a way of seeping slowly but surely out from the heart of a city, through the suburbs and into the countryside. And you know the rural heart of a place is really beating to a different rhythm when curious anomalies start to spring up in what might otherwise be provincial mediocrity.

In Portarlington, for instance, there is a cluster of new restaurants that has brought a touch of culinary cheer to a part of the world that, until now, has really only been able to offer counter meals, Aussie-style burgers and fish and chips. My favourites are Port Pier Café, the Spanish restaurant down near the pier; the Greek-ish Katialo up on the main drag; and the hip new reincarnation of The ol' Duke Hotel. All of these venues are being run by eager young people, and what they lack in budgets they make up for with plenty of energy and enthusiasm for what they are doing.

Port Pier Café, the first to arrive, brought a little touch of Spain to the Bellarine Peninsula. Run by Paul Perez and his Spanish partner Xeni Pages, it's located down on Portarlington's wide foreshore, next to the carpark and busy working pier. At first glance things don't look very promising. The building itself is a squat, low-lying brick construction, which looks rather like the small fish-processing factory it used to be. Inside, things are similarly low-key, and the only real clue that you are in a Spanish café comes from the couple of Picasso prints on the wall and the large poster of a Spanish bull above the cash register.

But rest reassured, everything is just as is should be in this unpretentious and very reasonably priced Spanish restaurant. Whether you sit inside or at one of the outside tables in warmer weather, your gaze is drawn inexorably out across the wide,

Bazils Café
Licensed

wide bay. If you are there during the day, let your eyes wander over the constantly changing seascape or check out the activity on the mussel boats moored at the end of the pier. And at night time, if you look carefully, you can make out the distinctive sweep of the West Gate Bridge, and even see the lights of the MCG.

The menu at Port Pier Café features traditional home-style dishes from Northern Spain, and like most informal Spanish restaurants, is fairly loose. At lunch time, many people prefer to nibble on tapas, perhaps with a light Spanish red or a chilled local chardonnay. You might choose crisp fried potatoes, drizzled with a wonderfully pungent aïoli. Equally delicious are tiny spicy meatballs and calamari in a rich tomato, as are Xeni's homemade chicken croquettes.

If you choose from the main menu, you might start with the very popular potato and onion omelette, pan-fried sardines with garlic and parsley or a platter of excellent Spanish jamon. Main courses lean heavily towards top-quality local seafood, and, unsurprisingly, mussels feature prominently on the menu. Most of the fish on offer comes from the excellent White Fisheries in nearby St Leonards, and for mussels, all Xeni really needs to do is open the kitchen window and shout out her order.

And it wouldn't be a real Spanish restaurant without paella, which Xeni makes entirely from scratch for each diner. You will have to wait around twenty minutes or so, but it is worth the wait. This is home-style paella, pungent with saffron and crammed full of tasty ingredients. It comes 'mixta' – with chicken, pork and seafood, or vegetarian – full of garlic, vegetables and fresh herbs from Paul and Xeni's own garden; or my favourite, 'marisco', with seafood.

When you have finished eating, take a stroll along the esplanade or out along the pier for a chat with the fishermen. On your way back, you can always stop back at the restaurant for a cup of good strong coffee and a slice of cake, and ponder some more about how good life can be.

Katialo

Katialo is, quite literally, something else. That's the translation of the Greek word, and very apt it is too.

When young owners Steven and Alex Souflas took over the premises in February 2000 it was a popular but rather old-fashioned Italian-style bistro, and one of the very few eating-out options in Portarlington. Katialo is their first restaurant together, and their enthusiasm and energy show. However, the transformation they have wrought about the place is not so much in the décor (which is still a little provincial 1970s), but in Steve's terrific Greek–Mediterranean food.

Above: Steven and Alex Souflas at Katialo Restaurant, Portarlington.

As is the case for many young operators starting out on a new venture, dollars were short. 'Rather than spend what little money we had on fancy decorations, we felt it was more important to spend it on good ingredients and to let the food speak for itself,' said co-owner and chef Steven, as we sat for a chat one midweek lunchtime. The place looks convincingly like a Greek taverna: the terrace out the front is lined with pots of aromatic herbs, and on sunny days, sipping on a glass of retsina, gazing out through the cypress trees over the sparkling blue of Port Phillip Bay, one could almost be in Paros.

The food, however, is way above your average Greek-island meal. Steven has deliberately avoided predictable tourist tucker, so don't expect to see souvlaki on the menu. Instead, the food might better be described as 'Greek influenced', and features simple, authentic, village-style fare. That day, for instance, starters included whole sardines with local figs and white pomegranates, and lemon gnocchi with Kalamata olives and thyme. Among the mains was a shoulder of local lamb roasted with lemon, garlic and oregano, and grilled loin of pork with allspice, pimentos and golden delicious apples. For dessert there was baklava roll with fresh fruit and Tsantali Mavrodaphne liqueur, or Gavin's local nectarines poached in dessert semillon.

Steven spent eighteen months at the wonderful Sunnybrae restaurant with chef, teacher and exponent of Victorian produce George Biron, and the influence shows. Steven shares George's passion for sourcing good-quality, seasonal, local produce, and even makes a feature of it. So, typically, the menu offers dishes such as the aforementioned Gavin's nectarines, or Peter 'Jerker' Jenkins' local calamari with braised bitter greens. Peter is a local fisherman who pulls his truck up outside the restaurant most mornings so that Steven can choose the best from that day's catch. 'It's not often you can buy fish that has only been out of the water an hour or so,' said Steven, smiling happily.

In the same vein, meat comes from a local butcher who rears his own cattle. Poultry comes from Glenloth and fruit and vegetables from nearby market gardeners. And then there are the Portarlington residents who come in with produce from their own gardens – one might have a box of figs, another a box of eggplant or tomatoes, and so on. The wine list is also proudly local, with just about every nearby winery represented. Steven and Alex also offer a couple of Greek beers, wines and liqueurs.

Katialo was one of the first of the new wave of good eating places in booming Portarlington and, for my money, is one of the very best. The blackboard out the front of the restaurant proclaims: 'Of course you can just have coffee'. But take a tip from me and make sure you stay for lunch or dinner. You'll be glad you did.

The ol' Duke

There's no doubt that Portarlington's newest culinary venture is a beautiful and stylish addition to the place, and a good litmus test of just how things are changing. Once a sleepy and little known corner of the Bellarine Peninsula, today it is once more becoming a desirable holiday destination, with stressed-out city folk coming down in their droves to find the perfect 'new' place for a weekender.

The old Duke of Edinburgh Hotel (known to locals as 'the family hotel') was one of the first pubs to be built in the town, back in 1855. In the early days it was said to offer 'superior accommodation' to the crowds of

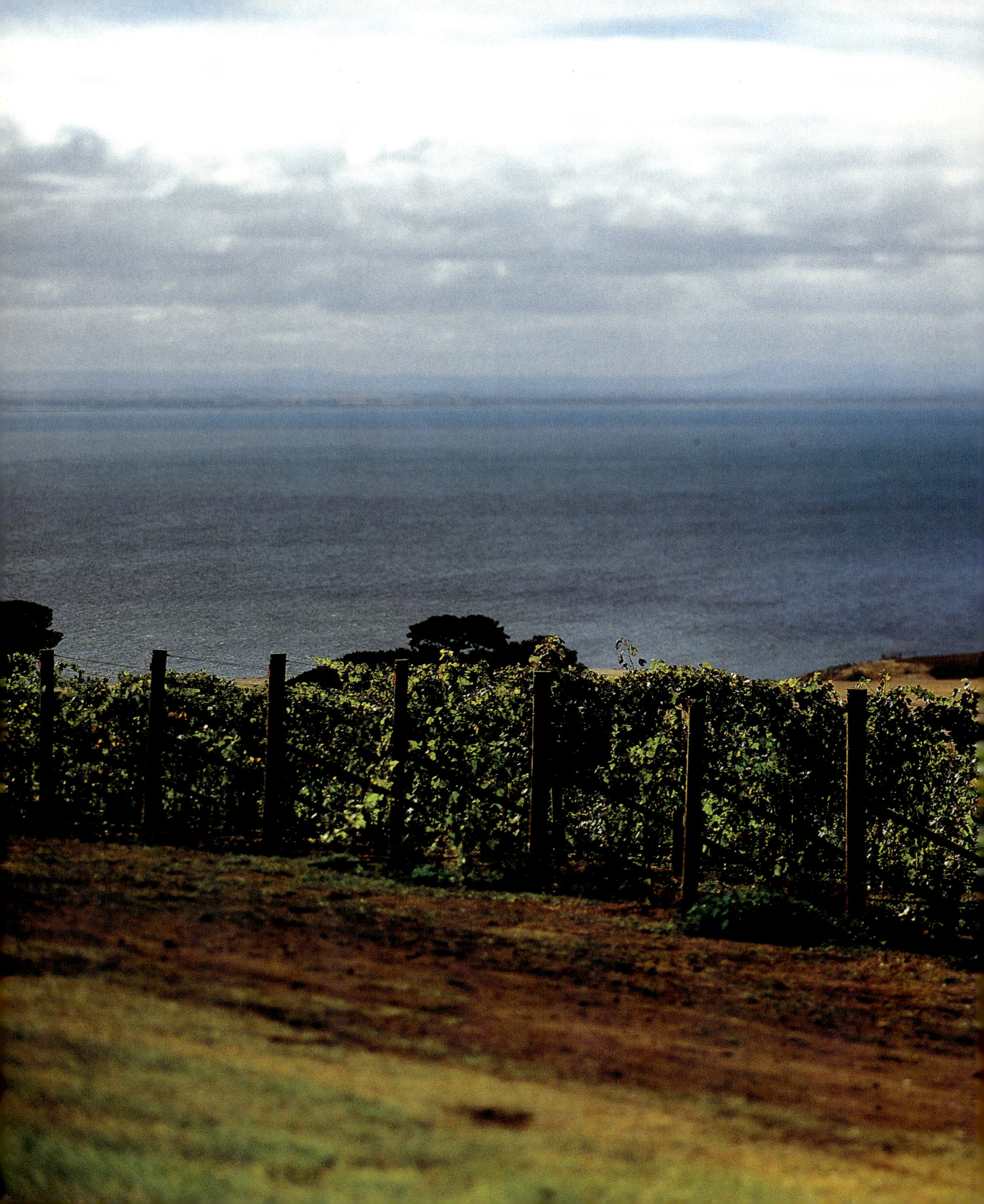

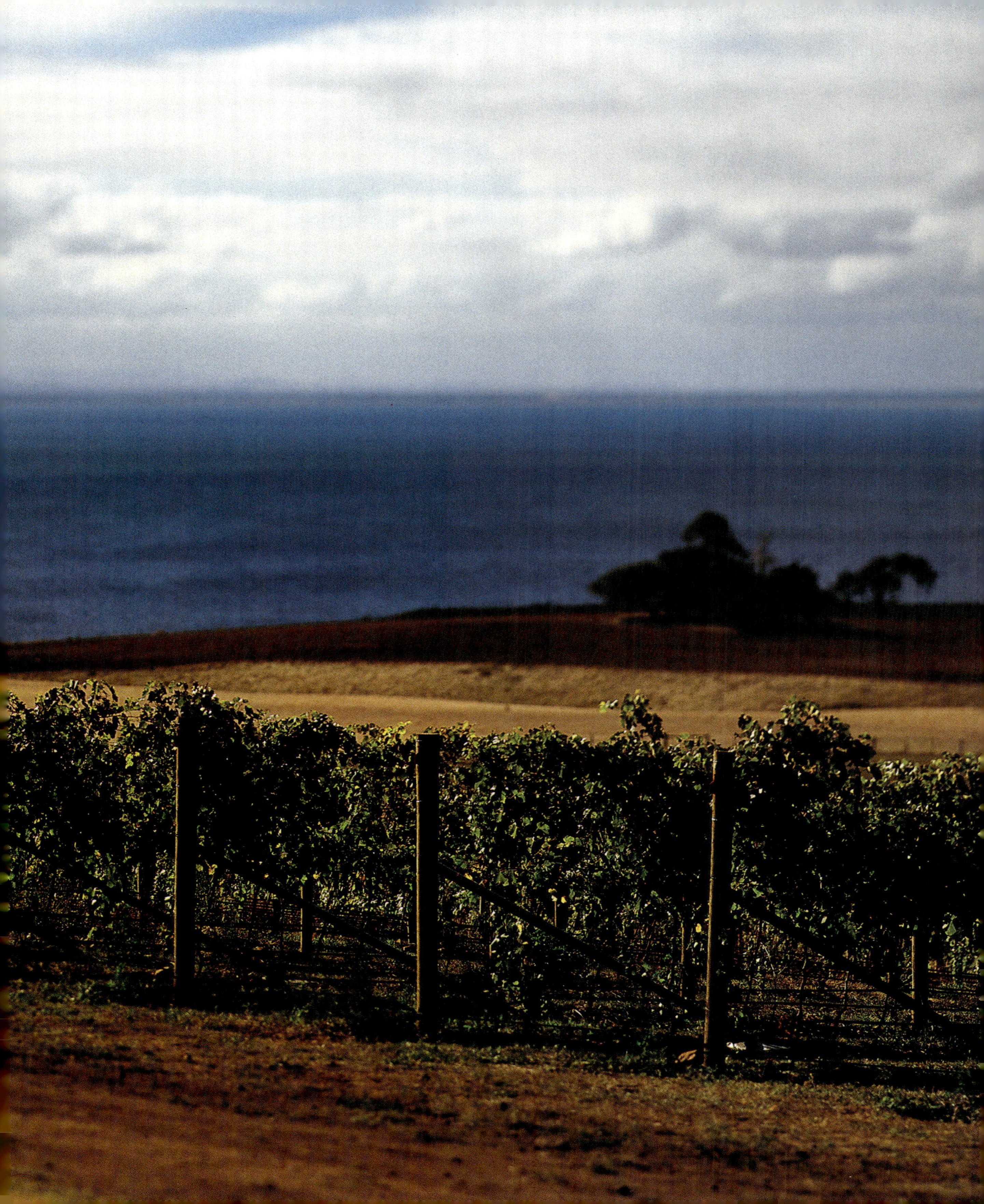

Melburnians who came across the bay by the ferry-load in the summertime to escape the city heat. It even boasted a ballroom, and one can have great fun imagining those Victorian ladies and gentlemen, dressed to the nines in their crinolines and dinner jackets, whirling away the hot summer evenings, and perhaps taking a stroll down to the waterfront after dinner for some reviving sea air.

After World War I things changed, and tourism went into a steady decline, exacerbated by the closure of both rail and ferry services to the peninsula. The family hotel was de-licensed in the 1940s and became a hospital (many locals were born there), and then an all-purpose police station, courtroom and gaol house. Over the past twenty-odd years the building has been just about everything from a pizza shop to a clothes shop, but it is only now, at the start of the twenty-first century, that a couple of bright young things have begun to breathe some life back into the place.

Energetic new owners Melanie Pitman and her partner Andrew Parker have resisted the temptation to restore the place to its original Victorian splendour. For a start, the building was never as upmarket as some of the grand historic hotels over the way at Queenscliff. Secondly, it was nigh on derelict when they took it over in July 2000. Instead, Mel and Andrew opted to create a stylish, modern and accessible place for locals and holidaymakers alike.

The ol' Duke is now all light-filled airy spaces, with contemporary touches. The main dining room boasts high ceilings, navy leather banquette seating and warm wooden floorboards. At the front, doors open onto a wide veranda with stunning views out through the cypress trees to the bay. Towards the rear, there is a lounge area with subdued lighting and comfortable sofas in squishy dark-brown leather; it's the perfect cosy spot for a late-night drink or a quiet coffee with a magazine.

And then there's that ballroom, which Mel and Andrew intend to use for functions and conferences. It is a simply stunning space; light floods in on all sides through tall arched windows set with brilliant blue stained glass, and it's not hard to imagine the room filled with music and dancing and happy revellers once more.

Mel and Andrew have been very keen to make The ol' Duke a relaxed and easygoing family hotel again. So the menu offers accessible and tasty food, which might be as simple as toasted focacce and BLTs (albeit upmarket versions of these favourites), and as stylish as lightly spiced oven-roasted vegetables with vermicelli noodles, or a seafood chowder chock-full of prawns, scallops and sweet local mussels. Their chef, Dean Matthews, has had plenty of experience feeding tourist tummies, from a stint at Chris Talihmanidis's wonderful restaurant at Beacon Point, and eight years working with Luigi Bazzani in Geelong and then at the Warrenmang Winery Restaurant.

In an interesting break from current trends, the wine list at The ol' Duke is not doing the 'local' thing. Instead, Mel has put together a small list of well-priced wines – seven reds and seven whites, all available by the bottle and the glass – and features one different local winery every month or so.

With grand plans afoot for development of the Portarlington foreshore and whispers about the reintroduction of a ferry service from Melbourne, it seems that it won't be long before Portarlington is once again the lively little town that it was a century ago. I, for one, will be keen to don my dancing shoes and trip the light fantastic in the ballroom at The ol' Duke.

Previous page: Ocean view from the Spray Farm.
Right: Owner Mel Pitman making coffee; inside The ol' Duke.

The ol'Duke – eat

The ol'Duke – eat

Spinach & Marscapone tart...
Lightly spiced oven Roasted v...
tossed w noodles
Duck leg confit risotto w s...
Mushrooms & Semi dried tom...
Pasta Marinara w garlic,
shallots & olive oil
Pork cutlet on mushroom
confit, caramelized apple & a...
Lemon & pistachio pesto
...fillet steak topped w...

The Queenscliff Hotel

'You always know when the squid are running down here,' said Patricia O'Donnell, as we sat chatting over a cup of coffee. 'All night long you hear the "zoom, zoom, zoom" of cars pulling up to the end of the pier. I don't know how the word gets around, but it seems to spread like wildfire.'

I'd been telling her about my walk the previous night, out to the end of the long pier in the pouring rain. And my strange encounter with fifteen or so men, women and children, clad from head to toe in wet-weather gear, excitedly hauling in the straggly, tentacled sea-monsters by torchlight.

It had been such a startling contrast to the elegant, gracious Queenscliff I thought I knew: the cosy world from my childhood, of buckets and spades and sunny afternoons spent fossicking in rockpools; the comfortable world I was currently enjoying; of tea in front of a roaring fire; and drinks before dinner at The Queenscliff Hotel.

But Queenscliff has always been much more than just a seaside resort. The residents have a long, working association with the sea and the creatures beneath the waves. For over a century, its young men have manned the lighthouses and sailed the tiny pilot boats that guided ships through the treacherous Rip. And until a few decades ago, there was a prosperous industry of boat builders and chandlers which serviced the busy local fishing fleet.

Things are changing though, gradually. In the mid-1970s the barracouta, which were the main catch in this part of the world, mysteriously disappeared. Since then, there has been an embargo on scallop dredging in the bay, and the fish are just getting harder to find. It's a hard, lonely life, being a fisherman, and it's one that fewer and fewer of the younger generation are willing to pursue.

Nevertheless, it is its history as a working town that makes Queenscliff so unique among Victorian seaside resorts. Unlike Portsea, its twin peninsula resort on the opposite side of the Heads, Queenscliff has always been a place for the people. At Portsea, visitors always feel like a bit of an outsider: there are grand private homes by the score, but no public buildings, shops or cafés. At Queenscliff, things are far more democratic. Its houses tend to be humble fishermen's cottages, and its facilities are there for everyone to enjoy. There are parks and piers and hot sea-baths (hopefully soon to be restored), there are beaches and steam trains and marine life to explore. And there is a wealth of cute little guest-houses, and smart hotels like the Vue Grand, The Ozone and The Queenscliff Hotel.

The Queenscliff Hotel is my favourite, probably because staying there feels more like being a guest in a large private home than a mere room number in an austerely elegant Grand Hotel. It's the little touches that make the difference. As owner Patricia O'Donnell puts it, 'We want people to feel welcome and comfortable, not intimidated.' So the furniture here is slightly shabby, rather than stylish or 'high-gloss'. The sitting

Right: Flowers at The Queenscliff Hotel.
Opposite: The Queenscliff Hotel's courtyard.

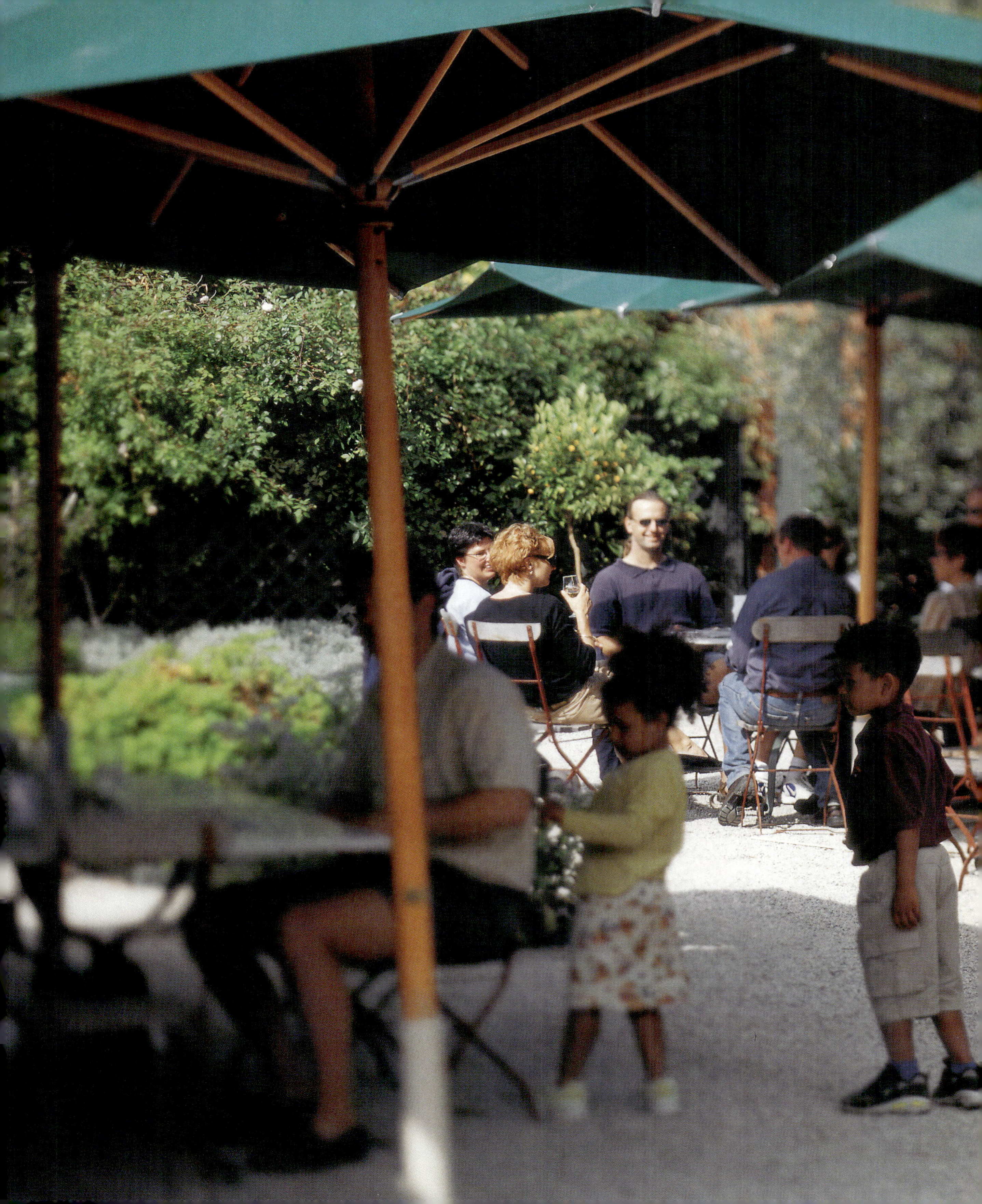

Seared Salmon with Olives, Anchovies, Vine Tomatoes and Green Beans

INGREDIENTS

200 G GREEN BEANS, TOPPED AND TAILED

20 SMALL VINE CHERRY TOMATOES

1–2 HANDFULS BLACK OLIVES, PITTED

12 ANCHOVY FILLETS

1 SMALL HANDFUL BASIL LEAVES

SALT AND FRESHLY GROUND BLACK PEPPER

50 ML EXTRA-VIRGIN OLIVE OIL

HERB PASTE

1 DRIED RED CHILLI

1 TABLESPOON CORIANDER SEEDS

1/2 CLOVE GARLIC

1 GOOD HANDFUL CORIANDER LEAVES

1 SMALL HANDFUL BASIL LEAVES

JUICE OF 1 LEMON

1 TABLESPOON EXTRA-VIRGIN OLIVE OIL

4 X 180 G SALMON FILLETS, PIN BONES REMOVED

50 ML OLIVE OIL

EXTRA-VIRGIN OLIVE OIL

LEMON WEDGES

JOSEPH'S RESTAURANT

Preheat the oven to 200°C.

Blanch the green beans in salted boiling water until tender. Drain them well, then put them in a bowl with the tomatoes, olives, anchovies and basil. Season with salt and pepper, toss in the olive oil, then place the mixture on a baking tray. Cook for 10–15 minutes.

To make the herb paste, grind the chilli and coriander seeds with a pestle and mortar, then add the garlic and fresh herbs. When well mixed, add the lemon juice and olive oil and season well.

Rub the herb paste all over the salmon. Heat the olive oil in a frying pan, and cook the fish for about a minute on each side. The salmon will still be pink in the middle, which is the ideal way to serve it, but if you like it a little more well done, then just leave it in the pan for a little longer.

To serve, divide the vegetables between 4 serving plates, place the salmon on top and serve with a drizzle of extra-virgin olive oil and a wedge of lemon.

Serves 4

areas are intimate and cosy, with shelves full of books and all the daily newspapers; the bedrooms are small, but charmingly appointed. It's the sort of place where your every comfort is catered for and your needs are anticipated, almost before you realise what they are yourself.

For the food and wine lover, the main appeal of The Queenscliff Hotel is the range of eating and drinking options available to suit one's mood. If you want the full-on experience, a meal in the grand dining room is truly memorable. This is the place to eat when you want to put on dinner dress and eat at tables set with gleaming antique silver, bathed in candlelight. Chef Xavier Robinson's set menu suits the surroundings.

The food is modern yet unquestionably 'fine dining'; complex without being overworked. For instance, galantine of duck, rabbit and pork comes with quince chutney and toasted brioche; veal loin comes roasted pink with lemon risotto, sweet and sour leeks and an intense port-wine glaze. Desserts might be as simple as a chocolate tart with caramelised oranges or as complex as a vacherin of hazelnut ice-cream with lemon curd and poached figs. The wine list is outstanding, with a strong emphasis on local Victorian wines, and also features a limited selection of older and Reserve vintages available from the hotel's cellar.

Lighter fare is on offer from the à la carte 'bistro' menu for lunch and dinner every day. This is simply executed food, with no extraneous fuss or frills, yet it still manages to be imaginative and bursting with flavour. Sugar-cured salmon, for instance, comes with a tangy apple and walnut salad; grilled kangaroo, with an intense raisin port and pink peppercorn glaze. Even the simple pumpkin soup I ate in front of the fire for lunch one day came fragrant with citrus shreds and thyme.

If you prefer, you can amble through the

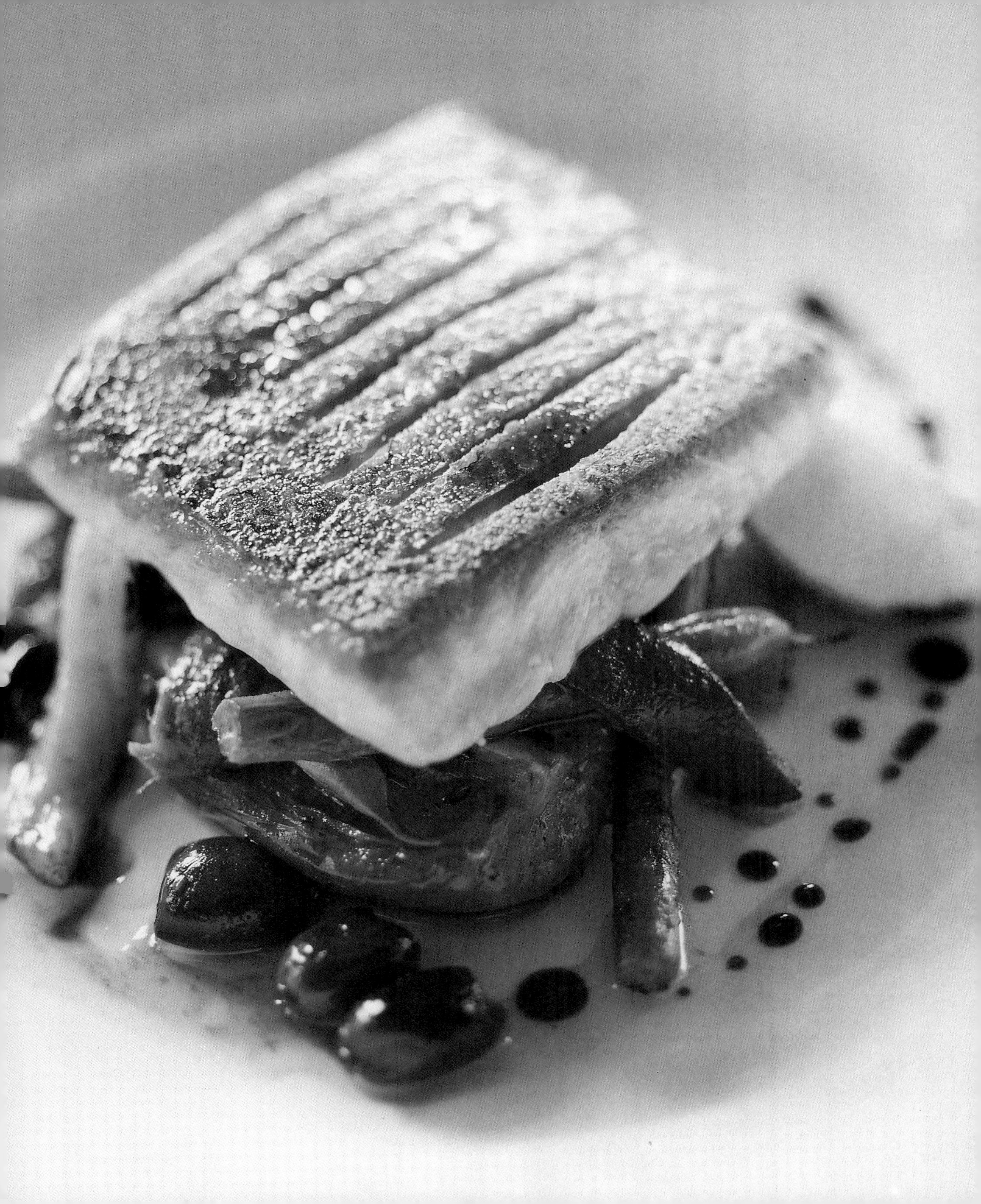

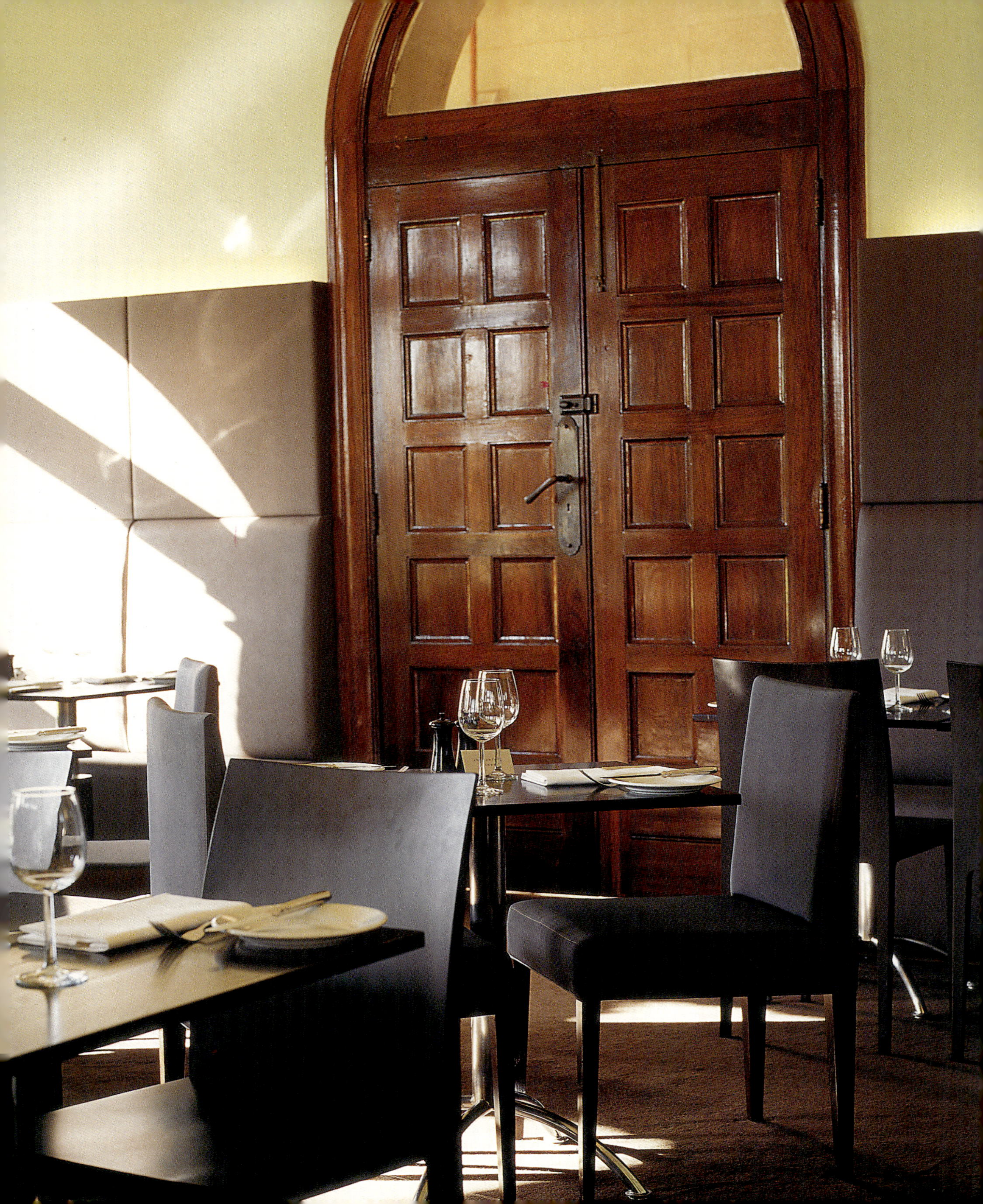

herb garden to the very attractive produce shop and browse among the produce, cookery and gardening books before settling down to a coffee and homemade tart. Simpler still is food in the side bar, where everything is gleaming brass, warm wood and strong nautical touches in the maps and boat pictures.

The Queenscliff Hotel has undoubtedly become a Queenscliff icon, due in no small part to its long association with the O'Donnell family (until very recently, it was even known as 'Mietta's' Queenscliff Hotel, to mark her early involvement with the place). Now in its twentieth year of operation, owner Patricia O'Donnell has decided to sell the hotel and move on. But the years of effort she and her family have put into creating such a uniquely warm and welcoming experience at the hotel will surely endure. The very distinctive charm of the place will undoubtedly ensure that visitors just keep on coming to enjoy the gracious, old-world ambience and extraordinarily attentive service. And my recommendation? Don't just go for lunch, but go and experience a weekend away. You won't want to leave.

Joseph's at The Mansion Hotel

It was a foggy Monday morning in early May when I set off for lunch at Joseph's. As I drove over the West Gate Bridge, red lights were flashing a slow-down warning, and I glanced quickly back at the magical sight of the city towers shimmering through the mist. Twenty-five minutes later I was turning off the freeway into the flatlands of Werribee South. This was market-garden country, dark, bleak and featureless, and the unmistakable odour of cabbage assaulted my nostrils as I turned down a boggy dirt road towards Werribee Park and The Mansion Hotel.

When I pulled into the carpark, sheltered among tall gum trees, I was taken aback to discover it was full. 'We've got three conferences on here today,' explained the friendly receptionist, as she directed me towards the restaurant. Apart from the cars, though, there was little sign of activity. The conferencees were obviously sequestered away somewhere, focusing on whiteboards. My mind was focused firmly on lunch, so I ambled slowly through the serene entrance lobby to Joseph's.

The Mansion Hotel is a stunning boutique hotel within the grounds of the old Werribee Park Mansion, the closest thing we Victorians have to a stately home. It has been skilfully incorporated into the Catholic seminary attached to the old mansion. The interior spaces are airy and clutter-free, and minimalist tones of taupe, cream and soothing woven metal fabrics emphasise a quiet air of restrained luxury.

The restaurant itself occupies a lofty wing of the old seminary, and looks out through tall, arched windows onto exquisitely manicured grounds. As I took my seat at a nicely positioned window table, the sun broke through the mist and flooded the dining room with light. Outside, a few gardeners were pottering about the grounds, and in the distance a small white buggy was chuntering off to the nearby golf course, with a couple of hotel guests on board.

I turned my mind to the job of eating. The menu in front of me bore the unmistakable stamp of former managing director, Martin Webb (he of the late lamented Georges, and mover and shaker within the legendary Conran empire). It featured the carefully composed, modern brasserie-style food that I had expected: simple, well-balanced ingredients and flavours, with no extraneous frippery.

My first course, a tomato tart with Persian fetta, was delectable. Four plump tomato halves sat on a bed of sweetly caramelised onion in a flaky puff pastry shell; perched on

Previous page: Seared salmon with olives, anchovies, vine tomatoes and green beans (see page 128).
Left: Joseph's Restaurant at The Mansion Hotel.

top, a blob of soft tangy fetta melted softly under a handful of peppery rocket leaves. As I savoured the intense tomatoey-ness of the dish, I sipped at a glass of Shadowfax pinot gris – the recommended accompaniment, with its appropriately sweet nougat tones.

My main course was a similar triumph of content over style. Two perfect fillets of crisply fried barramundi arrived, skin-side up, placed on a velvety smooth, well-balanced skordalia. It came with a salad of large parsley leaves, tangy lemon segments and a few flecks of lemon zest. To all appearances simple, but in its execution, just perfect.

For desserts, there were various simple delights on offer, like a sheep's milk parfait with drunken figs, a wicked chocolate tart and perfect local cheeses. Feeling greedy, I ordered the lemon crème brûlée, which was nicely lemony with an intense burnt caramel shell. I allowed myself to be talked into a glass of Moscato d'Asti to wash it down – it was light, petulant and delicately perfumed – and given my imminent drive back to Melbourne, appropriately low in alcohol.

As I sat in a kind of happy stomach-heavy stupor, Barry Vera, the newly appointed head chef came out for a chat. Barry was fresh off the plane from England, and his face was still washed with the grey pallor of jet-lag. But he was excited. 'I can't really believe I'm here,' he said happily. 'My wife's Australian, and we've been longing to come out here. I can't wait to finally start getting my hands on all the fantastic local produce.'

The hotel was equally excited about having Barry, who had spent the past six years working for such prestigious operations as The Conran Group (yes, there's a definite 'theme' here), the Marco Pierre White Group and, most recently, as executive chef of London's Waldorf Hotel.

I drove away from the hotel in a contented daydream. As I passed the open-range zoo, I gazed over fondly at a distant group of rhinos and a spindly giraffe, with its head buried in a tree. I felt a little bit like Barry Vera, that all this did seem like a rather wonderful dream. The drive back to Melbourne passed quickly, as I thought back happily over the day, and my good humour lasted until I hit the peak-hour traffic back in town.

Above: Chef Barry Vera at Joseph's Restaurant.
Over Page: Enjoying a glass of wine at Shadowfax Wines.

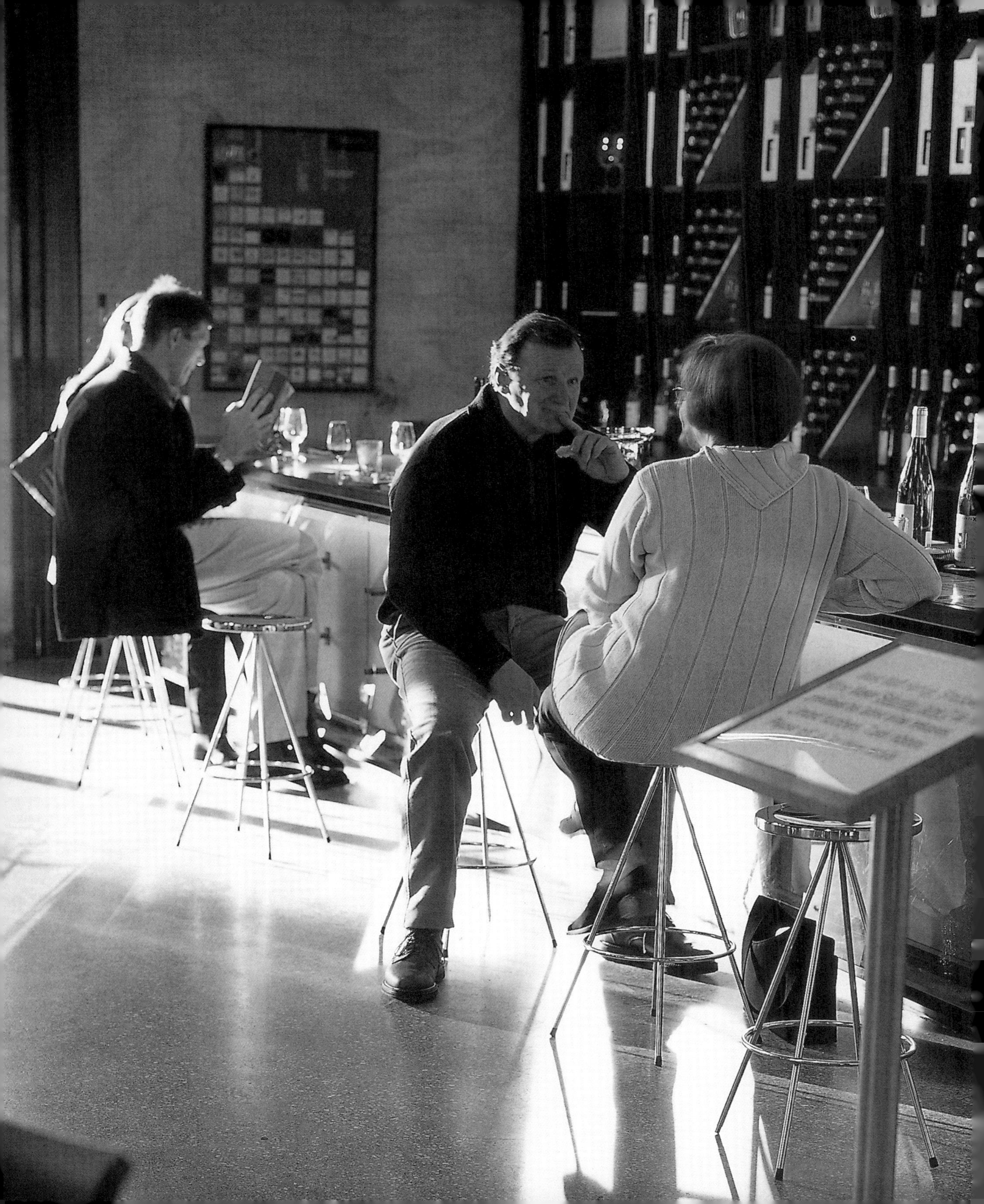

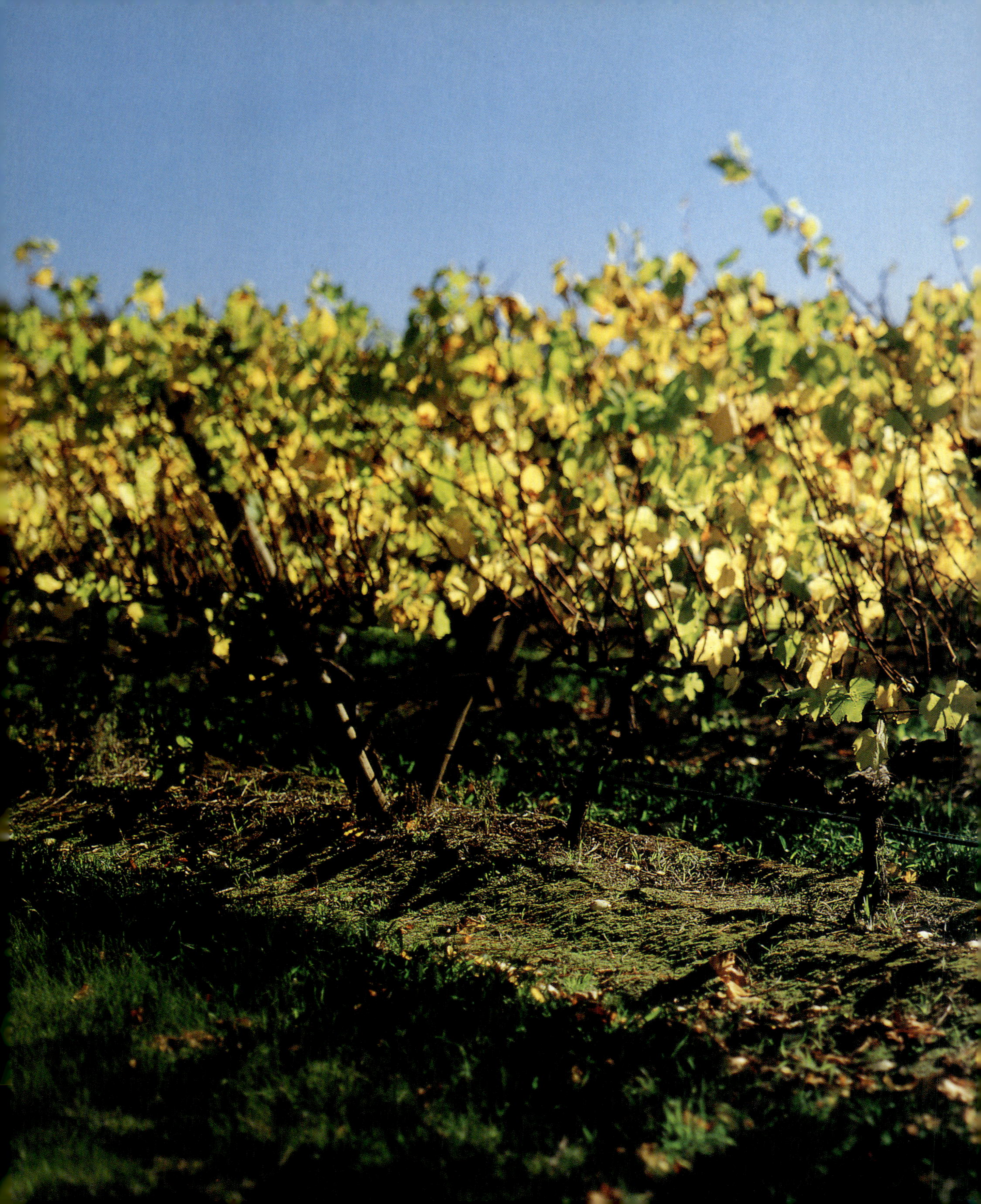

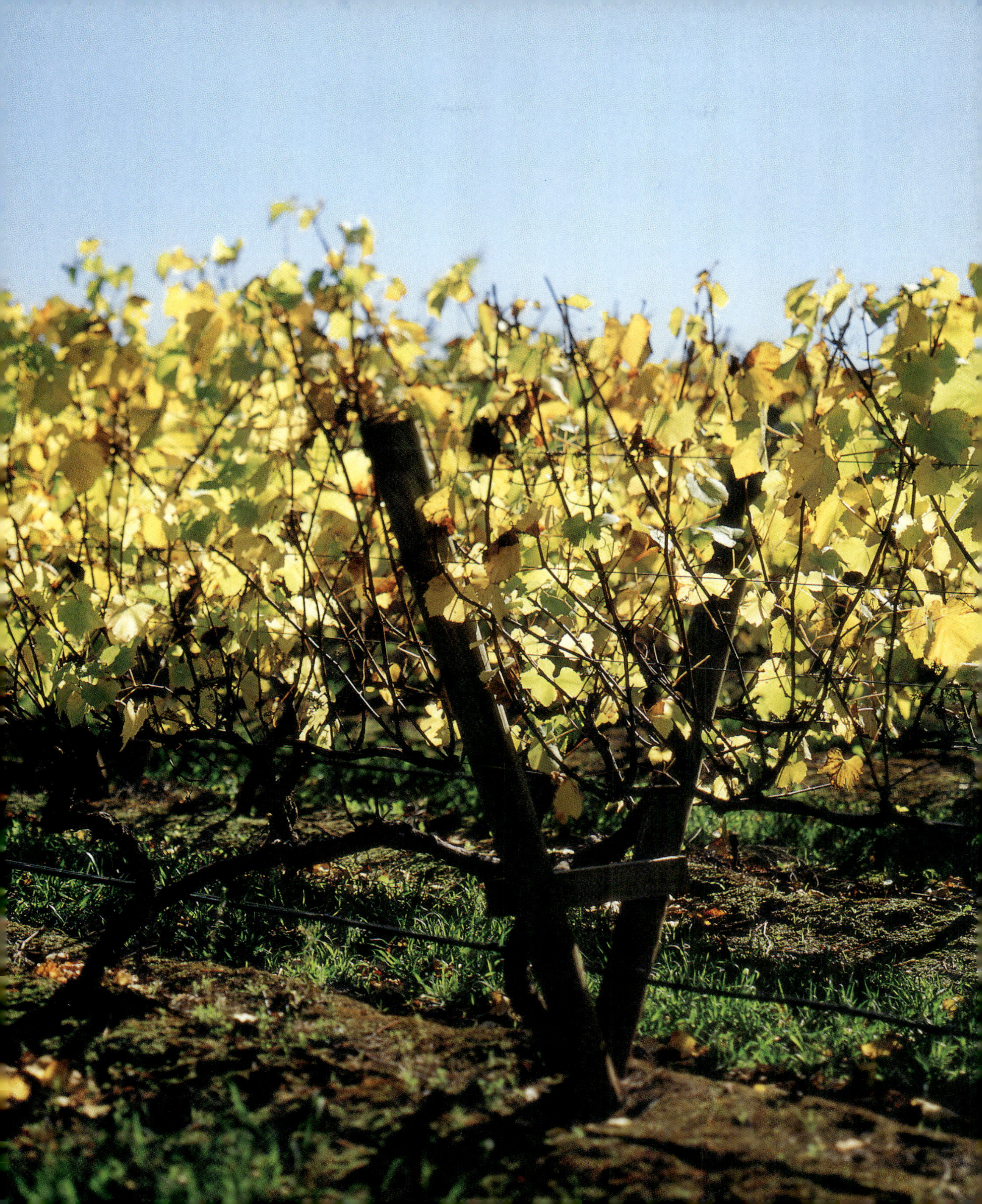

MORNINGTON PENINSULA

Accommodation

ELLISFIELD FARM
109 McIlroys Road
Red Hill Vic 3937
Ph: (03) 5989 2008
Fax: (03) 5989 2804
ellisfieldfarm@bigpond.com
s/c cottage

LINDENDERRY AT RED HILL
142 Arthur's Seat Road
Red Hill Vic 3937
Phone: (03) 5989 2933
Fax: (03) 5989 2936
Website: www.lindenderry.com.au

Lindenderry, a five-star country house hotel, restaurant and vineyard is the ideal retreat for food and wine lovers. The property includes forty bedrooms, several lounges, a wellness spa, meeting facilities, renowned restaurant, orchard, stone-walled herb garden, tennis courts and the pinot and chardonnay vines that produce its award-winning wines.

Produce

SUNNY RIDGE STRAWBERRY FARM
RMB 7320 Flinders Road
(cnr Shands Road)
Main Ridge Vic 3928
Phone: (03) 5989 6273
Fax: (03) 5989 6363
E-mail: info@thestrawberryfarm.com

The largest commercial producer of strawberries in Victoria, this U-Pick strawberry farm dedicates itself to flavour and quality. The strawberry centre offers homemade ice-cream, Devonshire teas, various strawberry desserts, a fresh fruit juice bar, a variety of fruit wines and liqueurs, as well as a range of locally produced gourmet delights.

Restaurants & Cafes

FLINDERS BREAD
58–60 Cook Street
Flinders Vic 3929
Phone: (03) 9768 2888
Fax: (03) 9768 3083
E-mail: flinders@hawley.com.au

Come and visit Flinders Bread being baked in the original oven (first fired in the 1880s), using old-fashioned baking practices and traditional recipes. The bread range includes wholemeal fruit cob and a multitude of gourmet-style breads, rich in natural flavour, which are available throughout Melbourne and parts of country Victoria.

MAIN STREET DELI
53 Main St
Mornington Vic 3931
Phone: (03) 5975 2403
Fax: (03) 9768 3083
E-mail: clb@hawley.com.au

The Main Street Deli serves gourmet sandwiches, healthy wraps, magnificent Mediterranean bruschetta on Turkish bread and pre-made baguettes and foccacia, all at reasonable prices. Homemade pies are a must, as are the rich cakes, pastries or jumbo cookies served with beautiful coffee or fresh juice. Open daily for breakfast and lunch.

Wineries

DROMANA ESTATE
25 Harrisons Rd
Dromana Vic 3936
Ph: (03) 5987 3800
Fax: (03) 5981 0714
E-mail: decellardoor@bigpond.com
Website: www.dromanaestate.com.au

Overlooking the picturesque lake and vineyard, this buzzing cellar door–restaurant not only serves wines of outstanding quality from the Dromana Estate, Schinus and Garry Crittenden's Italian ranges, but offers delicious light lunches made from fresh local produce. Open 7 days from 11am to 4pm. Melway reference 160 J6.

MOOROODUC ESTATE VINEYARD
501 Derril Road
Moorooduc Vic 3933
Phone: (03) 5971 8506
Fax: (03) 5971 8550
E-mail: moorooduc@ozemail.com.au
Stylish!

MORNING STAR ESTATE
Sunnyside Road
Mt Eliza Vic
Phone: (03) 9787 7760
Fax: (03) 9787 7160
E-mail: morningstarestate@bigpond.com

Morning Star Estate offers a cellar door–restaurant serving everything from coffee and cake to the most imaginative cuisine using all local produce. Our manicured gardens and private chapel play host to many weddings and receptions of which we are noted for our excellence. Accommodation and corporate facilities will be available in 2001.

MORNINGTON PENINSULA VIGNERONS ASSOCIATION
PO Box 282
Red Hill South Vic 3937
Phone: (03) 5989 2377
Fax: (03) 5989 2387
E-mail: mpva@bigpond.com
Website: www.mpva.com.au

The Mornington Peninsula Vignerons Association (MPVA) is the industry association for the winemakers and grape growers of the region. The region includes 174 vineyards and more than 40 wineries with cellar doors. Call the association for your free wine touring map and information on wine festivals and events in the region.

RED HILL ESTATE
53 Shoreham Road
Red Hill South
Victoria 3937
Phone: (03) 5989 2838
Fax: (03) 5989 2855
E-mail: info@redhillestate.com.au
Website: www.redhillestate.com.au

Red Hill Estate is a 50 acre cool climate property located on an elevated area of the Mornington Peninsula with sweeping views overlooking Westernport Bay and Phillip Island. Just over an hours drive from Melbourne, Red Hill Estate with its premium award winning wines and exquisite restaurant is a magical destination.

STONIER WINES • MERRICKS
362 Frankston–Flinders Rd
(cnr Thompsons Lane)
Merricks Vic 3916
Ph: (03) 5989 8300
Fax: (03) 5989 8709
E-mail: stoniers@stoniers.com.au
Website: www.stoniers.com.au

*Established in 1978, Stonier Wines is an award-winning producer of chardonnay, pinot noir, cabernet sauvignon and sauvignon blanc. The striking Stonier winery is open daily for wine tastings and sales, cheese platters, winery tours, and children's playground, and has Easter, Queen's Birthday and Cup Weekend festivals annually.
Mel ref 192 F9*

STUMPY GULLY VINEYARD
1247 Stumpy Gully Road
Moorooduc Vic 3933
Ph: (03) 5978 8429
Fax: (03) 5978 8419
E-mail: sguzant@bigpond.com

Located in the Moorooduc wine touring area and open from 11am to 5pm every weekend, this colourful cellar door offers premium wines. Stumpy Gully produces classic Mornington Peninsula chardonnay, pinot noir, cabernet and sauvignon blanc as well as the more unusual sangiovese, marsarne and pinot grigio, all estate grown and produced.

WILLOW CREEK VINEYARD
166 Balnarring Road
Merricks North Vic 3926
Ph: (03) 5989 7448
Fax: (03) 5989 7584
E-mail: admin@willow-creek.com.au
Website: www.willow-creek.com.au

Winery restaurant.

Other

AAA ALLDAY WINERY TOURS
PO Box 2142
Carrum Downs Vic 3201
Phone: (03) 9789 9913
Fax: (03) 9789 9913
E-mail: allday@satlink.com.au

AAA Allday Winery Tours have designed a number of personalised tours so you can have the best things in life – great wine, good food and fantastic countryside viewing. Tours include the winery, restaurant, BBQ or BYO lunches and tasting fees. Start and finish from your home, office or accommodation.

HERONSWOOD DROMANA
105 La Trobe Parade
Dromana Vic 3936
Phone: (03) 5987 1877
Fax: (03) 5981 4298
E-mail: info@diggers.com.au

*Visit our famous garden and enjoy our fabulous food. Stroll around two hectares of stunning gardens. Browse through the National Trust–registered garden bookshop. Indulge in delicious Mediterranean-style food at Australia's only thatched roof café. Open weekdays from 9.30am to 4.30pm. Closed weekends and public holidays.
Mel ref 159 C9*

MCCLELLAND GALLERY
390 McClelland Drive
Langwarrin Vic 3910
Phone: (03) 9789 1671
Fax: (03) 9789 1610
E-mail:mcclell@corplink.com.au

Established in 1971, McClelland Gallery is set within an 4.5 hectare sculpture park that features works by prominent Australian artists. The gallery hosts changing exhibitions, installations, lectures, floor talks, and concerts and also boasts a gift shop as well as a café which serves a range of light lunches. Entry is by donation.

MORNINGTON PENINSULA REGIONAL GALLERY
Civic Reserve
Dunns Road
Mornington Vic 3931
Phone: (03) 5975 4395
Fax: (03) 5977 0377
Website:
www.mornpen.vic.gov.au/gallery

MPRG – the region's premier art gallery – offers a dynamic program of nationally significant exhibitions of contemporary and historical art by Australia's leading artists, together with exhibitions that focus on the Mornington Peninsula's rich cultural life. For more information on our changing program of exhibitions visit our website.

MORNINGTON PENINSULA VISITOR INFORMATION CENTRE & BOOKING SERVICE
Pt Nepean Road
Dromana Vic 3936
Phone: (03) 5987 3078
Toll free 1800 804 009
Fax: (03) 5987 3726
E-mail: tourism@mornpen.vic.gov.au
Website: www.visitmornington-peninsula.org

Need accommodation or travel advice? Talk to a local! We'll advise you for free, on the right accommodation choice for you; what you can see and do; what events are on; what the weather is like – even if the dolphins are out! In fact, we are like having a good friend on the Mornington Peninsula – one that gives you the right advice, every time. Not to mention, we can book everything for you – and that's free too. So give a local a call today on 1800 804 009 or 03 5987 3078.

Accommodation

MELBOURNE'S PENINSULA GETAWAYS LUXURY ACCOMMODATION RESERVATION SERVICE
Freecall: 1800 153 114
Phone: 5985 1114
E-mail: enquiries@peninsulagetaways.com.au

A choice of luxury accommodation around the bay…just for you. We have a large range of luxury, yet affordable accommodation, to make your getaway memorable. Choose from self-contained cottages, apartments, houses, B & Bs and resorts, all offering something special.

TOP OF THE BAY

Restaurants

DONOVANS
40 Jacka Boulevard
St Kilda Vic 3182
Phone: (03) 9534 8221
Fax: (03) 9525 3595
E-mail: eat@donovanshouse.com.au

Waterfront dining is hard to resist when the ambience is as relaxed and the food is as good as Donovans. Gail and Kevin Donovan have got the mix just right at their St Kilda beachhouse. The style of food served is modern Australian with a Mediterranean influence.

BELLARINE PENINSULA AND GEELONG

Accommodation

BEACON RESORT HOLIDAY PARK
78 Bellarine Highway
Queenscliff Vic 3225
Phone: (03) 5258 1133
Fax: (03) 5258 1152
E-mail: book@beaconresort.com.au
Website: www.beaconresort.com.au

Complement your break by staying at our multi-award-winning five-star caravan park. Choose between budget and luxury self-contained park cabins, motel rooms, or spacious powered sites. Leisure facilities include heated indoor pool, tennis courts, movie/function room, BBQs plus lots more. Fantastic for families, great for groups, perfect for couples.

THE QUEENSCLIFF HOTEL
16 Gellibrand Street
Queenscliff 3225
Victoria
E-mail: www.queenscliffhotel.com.au
www.miettas.com.au
Tel: 03) 52581066
Fax: 03) 5258 1899

Modern Australian

THE MANSION HOTEL
K Road
Werribee Vic 3030
Ph: (03) 9731 4000
Fax: (03) 9731 4001
E-mail: mansion@bigpond.com
Website: www.mansionhotel.com.au

Just 20 minutes from Melbourne, The Mansion Hotel features 92 contemporary guestrooms, Joseph's Restaurant and luxurious spa complex. Read a book by the open fire in the library, enjoy a game of snooker and tennis or take a leisurely stroll through the gardens to nearby Shadowfax Winery. It's all at your doorstep!

THE OL' DUKE
40 Newcombe Street
Portarlington VIC 3223
Tel: 03 5259 1250
Fax: 03 5259 1237
E-mail: theolduke@bigpond.com
Contemporary

Restaurants & Cafes

ATHELSTANE HOUSE
4 Hobson Street
Queenscliff Vic 3225
Phone: (03) 5258 1024
Fax: (03) 5258 4930
E-mail: athelstane@bigpond.com
Website: www.lovehotel.com.au

Inside, Athelstane House is a contemporary restaurant and bar offering creative, seasonal food. Outside, enjoy great coffee, cake and a choice of over 15 wines in the courtyard and veranda areas. With professional and friendly service you may never wish to leave and for those who don't, there are 10 funky spa rooms to stay overnight in.

SPRAY FARM
2275 Portarlington Rd
Bellarine Vic 3222
Phone: (03) 5251 3176
Fax: (03) 5253 1743
E-mail: info@scotchmans.com.au

The historic homestead and gardens of Spray Farm, built in 1851 and restored to its original state by The Scotchmans Hill Group, offers a magnificent venue for corporate events, conferences, private functions and weddings. A restaurant is open on weekends for lunch, tastings and sales. With expansive water frontage, the property boasts spectacular views of the You Yangs, Port Phillip Bay and the city of Melbourne.

ZEN ARTISAN CAFÉ & BAKERY
153 High Street
Belmont Vic Geelong
Phone: (03) 5244 1488
Fax: (03) 5244 2864
E-mail: zenbread@pipeline.com.au

The Zen Artisan Café & Bakery invites you to enjoy a wide range of lunch choices from homemade soup and gourmet pies to cakes and pastries served with coffee. Grab the quintessential picnic stock of ciabatta, fresh croissants, crispy pasta dura and some of our delicious sourdough bread on your way to your coastal getaway.

Wineries

BELLARINE ESTATE
2270 Portarlington Road
Bellarine Vic 3222
Phone: (03) 5259 3310
Fax: (03) 5259 3393
E-mail: plkenny@bigpond.com

Surrounded by Port Phillip Bay and nestled in a picturesque north-facing slope in a valley on the Bellarine Peninsula, Bellarine Estate is a true maritime-climate vineyard. Here, the cooler bay-influenced temperatures create fruit of superior quality and unique character. All of our wines are produced using only the highest-quality, estate-grown fruit. Bellarine Estate produces premium quality chardonnay, shiraz, sauvignon blanc, pinot noir and merlot grapes. Our 1999 James' Paddock Chardonnay was a multi-award-winner on the 2000 Australian show circuit. The Bellarine Estate cellar door is open from 11am to 5pm weekends and public holidays.

BELLARINE PENINSULA PROVIDORE
Leura Park Estate Vineyard
1400 Portarlington Road
Curlewis via Drysdale Vic
Phone (03) 5253 3180

Regional wine tourism facility. New to the Bellarine Peninsula, the Providore offers comparative tastings of varietals flourishing in the area. Compare Geelong with Mornington, Bellarine with Burgundy. A meeting place for local vignerons with great espresso, wine trail snacks and an open fire for restoring winter wine tourers. Leura Park Estate wines exclusively.

DEL RIOS VINEYARD
2320 Ballan Road
Anakie Vic 3221
Ph: (03) 9497 4644
(03) 5284 1221
Fax: (03) 9497 4644
E-mail: sales@delrios.com.au
Website: www.delrios.com.au

Del Rios Vineyard is family-owned and -operated and is situated at Anakie, north of Geelong. Enjoy our premium wines of sauvignon blanc, chardonnay, marsanne, pinot noir, cabernet sauvignon and shiraz. Visit our website or cellar door by appointment.

SCOTCHMANS HILL
190 Scotchmans Road
Drysdale Vic 3222
Phone: (03) 5251 3176
Fax: (03) 5253 1743
E-mail: info@scotchmans.com.au

Established in 1982, the family owned vineyard and winery of Scotchmans Hill produces premium wine from vines planted in this cool maritime climate. The cellardoor is open 7 days for tastings and sales of internationally renowned wines.

SHADOWFAX WINES
K Road
Werribee Vic 3030
Ph: (03) 9731 4420
Fax: (03) 9731 4421
E-mail: shadowfax@mansiongroup.com.au
Website: www.shadowfax.com.au

Melbourne's latest winery, Shadowfax, is open daily from 11am and invites visitors to taste the wines, purchase from the cellar door, enjoy a leisurely lunch at the gourmet foodstore, stroll around the picturesque vineyard and visit the neighbouring Mansion Hotel. Shadowfax also provides the perfect venue for weddings and special events.

Other

QUEENSCLIFF VISITOR INFORMATION CENTRE
55 Hesse Street
Queenscliff Vic 3225
Phone: (03) 5258 4843
Local information

V & R FRUIT AND VEGETABLE MARKET PTY LTD
5 Pakington Street
West Geelong Vic 3218
Phone: (03) 5222 2522
Fax: (03) 5222 2515

As a family-run business for the past 22 years, we pride ourselves on stocking the finest-quality produce as well as supplying the local hospitality industry. Our range of speciality products (such as cheese, breads, oils, preserves etc) enhances our appeal to food lovers seeking a bounty of culinary delights.

INDEX

AAA Allday Winery Tours 137
Acland Street 80, 83–4
Albert Park 79–80
Albert Park Deli 80
Amaretti Chocolate Torte 116
Anakie 139
art galleries 137
Arthur's Restaurant 34, 59, 61, 63
Arthur's Seat 24, 61, 63
Athelstane House 138

Baked Westernport Mullet 45
Baker Boys 41
Bannockburn Cellars 97, 99, 108–9, 111
Barwon Heads 96, 101–4
Bazils Café 117–18
Beacon Resort Holiday Park 138
Beaumaris Pavilion 91–2
Bellarine Estate 111, 139
Bellarine Peninsula 96–132
Bellarine Peninsula Providore 139
Benbrook 73
Biron, George 111, 121
Bittern Cottage 59
Blazey, Clive and Penny 36
Brandon, Jan and Trevor 31–2
bread 41–2, 67, 76, 80, 87, 99, 101–2, 104, 105–6, 136
Bright, Jenny 48
Brighton 87–8
Brighton Food Store 87–8
Brockett, Robin 112, 113
Brown, Greg 80
Brown's Bakery 80
Browne family 112
Bryant, Graham and Rosemary 34
Bryant's Organic Vegetables 34, 36
Burgess, Greg 60, 61

Café Sweethearts 75
cakes 83, 88
  Amaretti Chocolate Torte 116
  Vanilla Slice with Candied Chestnuts 85
  see also tarts
Castellani, Robert 86
Centro Cafe 75
chair lift 61, 63
cheese 28, 31–2
cherries 34
chickens 110–1, 118
Chilli Mussels 117
Chinese Five-spiced Duck Breast on Warm Potato and Porcini Salad 77
Christofi, Terry 105–6
Cicciolina 84
concerts outdoors 111, 114
cooking classes 64, 67, 79
Crittenden, Garry 48, 55–6, 60
Crittenden, Margaret 60
Curley, Ian 91–2

Del Rios Vineyard 139
Delgany 59
Devil's Bend wine 61
Dexter, Todd 53
Diggers Seeds 36, 38
Donovan, Gail and Kevin 84, 86
Donovans 80, 84–6, 138
Dromana 48, 49, 136, 137
Dromana Estate 48, 49, 55–6, 60, 136
Drysdale 111, 112–13, 139
Dundas Place Café 80

Edelweiss 84
Einsiedel, Jodie and Peter 27–8
Ellisfield Farm 32, 34, 35, 136
Elwood 87
Emu Plains Market 27
Esipoff, Sasha 34, 64
est est est 75

Farr, Gary 109
Fegan, Matthew 74
fish 80, 99, 121
  Baked Westernport Mullet 45
  fish and chips 73, 97
  Seared Salmon with Olives, Anchovies, Vine Tomatoes and Green Beans 128
fishing 44–8
Fitzpatrick, Mike and Sandi 111
Fitzroy Street 80
Flinders 59, 136
Flinders Bread 42, 136
Fox, Paul 102
fruit 76, 79, 80, 87, 97, 99
  pick-your-own 32, 34, 36
Fruit Palace 79

Gaskell, Val 88, 91
Geelong 96, 97, 99–101, 114–18, 139
Gennaro's Table 64, 67
Golden Gate 75
Gray, Jane 100–1
Greek Vegetable Soup 100

Haig, Gill 27
Hampton 87
Hanns Creek 60
Harrop, Matt 114
Harry's 97
Harvest Café 36
Hastings 24, 44–6, 47–8
Hawley, Barry and Jan 42
Heath, Greg 112
Heirloom Cherry Tomato and Basil Tart 36
Heronswood 36, 38, 137
Hickenbotham, Stephen 48
Hodgson, Lisa 88
Hooper, Stuart 108–9
hotel resorts 59
hotels 60, 97, 118, 121, 124, 126–32, 136, 138, 118
Houghton's Fine Foods 42–3
Hutchins, Dalton and Neville 47–8
Hyett, Bruce 109

ice-cream 88, 91
Idyll Vineyard 108
Indented Head 97
Innisfail 111

Jenkins, Peter 'Jerker' 121
Jill's 34, 60
Joseph's 116, 128, 131–2, 138

Karklins, Dinah 102
Katialo 118, 120–1
Kilgour Estate 111
Kinsella, Lisa 38
Kowalyk, Helen and Mark 73–4

La Baracca 58, 59, 60
Langton, Stewart 114
Lawrence, Sharnell 38
Lechte, Louise 58
Lever & Kowalyk 73–5, 77
Lever, Rohan 73, 74
Lindenderry 59, 136

Main Ridge Estate 48, 49, 52–3
Main Street Deli 42, 136
Malouf, Greg 76
Mansion Hotel 114, 116, 128, 131–2, 138, 139
markets 27, 75, 42–3, 76–7, 139
Marshall, Stuart 53
Matthews, Dean 124
Max's 60
Mazzella, Gennaro 64, 67
McCarthy, Heather 104–5
McCarthy, Kevin 48, 58–9
McClelland Gallery 137
McIntyre, Jill and Richard 34, 48, 60–1
Melbourne Wine Room 80
Melbourne's Peninsula Getaways Luxury Accommodation Reservation Service 137
Mentiplay, John and Paul 41–2
Merricks 49, 53, 55, 113, 137
Merricks Estate 48
Mietta's 97, 126, 128, 131, 138
Mirabella Tim 44–6
Misuzu's 80

140

the food and wine lover's guide to Melbourne's Bays and Peninsulas

Moorooduc 136, 137
Moorooduc Estate Vineyard 34, 48, 60–1, 136
Morning Star Estate 136
Mornington 42–3, 49, 136, 137
Mornington Estate 56
Mornington Peninsula 24–70, 42–3, 49, 136–7
Mornington Peninsula Gourmet 27
Mornington Peninsula Regional Gallery 137
Mornington Peninsula Vignerons Association 48, 136
Mt Eliza 136
muesli 27–8
mushrooms 79
  Chinese Five-spiced Duck Breast on Warm Potato and Porcini Salad 77
mussels 106, 108
  Chilli Mussels 117
Mussels Fish & Chippery 73

Nelson, Sarah 100–1
Nelson Place 73

O'Connells Centenary Hotel 75
O'Donnell, Patricia 126, 128, 131
Ongarello, Deb 68
Opus 59, 68
organic produce 27, 32, 34, 36, 38
Osborne, Marilyn 117–18

Pages, Xeni 118, 120
Pako Street Festival 114
Paringa Estate 41, 60
Parker, Andrew 124
Peppercorn Foods 104–5
Perez, Paul 118, 120
Pettavel winery restaurant 111
Phillippa's products 76
Pickadelis 76
pick-your-own fruit 32, 34, 36

picnic hampers 38
Pitman, Melanie 124
Poffs' 34, 64
Point Lonsdale 97
Pontifex, Barry and Liz 34
Port Pier Café 118, 120
Portarlington 97, 105–6, 118, 120–5, 138
Portarlington Bakehouse 105–6
Portarlington Mussels 106, 108
Portsea 59, 126
Portsea Hotel 60
poultry 100–1
Prince Albert Vineyard 109

Quealy, Kathleen 48, 58–9
Queenscliff 97, 116, 126–32, 138
Queenscliff Hotel 126–32
Queenscliff Visitor Information Centre 139
quinces 34
Quince and Almond Tart 35

rabbits 77, 100–1
Raines, Sheryl 106
Red Hill 24, 59, 60, 61, 64, 67, 136
Red Hill Cheese 28, 31–2
Red Hill Cool Stores 27, 28
Red Hill Estate 48, 49
Red Hill Market 27, 28, 32, 67
Red Hill Muesli 27–8
Ricketts Point Fine Foods 88, 91
Robinson, Hugh and Isabel 56
Robinson, Xavier 128
Ryan, Tony 68

safi buluu 59
Scheherezade 80, 83
Schneider, Faye and Hermann 34, 63
Scotchmans Hill 111, 112–13, 139
SeaChange phenomenon 96, 101–2
Seared Salmon with Olives, Anchovies, Vine

Tomatoes and Green Beans 128
Sefton, Daryl and Nini 108, 111
Shadowfax Wines 111, 113–14, 139
Sirens 73
Smokehouse pizza restaurant 60
Sorrento 59, 68
Sorrento Hotel 60
Souflas, Alex and Steven 120–1
South Melbourne 75–9
South Melbourne Market 75, 76–7
Spray Farm 111–12, 138
Spray Farm Summer Festival 111
St Kilda 80–6, 87, 138
St Leonards 96
Starfish Bakery 100, 101–2, 104
Stokehouse 80
Stonier, Brian and Noel 48, 53
Stonier Wines 49, 53, 55, 113, 137
strawberries 25, 136
Stumpy Gully Vineyard 137
Sunny Ridge Strawberry Farm 27, 136
Swan Bay wines 112
Swords 76–7

T'Gallant winery 48, 56, 58–9, 60
take-home food 44, 74, 80, 87, 104, 106
tarts
  Heirloom Cherry Tomato and Basil Tart 36
  Quince and Almond Tart 35
Tedder, Andrew 114
Thatched Earth Café 38
The ol' Duke Hotel 97, 118, 121, 124, 138
The Ozone 97, 126
The Vital Ingredient 75, 77
tomatoes 27, 36, 41, 118
  Heirloom Cherry Tomato and Basil Tart 36

Seared Salmon with Olives, Anchovies, Vine Tomatoes and Green Beans 128
Top of the Bay 73
Tuerong Park 56

V&R Fruit and Vegetable Market 99–100, 118, 139
Vanilla Slice with Candied Chestnuts 85
vegetables 76, 87, 97, 99
  Greek Vegetable Soup 100
  organic 34, 36
  see also tomatoes
Veludo 84
Vera, Barry 132
Villa Primavera 64, 67
Vue Grande 97, 126

Warren and Hutch, Provenders 100–1
Water Rat 75
Waurn Ponds 109, 111
Werribee 112, 114, 116, 131–2, 138, 139
Werribee Park 111, 113, 116, 131–2
White, Nat and Rosalie 48, 49, 52–3
Williamstown 72–5
Wilson, Victoria 113–14
Winbirra winery 49
wine shops 87, 97, 99
wine tours 137
wineries 48–59, 97, 108–14, 136, 137, 139
winery restaurants 60, 111–12, 136

Zen Artisan Café & Bakery 139

REFERENCES

The Bays and Peninsulas, Tourism Victoria
Wine Regions of Victoria, Tourism Victoria
The Story of Geelong 1800–1990, N. Houghton, Geelong Historical Records Centre
From the Farmgate: A guide to farmgate sales in Australia, Sol Salbe, Vista Publications
The Goods, Allan Campion and Michele Curtis, Wakefield Press
Victoria's Mornington Peninsula, Malcolm Gordon, Loch Haven Books
The Early History of the Mornington Peninsula, Hunter Rogers
Lime, Land and Leisure, Charles Hollinshed, ECF Bird and Noel Goss
Wine Lovers' Guide to Australia, ed. Jill Sykes, Pan Macmillan Australia
Crush, The New Australian Wine Book, Max Allen, Hardie Grant Books
Wine Atlas of Australia & New Zealand, James Halliday, Harper Collins
Crushed by Women, Jeni Port, Penguin Books
'Location, location, location', Barbara Santich, Epicure, Age, 22 June 1999
From Antarctica to the Tropics: a snapshot of the Australian fishing industry, Fisheries Research and Development Corporation
Mornington Peninsula Vignerons Association, Report 2000, MPVA Inc

PHOTO CREDITS

Photography, Simon Griffiths, except as follows:

Authors' photographs:
Lucy Malouf: Matt Harvey
Simon Griffiths: Gail Donovan
Max Allen: Adrian Lander

pages 16, 97
Nepean Historical Society
page 24
Western Port Historical Society